ACHIEVEMENT OF PRIMARY SCHOOL PRE-SERVICE TEACHERS

ACHIEVEMENT OF PRIMARY SCHOOL PRE-SERVICE TEACHERS

By

Dr. V. GOVINDA REDDY
Teaching Faculty, Department of Education
Sri Krishnadevaraya University
Anantapur–515 003
(A.P.)

D P H

DISCOVERY PUBLISHING HOUSE PVT. LTD.
NEW DELHI-110 002

First Published - 2008

Reprinted - 2018

ISBN: 978-81-8356-318-5

Achievement of Primary School Pre-service Teachers

Published by:

DISCOVERY PUBLISHING HOUSE PVT. LTD.

4383/4B, Ansari Road, Darya Ganj

New Delhi-110 002 (India)

Phone: +91-11-23279245, 43596064-65

Fax: +91-11-23253475

E-mail: discoverypublishinghouse@gmail.com

sales@discoverypublishinggroup.com

web: www.discoverypublishinggroup.com

Printed at:

Infinity Imaging Systems

Delhi

PREFACE

Teaching is an art and many are to be trained in this art. Anybody can become a teacher but everybody cannot become an effective teacher. The quality of education in schools depends upon the quality of teachers. In olden days the requirements in terms of teacher education were limited but the present system requires only well trained teachers. A comprehensive teacher education programme may help in producing quality teachers. The quality of teachers depends upon the training that is provided to the teachers through the various teacher training institutions. A new type of educational institution called the District Institute of Education and Training (DIET) has been conceived within the National Policy on Education (NPE) and Programme of Action (POA) as one of the major steps towards the effective teacher education at the primary level.

Primary education occupies the most important place in the ladder of education. The progress and achievement in the higher stages of education depends upon the effectiveness of the primary education. Keeping the objectives of education and teacher education at primary stage the new Teacher Training Course of one year duration was started during the academic year 1975-76 as approved by the Government of Andhra Pradesh, vide G.O.Ms. No. 169, Education, dated 16th May 1975. This is an important change in the field of primary teacher education to raise the quality of teachers at primary and upper primary level. The Teacher Training Institutions are renamed as District Institutes of Education and Training (DIET) with effect from 28-10-1989. To strengthen the primary teacher training programme, National Council for Educational Research and Training (NCERT) and NCTE advised the state Governments to change the duration of the teacher training programme from one year to two years Course namely Diploma in Education (D.Ed.), vide G.O.Ms. No.502, dated 11-11-1998.

The DIET is designed to improve and enrich the academic background of elementary school teachers, non-formal and adult education functionaries and other personnel at the lowest level of the educational system.At present the DIETs are given the responsibility of providing pre-service training at primary level. Hence, there is every need to look into the status of DIETs from various angles and to study the achievement on the basis of Psycho-Sociological factors of student teachers.

The book has been divided into two parts. The first part is the various aspects of Teacher Education, detail report on Primary School Education in Andhra Pradesh which includes brief review of the previous studies and its foundation for the present investigation.

The second part is related the various aspects of the present study and methodology of the study and results obtained etc. The tables and graphical representations are placed in the main body of the book.

V. GOVINDA REDDY

CONTENTS

1

TEACHER EDUCATION

Education, according to Indian tradition, is not merely a means to earn a living, nor is it only a nursery of thought or a school for citizenship. It is an initiation into the life of spirit, a training of human soul in pursuit of truth and the practice of virtue. Aristotle, however, held that education exists exclusively to develop man's intellect in a world of reality, which men can know and understand.

The word 'education' has a very wide connotation. It is hard to define. There is no single objective, which can cover the world of life with its various manifestations. The two poles of our concern; the temporal and the world of spirit are widely apart. Philosophers and thinkers from Socrates to Dewey in the West and from Yajnavalkya to Gandhi in the East have defined education in accordance with their philosophy of life with the result that there emerged divergent concepts and definitions of education. The concept of education is like diamond, which appears in different colours when seen from different angles.

The essence of education lies in stimulating the growing generation with a consistent, compelling and creative system of values around which cultural heritage, both spiritual and material of the community is transmitted, to the tender souls so as to develop them into civilized, creative and productive members of a progressive society. Sets of various institutions are involved in this task, in so far as Teacher Education is concerned.

THE CONCEPT OF TEACHER EDUCATION

Teacher Education has been defined as "all formal and informal activities and experience that help to qualify a person to assume the responsibilities as a member of the teaching profession and to discharge his responsibilities more effectively". The concept of "Teacher Education" is not new. However, Scholarliness was considered the sole criterion for becoming a teacher. The concept that teachers are born and not made was also prevalent in those days.

It has been aptly remarked, "If you educate a boy, you educate one individual. If you educate a girl, you educate the whole family and if you educate an individual as a teacher, you educate the whole community".

The contention that teachers are born, not made, can be true only in a few rare cases. It is also not contended that training, by itself, is sure to make a good teacher. But it is generally observed that a teacher with training becomes more mature and confident to perform his task more efficiently. Proper training and education enables the teacher to have knowledge of how children grow, develop and learn how they can be taught best and how their innate capacities can be brought out and developed.

According to Monroe Encyclopedia of Educational research "Teacher education refers to the totality of educational inputs, which contribute to the preparation of a person for a teaching position in schools". But the term is more commonly employed to designate the programmes of courses and other experiences offered by an educational institution for the announced purpose of preparing persons for teaching and other educational services.

W.S. Kilpatrick, the famous American educationist once remarked, "One trains circus performers and animals, but one educates the teachers", consequently the new term "Teacher Education" has been adopted replacing the term "Teacher Training".

Teacher education is not mere pedagogy or acquisition of a training qualification. It is preparation of persons for family, for society and for the country. It is nurturing of creativity, inculcation of commitment and generation of a strong will to contribute at the highest level of efficiency through a value-based approach. Teacher education is a process of unearthing the treasure within every teacher and subsequently within every learner in each and every learning centre. It is the process, which makes the individuals realise the magnitude and potentialities, which, if nurtured and inculcated in the right direction, could make significant contribution to the identified sectors.

NEED AND SIGNIFICANCE OF TEACHER EDUCATION

Teacher education is needed for kindling the initiative of the teacher, for keeping it alive, for removing the evils or 'hit and miss' process, for according a process, for according a professional status to the teaching profession and above all for making the optimum use of time and energy of the teacher and the taught.

The Education Commission (1964-66) observed: "A sound programme of professional education of teachers is essential for the qualitative improvement of education. Investment in teacher education can yield very rich dividends because the financial resources required are small when measured against the resulting improvement in the education of millions".

National Policy on Education (NPE) 1986 calls for the overhaul of teacher education as the first step towards educational reorganisation.

In this context effective teacher education becomes a core condition to ensure high proficiency and quality school education. In other words effective school education anticipates effective teacher education.

AIMS OF TEACHER EDUCATION PROGRAMMES

Following are the some of aims of teacher education programme. The perspective teacher trainee:

1. Enable to acquire the capacity to manage a class with pupils of varying abilities.
2. Communicate ideas logically.
3. Use the technology available to make teaching effective.

4. Organise educative experiences outside classroom.
5. Learn to work with the community and help the students to do so.
6. Learn to communicate to his pupils the importance and the feeling of national integrity and unity.
7. Develop among the pupils a scientific attitude, a commitment to excellence in standards of work and action and a concern for society.
8. Have an understanding and appreciation of human predicament; population explosion, environment pollution, the threat of a nuclear holocaust and the quest for world peace.
9. Imbibe the right attitudes and values, besides being proficient with the skills relating to teaching.

TEACHER EDUCATION IN INDIA—HISTORICAL PERSPECTIVE

The way in which the teacher education was initiated and evolved in the pre-independent India (i.e. before 1947) and post-independent period have been summarized below:

PRE-INDEPENDENT PERIOD

Teaching has been one of the oldest and most respected professions in the world. When a systematically organised human society came into existence the need to mould its children on proper lines arose requiring persons who could perform this role, that is, teachers. The task of shaping the future citizens is noble one and also the teacher has always occupied a place of honour and reverence in the Indian society over the ages.

In the ancient period when knowledge was transmitted orally (since writing developed later) the students memorized the spoken lessons and repeated them orally. Teachers gave explanations whenever required by the pupils. For instance, the *Sutras* were written in a language so condensed that without explanation they could not be comprehended. The teacher used parables from nature, and stories such as *Panchatantra* and *Hitopadesa* to explain the deep philosophical concept of the Upanishads. Thus, teachers in ancient India used various methods to explain and expound difficult philosophical concepts.

With the advent of the Western powers in India a new type of educational system, quite different from the existing indigenous system came to be established. European missionaries took lead by starting schools first and teacher training institutions later. The Danish Mission under the inspiring leadership of Zienbalg and his colleagues opened an institution for the training of teachers at Tranquebar in 1716, and opened two charity schools in 1717, one for the Portuguese and the other for Tamil children.

As early as 1802, William Carey set up a normal school for primary teachers in Serampore. In June 1826, the first normal school was started under the management and with the finance of the Government in Madras. Initially, it prepared teachers for the District Schools (secondary schools). Later, this normal school developed into the Presidency College. The Calcutta Ladies Society also organised a training class in 1828 for women teachers in the Calcutta Central School for girls.

In August 1828, the Committee of Public Instruction in Madras suggested an increase in the salary of teachers and an improvement in their training. In 1829 the Native Education Society of Bombay started a training class for primary teacher. In 1847, Bombay started a normal school in the Elphinstone Institution, and in 1849, Calcutta too had a normal school. Normal schools were also started in Poona, Agra, Meerut and Benaras during 1850-57. Mass education gained momentum with the recommendation of Wood's Despatch, 1854.

The Indian Education Commission 1882 provided some definite direction for furthering teacher education in India. The commission not only approved teachers training programme for both elementary and secondary teachers but also recommended a separate programme for secondary schools, distinctly higher in level, form and method. As a result of this, training colleges for graduates and undergraduates were established for the first time; six training colleges at Lahore, Madras (1886), Allahabad, Jabalpur

(1890) and Rajamundry (1894) are worth mention. By the end of nineteenth century, teacher education became established as a substantial structured setup.

Lord Curzon (1902-05) took several significant steps to improve the quality of education. His emphasis was on improvement of quality and not quantity at the university level, better control and improvement at the secondary level and expansion and quality at primary level. He highlighted these concerns in his Resolution on Education Policy (1904), which is more commonly known as the "Government of India Resolution 1904". The Resolution presented conditions to be satisfied by school to be eligible for receiving grant-in-aid and recognition by the government. The Resolution emphasized the necessity of providing a large number of training institutions for primary teachers; the duration of training being a minimum of two years.

The other recommendations relevant to teacher education in the Government of India Resolution 1904 were:

1. The equipment of a training college should be as important as that of an arts college.
2. The training courses should be one year for graduates, leading to a university degree, while training courses for under graduates should be of two years.
3. The theory and practice of teaching should be included in training courses.
4. A practicing school should be attached to each training college.
5. Every possible care should be taken to maintain a connection between a training college and schools.

Based on Minto-Morely reforms of 1909, the government passed another Resolution on Education Policy in 1913, which among other things declared that under the modern system of education no teacher should be allowed to teach without a certificate that he is qualified to do so.

The Calcutta University Commission (1917-19) recommended that a Department of Education should be created in the University of Dacca (Dhaka, now the capital of Bangladesh) and Calcutta and that education should be included as a subject of study in intermediate, B.A. and M.A. degree examination.

Hartog Committee (1929) recommendations about the training of primary school teachers:

1. Raising the standard of general education of Primary School Teachers;
2. Lengthening of the duration of training courses;
3. Provision of adequate staff for training institution;
4. Improvement of service conditions of primary school teachers to attract and retain better quality of teachers.

As a result of the recommendations of the committee the following developments took place:

- Setting up of in service education programmes for primary school teachers.
- Training institutions were equipped with laboratories, libraries and practicing schools.
- Efforts streamline training and working conditions of the teacher were made.

The next noteworthy contribution in the field of teacher education took place as a result of Sargent Committee in 1944; significant among them are:

- Provision for training different categories of teachers for two years for the pre-primary and junior basic teachers; three years for senior basic teachers; two years for undergraduate teachers in high schools; and one year for graduates.
- In-service training in the form of short courses, evening classes, summer school courses etc, were started in Madras, the United Provinces, the Northern Provinces, Bombay and Jalandhar.

These developments achieved at the instance of the colonial Government of India during 1902-45, Indicate the growing concern about teacher education in respect of not only making it a necessary equipment for a school teacher, but also presenting adequate administrative and organisational specification as to the content, components duration and relevance of training made available to school teachers.

A general attitude of suspicion and distrust towards colonial government became increasingly widespread among Indians and as a result any effort by the government to regulate educational institutions through quality control met with strong criticism from educated Indians. National leaders like Gokhale and Annie Besant voiced these growing public sentiments in strong terms. 'National education' as started by Annie Besant should be totally 'Indian' in order to meet the national temperament at every point.

In response to Gandhiji's call for boycott of anything English, which included English run schools and colleges, teams of students came out. In Aligarh University a breakaway group of students formed itself into a new institution namely Jamia Millia Islamis. Other groups followed suit in other parts of the country by opening national universities, national colleges and national schools.

In addition to national educational institutions, the concept of 'Basic Education' as propounded by Mahatma Gandhiji, gained popularity as the Wardha Scheme. It emphasised economic self-sufficiency to be promoted in each individual through education which would be 'work centred'. In order to provide such education, teachers had to be trained differently. Experimental training for this was provided in some places like Wardha and Gandhigram. This was perhaps the first time that anyone had streamlined an educational programme in such a comprehensive manner, explicitly relating it to nation-building and social reconstruction. *"Buniyadi Shiksha as Nai Talim"* represented the first significant effort to develop an indigenous national system of education in conformity with the needs and aspirations of the people.

On the whole, by the time of Independence, teacher education has been established as one distinct component of the educational system. It was recognised as necessary for school teacher, both elementary and secondary.

POST-INDEPENDENT PERIOD

A fairly evolved system of teacher education was one of the several 'colonial legacies' to free India. The system comprised several institutions engaged in training teachers of primary and secondary schools. Certificate, diploma and degree-level courses were available for study. Government and non-government initiatives have been mobilised for offering these programmes. A trained teacher had come to be recognised as more effective than without training. The initial concepts of normal schools that provided 'on the job' training had given way to training as a desirable pre-condition for teachers' employment. The need for systematic effort to understand training practices and processes to enhance their potential for impact had been perceived. At the same time, the actual number of trained teachers in primary and secondary schools was dismally low and there was an ever-growing bulk of untrained teachers.

Immediately after independence several efforts were simultaneously made to tackle these problems. Looking back on the development over the years three streams of action seem to have been undertaken:

- Expansion of pre-service teacher education;
- Opening of supplementary channels for clearing the backlog of untrained teachers;
- Stabilization and expansion of in-service teacher education.

The expansion of pre-service teacher education is impressive if one looks at the continuous growth in the number of teacher education institutions. From a mere 10 secondary teacher-training institutions in 1948, the number increased to 50 in 1965 and 633 in 1995.

The incidence of 'untrained' teachers is a problem that has persisted from pre-independence times. It has in fact, increased during the post-independence period. One measure adopted during the early years of independence was the practice of "deputing" untrained schools teachers to training colleges and institutions. The Education Commission (1964-66) recognised in strong terms the urgent need to clear the backlog of untrained teachers and recommended opening supplementary channels, which would hasten the process. The commission suggested summer courses, part time courses and correspondence courses as effective possibilities. The correspondent-cum-contact mode was considered suitable especially for teachers of the secondary school stage. In order to institutionalize this mode of teacher training, the Central Institutions of Education, which was a constituent unit of National Council for Educational Research and Training (NCERT), started in 1966 a B.Ed. programme through correspondence-cum-contact mode. The regional Colleges of Education at Ajmer, Bhopal, Bhubaneshwar and Mysore started this programme in 1976. However, these programmes were stopped subsequently when it was found that there was no backlog of untrained teachers regionally.

The year 1986 may be considered as a landmark in the history of teacher education–the National Policy on Education (NPE) with major emphasis on quality in education has got not only the approval of parliament but a Programme of Action (POA) was also chalked out which was implemented with great seriousness all over the country. The policy declared: "Of all the different factors which influence the quality of education and its contribution to national development, the quality, competence and character of education of teachers are undoubtedly the most significant".

As a result of this, a variety of institutions were established for teacher education. These include:

- District Institutions of Education and Training (DIET) for the training of teachers for elementary schools (Upgrading TTI).
- Colleges of Teacher Education (CTEs) – (upgrading Teacher Training Colleges).
- Institutions of Advanced Study in Education (IASE).

When training was accepted as a requisite qualification for teachers at the school stage, teacher education programmes became diversified, separate programmes for separate states were developed. Based on the nature of training, the training institutes in our country may be broadly stated as follows:

Pre-primary Training Centers

Pre-primary education is in its early steps in our country. Consequently the provision of training of teachers of pre-primary schools is also made. Pre-primary education training centres impart training to the metric and upper primary pass students for a period of one year. The curriculum of the training centres is different. These centres fulfill the needs of different pre-primary schools such as kindergarten and Montessori schools.

Primary Training Schools

There were two types of primary schools in India. (i) basic and (ii) non-basic; consequently there were two types of training schools—Junior Teacher's certificate was conferred on those students who take admission in these school after passing upper primary, Senior Teachers certificate was awarded to the students taking training in these centres after passing matriculation. There was wide difference in the curriculum of these training schools. Agriculture (for men), sewing (women), spinning and weaving, drawings were compulsory; wood work, scientific processes and activities (including making of paper, soap, candle, chalks etc.) were optional. There were seven papers under theory; theory of basic education; preliminary education of psychology; school organisation; and 4 papers under teaching methods. Practical teaching includes 30 teaching lesson, use of exhibiting materials and physical training. However, based on the development in the field of teacher education, these training institutions gradually disappeared.

Secondary Training Schools

Intermediate pass students were admitted in these schools. The training period in such schools was one year in some states and 2 years in some other states. The successful students were conferred a certificate or diploma by the University or Education Department. The teachers trained in these institutions perform teaching work in middle schools. Now primary training institutions are merged with secondary and are called elementary teacher training institutes. Based on the recommendations of NPE 1986 and National Council for Teacher Education (NCTE) norms, the duration is enhanced and competency based and commitment oriented curriculum is introduced for pre-service teacher education at elementary level and the training is imparted through DIETs.

2

PRIMARY TEACHER EDUCATION IN ANDHRA PRADESH

HISTORICAL PERSPECTIVE

The State of Andhra Pradesh came into existence in 1956 by readjustment of the former Nizam's dominions with the newly formed Andhra Pradesh, which had its capital at Kurnool. The Andhra regions of the state extended to Nellore in the south, Godavari district in the east and Vijayanagaram in the north. The south and the north western parts up to Aurangabad and the southern districts upto Raichur were added to Maharashtra and Karnataka respectively.

Teacher education courses of one and two years existed in the Nizam's dominions in the four divisions called *'Subas'*, with their headquarters at Hyderabad, Warangal, Gulbarga and Aurangabad for the matriculates and the middle passed primary school teachers to begin with. The middle passed teachers were required to undergo a two years' training course in which the first year was mostly devoted to further academic courses such as Telugu, Urdu, Mathematics, History, Geography to raise their academic level. Part of the first year training course was devoted to the subjects like Principles of Education, Educational Psychology, and History of Education from the teacher education point of view and methodology. The courses used to be conducted through regional languages such as Telugu, Urdu in the Maharashtra area to improve the understanding and development of communicative skills in the regional languages. The second year of their training concentrated on the methods of teaching of any two subjects of the primary and lower secondary school curriculum with a minimum of fifteen practice teaching lessons in each subject, supervised by the lecturers concerned after a model lesson by them in each subject.

In the case of matriculates, the training course in the normal schools was of one-year duration only, as in the case of graduates who were admitted to the then B.T. and L.T. courses throughout the country. They required undertaking any two curricular methodology subjects, through the media of Urdu and regional languages of the areas concerned.

The above pattern was more or less uniform throughout India before Independence, say, from 1882 to 1947. There were about 34 teacher training schools in the country by 1947 for the secondary school teachers also during this period, along with a good number of normal schools both for men and women teachers separately. The teachers in charge of giving training in normal schools were trained graduates in the subjects concerned with methods of teaching.

BASIC TEACHER TRAINING SCHOOLS

A new chapter of primary education started in 1937 under Mahatma Gandhi's scheme. Spinning was the main craft all through in schools supplemented with field agricultural work, woodcraft and work culture also in some schools. As a result of this scheme, the primary schools all over the country were divided into two kinds—namely basic and non-basic—the later schools were merely a continuation of the former primary schools where the craft arrangements could not be made owing to different administrative and personnel non-availability conditions.

As a result there arose the need of basic teachers' training schools in the country. In the Nizam's dominion, Biknoor was one of such well-known centres in the district of Nizamabad. The teachers of the school were trained graduates with special expertise in different basic crafts required in the basic primary schools, mainly spinning and weaving coupled with agricultural work, where the government was able to provide the necessary facilities including the staff. In the Andhra region, the Government Training College at Rajamundry was the first to be started as early as 1901-02, affiliated to Madras University. A basic training college was run at a place called Pentapadu to cater to the needs of basic school teachers.

The basic teacher training schools gradually disappeared after short existence as the government converted the then basic schools into Basic type of primary schools, which term also disappeared from the field of primary education in a brief course of time. The terms 'Basic' was converted to 'Work Experience' as a common feature of education at all stages, including university education, with workshops attached to schools and colleges to give practical training to students on different vocations. No special coaching or training for teachers was offered systematically and, therefore, this type of basic education training also disappeared from the field.

TEACHER TRAINING INSTITUTES (TTIs)

The Teacher Education at Primary stage, namely the new Teacher Training Course (TTC) of one-year duration was started during the academic year 1975-76. The institutions offering this revised course were called Teacher Training Institutes (TTIs). A pass in the Intermediate examination with a minimum of 45 per cent of marks in aggregate was prescribed as a minimum qualification for admission. This is an important change in the field of Primary teacher education to raise the quality of teachers at Primary and Upper Primary levels. The duration of the course is one academic year after a pass in the intermediate examination. These institutions were working for 220 days a year with 5 ½ hours of work a day. Twelve Institutes were established (seven in Telangana region and five in Andhra region) in Andhra Pradesh state.

In Teacher Training Course Examination, the total marks allocated to theory were 400 and 600 marks for practicals. Thus, the total marks for the purpose of deciding the grade was 1000.

DISTRICT INSTITUTE OF EDUCATION AND TRAINING (DIET)

A new type of educational institution called the District Institute of Education and Training (DIET) has been conceived within the National Policy on Education (NPE) and Programme of Action (POA) as one of the major steps towards the effective teacher education at the primary level. The DIET is designed to improve and enrich the academic background of elementary school teachers, non-formal and adult education functionaries and other personnel at the lowest level of the educational system.

Thus, facilities for qualitative improvement of teachers are made available at the very doorstep of the teachers and others involved. DIET's aim is to extend to the remotest parts of the country, with relative ease, the advantages of the educational knowledge available about management and planning, research and experimentation and the existing variety of rich resources and learning materials. The DIETs provide academic support to the District Boards of Education.

The DIET is a step towards the decentralization of opportunities of professional preparation and extension of excellence from 'urban' to 'rural' areas, from the 'elite' to the 'general' population of teachers, from 'higher' to 'lower' levels of education, and from the 'academic' to the 'teacher'. It will provide guidance and leadership to ensure that effective measures are adopted in the four aspects of the Universalisation of Elementary Education (UEE) through access, enrolment, retention and standards. The DIET should be in a position to devise, for local situations, specific ways to increase enrolment and more importantly, drastically reduce the alarming drop-out rate at the primary school level. It should also facilitate the education and literacy of adults and others who, unfortunately, drop out of the formal system due to economic and social handicaps.

The DIET has been conceived as a vibrant instrument for bringing about qualitative change in quality of life of the community through education. It aims at energizing the educational climate of the district by providing rich training and resources and improving the professional competence of teachers and other educational functionaries. It has the following major objectives:

- To provide pre-service and in-service education of elementary school teachers;

- To provide teacher education and continuing education of instructors and supervisors for non-formal education, and the provision of resources to support them;
- To provide planning and management support for District Boards of Education (DBE), school complexes and educational institutions;
- To serve as an evaluation centre for primary and upper primary schools, as well as for non-formal and adult education centres;
- To act as a resource and learning centre for teachers and instructors;
- To act as a centre of experimentation and research; and
- To support educational technology and computer education programme in the district.

To effectively perform their major functions, the DIETs have the following seven academic branches:

- Pre-Service Teacher Education (PSTE).
- In-Service programmes, Field Interaction and Innovation Coordination (IFIC).
- District Resource Unit (DRU) for Adult and Non-Formal Education.
- Work Experience (WE).
- Curriculum, Material Development and Evaluation (CMDE).
- Educational Technology (ET).
- Planning and Management (P&M).

Past Basic training schools, later called Teacher Training Institutions (TTIs) used to play an important role in producing required teachers for elementary schools. Now, in the place of TTIs, the DIETs have come into existence to produce effective teachers for primary and upper primary schools. At present there are 23 DIETs in 23 Districts of Andhra Pradesh. Apart from these, there are two sub-DIETs located one at Araku Valley (Visakhapatnam District) and another one at Utnur (Adilabad District). These Two sub DIETs are established to provide training for tribal students under Integrated Tribal Development Agency (ITDA) areas for their requirements. Hence, there are 25 teacher education institutions for primary school teachers in Andhra Pradesh. The state government is providing financial support to these DIETs.

GENERAL SCHEME OF THE DIETS (D.Ed. Course)

Quality education is the cherished goal, which mainly depends on the nature of pre-service Teacher Training they receive before entering into teaching profession. In the document, "Challenge of Education, a policy framework" it is envisaged that the teacher education curriculum should be able to prepare self-directed professionally motivated and creatively alert teachers who will be fully equipped with all necessary skills and techniques to be efficient.

Pursuance to the provision of NPE-1986, DIETs have come up in every district in Andhra Pradesh to provide academic and resource support to achieve laudable objective of providing Education for All (EFA). Activity based approach has been introduced in primary schools of Andhra Pradesh. Minimum levels of learning (MLLs) a concept at National level are being adopted in all States.

Pursuant to POA of NPE-1992, District Primary Education Project (DPEP) programme is being implemented in various districts. The recent legislation brought about in A.P. Legislature Assembly empowers the community to participate in school development. All these sweeping changes emphasise the urgent need for radical change in the present curriculum of Pre-Service Teacher Education in DIETs.

Based on this ideology and consequent on prescribing norms by NCTE for a two year D.Ed. course and in the light of Government G.O. No. 502, Education, dated 11-11-1998, it has been decided that the existing scheme and syllabus of TTC course may be revised to a two-year D.Ed. Course with effect from the academic year 1999-2000.

AIMS OF THE B.Ed. COURSE

The two year course which is competency based and performance oriented aims at enabling the prospective teacher trainee to understand the aims and perspectives of Elementary Education including pre-school education. Following are the aims of the two year B.Ed. programme.

1. Develop necessary professional skills and attitudes especially in handling classes in multigrade and multi-level schools.
2. Understand the cultural diversity and social needs of secular democratic and socialist society in the scientific era.
3. Understand the factors, which influence education growth and development of emerging Indian society.
4. Provide necessary knowledge and skills for ensuring quality education for all.
5. Acquire managerial and planning skills needed for effective management of classroom and the school plant.
6. Conduct empirical child study in order to identify child's innate abilities, needs and urges.
7. Adopt learner centered competency based teaching strategies by providing natural learning experiences through creative and productive activities.
8. Enable the trainee to have hands on experiences of information technology especially of computer assisted learning.
9. Provide necessary inputs needed to build the capacity of the trainee to plan, execute and evaluate programmes under creative art, work-experience, health and physical education.
10. Possess necessary skills needed for teaching mother tongue, English, General Mathematics, General Science and Social Studies.

Here After DIETS that are Offering One Year Teacher Training Course shall be of Two Year Duration Leading to DIPLOMA IN EDUCATION (D.Ed.)

In addition to the theoretical and pedagogical orientation the course is predominantly school experience based with due emphasis of information technology and Pre-school Education. The DIETs and TTIs shall work for 220 working days in each year.

The curriculum is competency based, commitment oriented and performance related. In the first year course, trainee shall be exposed to content course upto class VII. All the subjects taught at the elementary school level shall become methodology subjects.

The subjects are as follows:

- Methods of Teaching Mother Tongue—Telugu/Urdu
- Methods of Teaching English
- Methods of Teaching Mathematics
- Methods of Teaching General Sciences
- Methods of Teaching Social Studies

These five methodology subjects which help in shaping the strategies in teaching and learning process at school level shall be called as **"strategy oriented subjects"**, or **"strategies"**.

THEORY

In the recent years, due to demands such as planning and management issues of primary education, community participation, pre-school education Early Child Education (ECE), potential quest for education as a process of human enlightenment and empowerment for achieving better and higher quality of life of constitutional commitment, Universalisation of Elementary Education (UEE) with an explicit aim of providing quality education for all, the scope of elementary education has widened. These concerns necessitated to include in the two year curriculum all components which relate to the challenges of education like achieving UEE, teacher empowerment, values in education, environmental concerns and early childhood education as a basic paper under the title: "Perspectives in Elementary Education".

In order to cater to the socio-cultural changes that are taking place in Indian society and in order to help the prospective teacher to develop insight into the bahaviour of the learner, subjects like (i) Education in emerging India and (ii) Educational Psychology are included. As these teacher trainees ought to work in wide variety of rural schools in multigrade situations where large number of first generation learners seeks admission, quality concerns of primary education drag the attention of educational planners and administrators.

In this context the functions of the teacher have become critical and challenging. Hence, a paper on "Elementary Education, Planning and Management and Teacher functions" is introduced. As all these subjects form the basics in empowering the prospective teacher, they form part "A" of Theory under the heading "Basic oriented subjects" or "Basics".

The subjects are as follows:

- Education in Emerging Indian Society
- Education Psychology, Measurement and Evaluation
- Elementary Education, Planning, Management and Teacher functions.
- Perspectives in Pre-Primary and Primary Education
- Capacity Building and Computer Education
- Computer Education
- Health and Physical Education
- Work Experience and Art Education

PRACTICUM

The two year professional presentation of teacher needs a theoretical background vis-à-vis intensive exposure to a wide variety of School Experience Programme (SEP). Therefore the component 'practicum' is organised in two units.

School Experience Programme is organised during the first year for 4 weeks in different intervals where the prospective teacher trainees shall have exposure to all types of schools such as pre-primary, primary, upper primary, NFE/alternative schools and this exposure shall be under the supervision of DIET faculty. During the second year, trainees shall be under internship for 80 working days in different intervals of which 40 days of attachment to a primary school; 15 days to a pre-primary/Early Child Education; 15 days to Upper Primary School; and for the rest of the days in alternative systems of education. During this period the teacher trainee shall work intensively with all the school activities related to child development.

RECORDS

In addition to School Experience Programme which is regarded as the only activity programme through which the teacher trainee acquires professional competency, the teacher trainee shall maintain and submit the following records which shall be evaluated internally by the DIET faculty and shall be assessed by an external board as nominated by Director, SCERT.

The following records are prescribed:

(a) Child Study

(b) Project work (related to Child/School/Community Development)

(c) Organisation and Participation in Physical Education and Health Education activities

(d) Computer Education

(e) Achievement test records for strategic subject

(f) Activity packs for strategic subjects

(g) Working with Community (Janma Bhoomi)

(h) Practical Record of Educational Psychology

(i) Work Experience (SUPW)

(j) Art Education

(k) School Observation Record

(l) Mandatory Literacy Activities of literating 2 adults and enrolling two dropouts/unenrolled children.

Participation of trainees in all the practical activities including participation in community activity namely literate the two illiterates are mandatory. Reports of each item should invariably be submitted and evaluated. Non-fulfillment of participation of the trainees shall amount to declaring the candidate ineligible to appear for theory examination. DIET faculty shall provide necessary guidance to all the trainees to take up projects, work experience activities, working with community and preparation of practical activities related to strategic subjects. Faculty shall guide the trainees to attain mastery over 12. Identified practical areas in the form of the records specified above.

THE PRESENT STUDY

Pre-service training for the teachers is not an end in it self. Its target is the effectiveness and the quality. The character of the school programmes should be reflected in the pre-service teacher education especially in its curriculum.

In the curriculum, equal priority is given to both theory (1000 marks i.e., 300 marks for internal assessment and 700 marks for external assessment) and practicals (1000 marks i.e., 500 marks for teaching practice and 500 marks for practicum and field work records). Due to these modifications in the DIET curriculum the investigator is interested to take up the present study in depth.

The present study entitled, *"Achievement of Primary School Pre-Service Teachers"* is a survey type research. The investigator collected the necessary information and made a statistical analysis and has drawn inferences so that the educational training can be modified to estimate the short coming to strengthen the system.

3

REVIEW OF RELATED LITERATURE

Academic achievement refers to the achievement of something that requires accurate repetitions acquired by the students. One can study this problem by analysing a number of possible related factors to see their effect upon the Achievement. Review of literature gives us the relevant material published in the problem area under study. The studies conducted during the last few decades in the field of Achievement that are more relevant and pertinent to the present investigation are discussed in this chapter.

NEED TO KNOW ABOUT RELATED LITERATURE

According to Best (1959), "Practically all human knowledge can be found in books and libraries. Unlike other animals that must start a new with each generation, man builds upon the accumulated and recorded knowledge of the past".

In the field of education, as in other fields too, the research worker needs to acquire up-to-date information about what has been thought and done in the particular area from which he intends to select a problem for research. But it is formed that generally the extent of important, up-to-date information regarding educational research and ideas possessed by educational workers, is very limited (Sukhia, 1980).

Availability of adequate information about educational thought and research doesn't by itself result in possession of its knowledge by the investigator. The investigator may be very keen to possess up-to-date information regarding his field, and may try hard to be posted up-to-date, and yet fail to get enough information due to the non-existence of sources of such information (Sukhia, 1980).

RELATED LITERATURE ON THE PRESENT STUDY

There are number of studies relating to the Academic Achievement (Scholastic Achievement) done in the past. However, only the literature pertaining to the independent variables used in the present study is referred in the next few paragraphs.

Hugh (1931) showed that the students' grades and study time was correlated and the Pearson 'r' was 0.317. In Wrenn's (1933) first study habits inventory, the items were based on the responses of the high achieving and the low achieving pupils, who were matched with regard to their intelligence and major fields of study. Cuff (1937) used a questionnaire to survey the study habits of grades IV to XII students. Half of the total students (samples) were defective in their achievement due to lack of study habits. Socio-economic status of the family plays an important role in boosting up the educational proficiency of children (Burt 1937, Vane 1960, Jammur 1963, Chopra 1966 and Gurman 1969).

Gordon (1941) found that the validity correlation coefficient between scores on study habits and course grades was higher when students were tested late in the semester than when tested at its beginning. Wrenn and Humber (1941) showed that the study habits are associated with scholastic achievement. Mary Esthar (1945) analyzed the study habits of catholic high school students by employing the Otis advanced examination and the Enrich study habits inventory. Statistically significant differences were reported between the study habits of the most successful and the least successful students and between the bright and the dull students. Carter (1948) administered a new test on 600 IX grade students. The items that discriminated significantly the 100 high achieving and the 100 low achieving pupils were included in the inventory. The test had further validity in fresh sample and it proved to be a valid predictor of grades. A number of studies have clearly established a definite positive relationship between SES and academic achievement (Chopra 1966, Verma 1971, Abraham 1974, Saini 1977 and Ganapathy and Singh 1981). Carter (1950) conducted two study method tests on 800 Educational Psychology students. He compared the study habits score with the composite measures of achievement. The correlation ranged from 0.46 to 0.51.

Burnett (1951) reported that the students taking how to study course increased their cumulative grade point averages. Vedavalli (1953) found that there was no significant difference between degree and non-degree students in respect to their study habits. Carter's (1953) study method test was administered on 130 Educational Psychology students and 129 seniors in a California College preparatory high school. In pre-instance, a correlation with mid-term test score was 0.40 and in the post instance the correlation with the senior year grade averages was 0.60. A survey of study habits and attitudes (1953-67), reports that the reliability of the scales is high although some sub scales give low correlation and that there is difficulty in predicting achievement especially for college or university students. Brown and Holtzman (1955), Patel (1981) and Chauhan and Singh (1982) found a positive relationship between study habits and academic achievement of school going children. Carter (1955) found a moderate linear relationship between study methods and academic scores. Brown and Holtzman (1956) constructed and validated a self-rating questionnaire that measured "A student aptitude and motivation towards studying as well as his study habits". The questionnaire was validated on a fresh sample of 219 men and 176 women. Correlation of 0.50 and 0.52 were obtained for the sample of men and women respectively. Krishnan (1956) showed that the Junior B.A. students had better study habits than Senior B.A. students. Ahmann, Smith and Glack (1958) reported that the raw scores yielded by SSHA failed to correlate significantly with the first semester grade point averages. It made no significant contributions to the prediction of these averages when included in a Battery of tests. Norton (1959) made an investigation on the relationship of study habits and achievement in IX grade general sciences. He found that the achievement in general sciences was not associated with study habits. Diener (1960) obtained the similarities and differences between over achieving and under achieving students and also observed that the two groups differed significantly in respect of their study habits. The over achieving males had better study habits. McCuen (1960) analysed the results and found that the socio-economic class and personality factors are important in determining children achievement.

Jammur (1961) found a correlation of 0.51 between study habits and achievement. Mc Clelland (1961) has found high correlations between academic achievement and need for achievement. Brown and Dubois (1964) found that SSHA scores are moderately correlated with academic performance of the students. Pavithran and Feroze (1965) have done research work on influence of socio-economic factors on the scholastic achievement of tenth students of Pathanamthitta educational district. The results came from the study are:

1. There is no significant relationship between the scholastic achievement of the pupils and the educational status of the families. The relationship between the economic status of the family and the scholastic achievement of pupils is extremely low and almost negligible. There is no conclusive evidence of either favourable or unfavourable influence of economic status of the family on the scholastic achievement of the pupils.
2. Occupational status of parents highly accelerates scholastic achievement in pupils.
3. There is no marked difference between boys and girls in scholastic achievement in pupils. Both are more or less on the same levels of achievement.

There were certain parallel studies which found very little negligible impact of SES on academic achievement in certain specific cases (Rao 1965, Srivastava 1967, Bernstein 1968 Sudamma 1973, Ahuliwalia and Shyam 1975 and Sharma and Bhargava 1980).

Cattell, Sealey and Sweeney (1966) claimed that the High School Personality Questionnaire (HSPQ) was predicting the school achievement of the students. The review of the studies on the relationship between academic achievement and age or sex has been very much limited in the sense that only one study each has been reviewed with respect to the relationship between academic achievement and age or sex. It was found in Srivastava's (1967) study that the relationship between academic achievement and age is insignificant. Spaights (1967) have found that the academic record of students intricately involved in their behaviour with the teacher. But almost all the studies agree that a teacher's own behaviour is the major deciding factor in creating a pattern of behaviour in the class. Richard and Virginia (1967) showed that the degree of knowledge of good study habits predicted academic achievement better than ability measures. Samuel and Rao (1967) conducted a study on a sample of 500 Pre-University College students and found that there is significant correlation between the habit scores and academic achievement of the students. It is clear that the achievement shows positive relationship with the study habits. Ved Prakash Gupta (1968) conducted a study on 100 school students (aged 12 to 16 years) studying 9th class in Patiala (Punjab, India) on intelligence, economic status, sex and academic status. The results found that the students who are higher on economic status and mental ability are significantly better in academic success than those who are lower. It was found that the academic achievement correlated + 0.34 with economic status. Comparing the boys and girls, it was found that there were no significant differences between the two groups in any of the three variables under study, viz., academic achievement, intelligence and economic status. The Co-efficient of correlation between the study habits' score and the scores on achievement in Mathematics when computed came to be + 0.14. It was found to be significant at the 0.05 level of confidence. The poor correlation does not imply that study habits are not important and do not help in achievement. Ford (1970) found that the employment of mothers had no effect on the achievement of children, either in a positive or negative direction. Ramkumar (1969) came out with the finding that sex and academic achievement are significantly related to each other. Aggarwal and Saini (1969) found that poor correlation doesn't however imply that study habits are not important and do not help in achievement. Krishnamurthy and Raja Rao (1969) conducted a study on 300 children in Coimbatore. They observed that there is significant correlation between the study habits and academic achievement of the urban students and also there is highly significant correlation between study habits and academic achievement of sub-urban students. Sten (1970) found that the study skills are an important factor in achievement of degree first year students in Mathematics. Results of Elliott (1972) and Entwisle (1972) showed that the personality variables significant effect in school achievement. Finlayson (1970), Desai (1971), Bhatia (1976-77) and Reddy and Basavanna (1978) were using different measures of achievement, have found it to be positively associated with academic achievement.

Achievement motivation has also been taken as one of the correlates of achievement in many studies (Desai 1971). Richard, Donald and Morley (1971) observed that the feasibility and applicability of combining Psychological conditioning techniques with a study technique in terms of its effect upon the academic performance of "high risk" college students. Florence and Ronald (1971) revealed that in the case of boys, the total SSHA score and attitudes subset predicted reading achievement and in the case of girls, the attitude subset did predict a different criterion mathematics achievement. Reddy (1972) reported that study habits didn't differ from pupils studying in one class to another. Goldfried and D'Zurilla (1973) found that influence of study habits and attitude towards teaching significantly effect academic competence. Goldfried and D'zurilla (1973) found that the correlation between grades and study habits was 0.16. Mc Causland and Stewart (1974) found that females obtain higher grades than males because females study more efficiently and accept academic standards more willingly. Kathleen Orme, (1974) found positive relationship between study habits and scholastic achievement of IX class pupils. Mc Causland and Stewart (1974) showed that academic aptitude, study skills and attitudes contribute to college success. Silverman and Riodens (1974) investigated that there was positive relationship between study habits and first semester grades of college freshman. Girija, Bhadra and Ameerjan (1975) showed that there was no significant difference among the first and final year undergraduate students in their study habits. Girija, Bhadra and Ameerjan (1975) made a study on the relationship between study habits and academic achievement of first and final year students of the undergraduates of University of Agricultural sciences, Bangalore. The two groups differed significantly with regard to their study skills and achievement. Benerjee and Papneja Geetha (1975) found that there is a positive relationship of study habits of college students to their academic achievement. Lynn (1976) showed that the lessons on note taking and study skills are directly related to the achievement. Patel (1976) showed that there is positive correlation between study habits and achievements in school subjects. Patel (1976) found that the study habits had significant relationship with reading ability. Best (1977) found that there is a relationship between study habits and academic achievement. Rangaswamy and Visvesvara (1977) conducted a comparative study of the academic achievement of high school sports men and other students in Coimbotore District and found that there was no significant different between the academic achievement of sportsmen and non-sportsmen in the S.S.L.C. Public Examinations. The girls who participate in sports are significantly better achievers than boys. Sex difference is however not significant in the case of non-sportsmen. No definite pattern of correlation could be noticed between academic achievement and factors like family economic status, education status or occupation status. Roach (1979) conducted a study on 206 boys and 212 girls from 5 urban elementary schools in Jamaica and found that the girls scored significantly higher than the boys did on the Mathematics achievement test. Asha Bhatnagar (1980) observed 600 X class students of Delhi and found a positive relationship between involvements in studies with their academic achievement. Tuli (1980) observed that study habits are correlates of achievement in Mathematics.

Patel (1981) found that there was a positive correlation between the study habits and their educational performance. Tiwari (1982) and Shanmugasundaram (1983) indicated a positive relationship between the study habits and academic achievement. Gupta (1983) have shown that 9th class girls have on the whole, greater achievement motivation and higher academic achievement than 9th class boys. The relationship between achievement motivation and academic achievement is positive and significant.

Skaalvik (1983) conducted a study on 348 children in five different class levels and found that the 4th to the 8th class level low academic achievement was associated with low self-esteem and with strong perceived parental pressure for boys, but not for girls. At the 8th class level low achievement was associated with low perceived value of the school for the girls while there was no such relationship for boys. The results supported the hypothesis that academic achievement has different effects for boys and girls. Singh (1984) found that the study habits of boys and girls differed significantly at different levels of academic achievement. Gadzella Bernadelta and James David (1984) found that effective study skills lead to academic success. Premalathasarma (1984) in a study on achievement of rural girls found that poor study habits were highly associated with under achievement. Watkins, Hattie and Astilla (1984) showed that significant interaction with variables such as sex, self-concept and intelligence have influence on achievement of pupils. Rama Mishra (1985) conducted a study on 200 secondary school teachers of Indore City and found that there is a significant relationship between achievement and their behaviour. Quraishi and Bhat (1986) conducted a study on 200 undergraduate students of M.S. University of Baroda and found that the variables SES and Sex have a significant effect on academic achievement. But there was non-significant relationship between age and academic achievement. Jagannadhan (1986) conducted a study and found that the SES factors viz., father's income, father's education and occupation has got much impact on the academic performance of their wards. Singh (1987) conducted a study on 300 ST students from class X of high and senior secondary schools of Kinnar and Lahaul and Spiti districts. Results showed that Sex and self-concept interaction significantly in relation to study habits of students. Stock (1989) conducted a study on 141 undergraduates and found that study times in the high performance expectation conditions would exceed those in the minimum performance expectation conditions the manipulations didn't affect study time. Praveena (1990) conducted a study on 737 secondary school students of Rajkot City and found that the student's attitudes towards mathematics have significant influence on the achievement in mathematics. Students of favourable attitude group had higher achievement than that of students of unfavourable attitude group. Kamala (1990) has shown that the attitudes of secondary school students towards science differ significantly in their biology achievement. Anuradha Joshi (1990) found that personality significantly effected the academic achievement. The extroverts were found to benefit significantly more through the developed instructional strategy, as compared to the introverts. Deb and Grewal (1990) revealed that after their investigation on B.Sc. Final year Home Science students, the component of study habits are positively correlated with the academic performance of students (r = 0.39). Students with good study habits do better academically. Therefore parents and teachers should help to promote good study habits in their children right from the beginning. Gary Lee (1990) indicated that there were significant differences between study habits and achievement in the subjects. Ramaswamy (1990) observed that there is significant difference between high and low achievers in study habits among boys and girls.

Carol (1991) evaluated the effectiveness of study process questionnaire (SPQ) in examining conceptual issues in the learning approaches of 374 Australian teacher education students, indicated that internal coherence of the surface strategy sub-scale was unsatisfactory. There was no relationship between surface deep and achieving strategy scores on the SPQ and performance on basic and complex tasks. Patnaik and Basavayya (1991) reported that there was no significant relationship between study habits and achievement in mathematics. Ekins Judith (1992) investigated on study approaches of distance learning students, studying in a second language. He reported that command of English is related to the study approaches and skills and it is likely to lead to academic success and persistence. Ruth Lee (1992) conducted a study on development of a study skill to improve grades in IX and X class students. It is found that development of study skills, increased student achievement. Stella and Purushothaman (1993) showed that there is no significant difference between the study habits of under achieving boys and girls. Adinarayana Reddy and Indira (1993) found that the study habits of the neo-literate were not similar to the literate. On Tse Ka and Watkins (1994) found that the study habits are significantly correlated with the school grades of first year school students in Hong Kong. Aruna (1994) concluded that scholastic achievement of the IX class pupils had significant influence on their study habits. Rawat Leela (1995) showed that there was no significant difference between the study habits of boys and girls and their academic achievement. Fruntera, Lucy and Rosalind (1995) found that the students study behaviour was significantly related to their success. Richardson (1995) examined 227 American university students (Group 1) responses to a shortened version of the approaches to studying inventory with the responses of British students (Group 2). Results indicate that this basic study orientation is interpreted in a manner that is distinctive to each particular cultural context. Verma, Sheikh and Sangita (1996) found that the level of academic motivation and test anxiety had a significant impact on the study habits of adolescent students. Narayana Koteswara (1997) showed that the study habits total score significantly influenced on reading achievement of high school students. Al-Hilawani, Yasser and Aziz (1997) investigated the influence of GPA, academic majors and academic levels on the study skills and habits of 480 female (Average Age 21 years) students from all majors in the faculty of education at the United Arab Emirates University. Results showed that there was no significant difference on study skills and habits due to student's academic levels. Al-Hilawani, Yasser and Aziz (1997) investigated the influence of GPA, academic majors and academic levels on the study skills and habits of 480 female (Average Age 21 years) students of United Arab Emirates University and found that students majoring in special education and educational psychology obtained a significantly high score than did students in the 'other majors'. Mavi and Iswar Patel (1997) conducted a study on tribal students and found that there is a significant positive correlation between academic achievement and personality adjustment. The male and female tribal students do not differ significantly on academic achievement. The tribal and non tribal differ significantly in relation to their academic achievement. Gordan (1998) found that the students having good study habits possessed good achievement. Vanden Hurk (1998) showed that the study habits of medical students were correlated with their academic achievement. Viswanadhan Nair and Bindu (1998) conducted a study on 879 pupils studying 9th standard of the schools of Kerala. The results found that Sex of pupils are associated the phenomenon of discrepant achievement in Mathematics and Social Studies. Ages of pupils are associated with phenomenon of discrepant achievement in Malayalam, Hindi, English and Social Studies. The demographic variables are not significantly associated with discrepant achievement in any of the school subjects. Palaniappan (1999) conducted a study on 50 teachers teaching 4th class in Coimbatore district and found that the achievement of the students improves as results of their teachers attending in-service training programmes. Lindblam-Yalamne (1999) showed that the students individual study orchestrations were related to their success. Nanda (2000) showed that advantaged group of students have greater mean score than the disadvantaged group of students.

Balasubramanian and Sivakumar (2001) conducted a study to find out the academic achievement of primary teacher training students in DIETs and found that there is no significant difference in the academic achievement of male and female primary teacher training students. Gaur, Amrith and Nathawat (2001) conducted a study on 240 school going teenagers. Results disclosed that boys were found to have lesser stress as against to girls. Furthermore adolescents high on intelligence and achievement had also disclosed significantly lesser stress but high level of adjustment than low intelligent and low achievers. Interaction of gender and intelligence as well as intelligence and achievement did influence either stress or adjustment in an expected manner. Archana and Mona Sharma (2002) conducted a study on 26 V grade children in Indore. The result found that the instructional material on thinking skill of classification could positively influence the achievement of students on the criterion test. Selvam and Soundravalli (2002) conducted a study on 300 higher secondary students on Nammakal district and found that academic achievement of higher secondary students had significant relationship with their economical, educational and vocational problems.

The above studies on study habits and academic achievement have shown that they are both relevant variables, which influence the quality and quantity of work output. Academic achievement can be improved by creating good study habits, which students can stimulate towards study. Besides, Academic achievement also depends on the personality factors and demographical variables of the students.

APPRAISAL

It may be seen from the brief review of literature presented in the foregoing pages that a few studies have been carried out in the area of academic achievement. But by and large except on a few variables, the results obtained are not coinciding and hence warranting further exploration. Further, studies on the relative impact of each of the several independent variables that affect academic achievement are rare to find. The precise-product studies in the area of academic achievement are rare to find.

Selection of certain important demographic variables, sociological variables and psychological variables are supported by many other studies, even though, they are not exhaustive for obvious reasons.

Reviews of Literature reveal that an extensive study of the influence of academic achievement is very rare. It is an attempt to see the relationship between the academic achievement and Psycho-Sociological variables. The area under investigation is novel and unexplored one with respect to population of DIET student teachers and their nature of work.

Further the study aims at providing some mathematical models with which it can be possible to predict the academic achievement of the student teachers. The need for research on the area of academic achievement of the DIET student teachers is warranting.

4

PRESENT STUDY AND METHODOLOGY

This chapter deals with the present study, objectives, hypotheses, various procedures implemented in the construction and standardization of data gathering instrument to measure the different variables which are included in the study; the methods adopted in selection of the sample, selection of data and statistical techniques employed.

INTRODUCTION

The present study aims at finding out the relationship between certain Psycho-Sociological factors on one hand and achievement of DIET student teachers on the other hand under the existing conditions of teacher training programme in the District Institutes of Education and Training of Andhra Pradesh. The present study is a "survey type" of research and attempts to find out the relationship between certain Psycho-Sociological factors and Achievement.

The present study is concerned with the "Achievement of DIET Students". It examines the differences in the performance of students residing in three regions i.e. Andhra, Telangana and Rayalaseema; Boys and Girls. It establishes the relationship between the Academic Achievement and other variables namely; Attitude towards teaching, Personality factors, Study habits, Objective achievement test and Socio-Economic conditions of the students studying in DIETs of Andhra Pradesh State.

NEED FOR THE STUDY

Since the DIETs have started offer the two year D.Ed. Course only from 1999, there is a need to identify the factors which influence the achievement of DIET students in order to draw up conclusions and to suggest remedial measures for them at this early stage itself so that the course can be recognized if necessary.

Recently the government of Andhra Pradesh enlarged the scope of the course, increased the duration of the course from one year to two years and designed the syllabus and curriculum for DIET students so as to achieve the objectives of its design as described in Chapter–2. Equal priority was given to Practical (1000 Marks i.e., 500 marks for teaching practice and 500 marks for field work and records) and Theory (1000 Marks i.e., 300 marks for internal and 700 marks for external assessment). With these modifications, the investigator is interested to study whether there is any differences in their academic achievement of DIET students due to this increased field work component and other Psycho-Sociological factors.

The above crucial conditions lead the investigator to make an analysis of the problem based on data collected from DIETS, draw conclusions in the influence of various factors on the scholastic achievement of students and suggest the suitable measures for remedial action.

DEFINITION OF THE TERMS

The definitions of some of the important terms used in this study are:

Academic Achievement

Academic achievement is the accomplishment or proficiency of performance in a given skill or body of knowledge.

Attitude

Attitude is a "personal disposition common to individuals but possessed to different degrees which impels to react to object situations or positions in ways that can be called favourable or unfavourable". Guilford (1954).

Study–Habit

"For all our practical purposes, all activities regularly pursued in relation to school work".

"The evaluation of pupils behaviour in terms of attitudes, appreciation and habits of work is fundamental to a well rounded study of the out comes of the teaching"(NSSE, 1935).

"Study habits include student habits of concentration, note taking, time-budgeting and study methods" (Smith, 1961).

Region

Defined portion of the earth's surface now especially as distinguished by certain natural features, climatic conditions, a special fauna or flora, or the like. A separate part or division of the world or universe, as the air, heaven etc. (Vivian Ridler, 1961).

OBJECTIVES OF THE STUDY

The study is designed:

1. To compare the Academic Achievement of DIET students studying in Rayalaseema, Andhra and Telangana regions, in boys and girls and to examine the significance or otherwise of these differences.
2. To compare the performance in academic achievement with their attitude towards Teaching.
3. Tc compare and contrast the Academic Achievement with personality factors of the DIET students.
4. To compare and contrast the performance in Academic Achievement with their Study Habits.
5. To compare the performance in Academic Achievement with the Objective Achievement test of the DIET students.
6. To establish relationship between Academic Achievement of the students and other variables namely Demographic and Socio-Economic factors.
7. To develop multiple regression equations to predict the academic achievement in Theory, Practicals and in total achievement of the DIET students.

HYPOTHESES OF THE STUDY

In the light of the above objectives, the following major null hypotheses have been set up for the purpose of this study.

1. All the DIET students do not have same academic achievement abilities.
2. Sex does not have any influence on academic achievement (i.e. in theory, practical and total score of the DIET students).
3. Region would not have significant influence on academic achievement.
4. Attitude towards teaching does not have any significant influence on academic achievement.
5. There would not exist any relationship between the personality factors and academic achievement.
6. Study habits of the pupils do not have any impact on academic achievement.
7. There would not be any relationship between objective achievement test score and academic achievement.
8. Demographic and Socio-Economic variables would not have any significant influence on academic achievement.
9. The variable sex and region individually would not have any significant influence on academic achievement
10. None of the 69 independent variable in this study turns out to be significant predicator of academic achievement of the DIET students.

VARIABLES INCLUDED IN THE STUDY

The list of variables is given below:

Dependent Variables

(a) Total achievement.

(b) Achievement in Theory.

(c) Achievement in Practicals.

Independent Variables

1. Teacher Attitude Inventory (TAI)
   - (a) Attitude towards profession.
   - (b) Attitude towards training
     - (i) Need for content
     - (ii) High conceptual level
     - (iii) Low conceptual level
     - (iv) High social approach
     - (v) High intrinsic motivation
     - (vi) Acceptance of values
     - (vii) Preference and visual and auditory presentation
     - (viii) Attitude during practice teaching
     - (ix) Classroom practice
2. Study Habits Inventory (SHI)

   Home environment

   Reading, listening and note taking techniques
   Planning of work and subject

   Habits of concentration

   Preparation for examination

   Social relationship in study

   Audio-Visual programmes

   General habits and attitude to work

   College environment
3. 16 Personality Factors (16PF)
4. Objective Achievement test (200 Multiple-choice questions)
5. Demographic and Socio-Economic variables

TOOLS USED

For the purpose of gathering data, the following tolls are employed in the present investigation:

1. Teachers Attitude Inventory (TAI)
2. Study Habits Inventory (SHI)
3. Objective Achievement Test (OAT)
4. 16 Personality Factor Questionnaire (16 PF) of Cattell's Form-C of 1969 and
5. Demographic and Socio-Economic Status Scale (DSES).

DESCRIPTION OF THE TOOLS

An attitude is an affect, a dynamic trait, a behaviour pattern, an anticipatory set or tendency, predisposition, conditioned response, implicit response, disposition, and mental and neural state of readiness. Many of the aforesaid terms described the nature of attitude as a mental state of readiness or feeling of an individual towards a certain object.

G.W. Allport (1949) defines attitude as "a mental and neural state of readiness organized through experience exerting a directive or dynamic influence upon the individual's response to all objects and situations".

Cattell (1950) defined it as "a dynamic trait commonly arising from some deeper sentiment or innate drive which it seeks to satisfy. It is a readiness to implement a certain course of action in regard to some object".

Guilford (1954) defined attitude as a "personal disposition common to individuals, but possessed to different degrees, which implies them to react to objects, situations or propositions in ways that can be called favourable or unfavourable".

Finally it may be said that an attitude is a mental set or state of readiness, which an individual holds in relation to his society towards a psycho-social object. Thus the study of attitude is the study of relation or correspondence of mental and social feelings of individuals in a society, and the object towards which the feeling is held is a psycho-social object.

Thus, if the student is asked whether he likes or dislikes a certain object or course of action, his endorsement measures the strength of the attitude vector. The direction of the attitude vector is fixed to some extent by the description of course of action of which the person is for or against.

Moreover, two individuals having equal favourable attitude towards an object may not act in the same way because they may arrive at the same level of attitude by entirely different routes and their factual association with the psychological object may also differ.

CONSTRUCTION OF TEACHER ATTITUDE INVENTORY (TAI)

A Teacher Attitude Inventory (TAI) is constructed to measure the attitude of the student teachers. To become a teacher in future it is better to have a favourable attitude towards the teaching profession and teacher training. Teacher training programme is that kind of an experience which should give sufficient and suitable theoretical and practical experiences to the student teacher for his becoming a teacher. In this connection, it may be stated that instead of admitting a candidate with unfavourable attitude or neutral attitude towards profession and training, it is better to take a candidate with a favourable attitude. Then, the training gives better results than in the former case.

The Teacher Attitude Inventory is divided into two sub-sections to measure the attitudes of DIET student teachers i.e. attitudes towards profession and attitudes towards training.

ATTITUDE TOWARDS PROFESSION

The first step of an attitude scale construction is 'collection of items'. For the purpose of attitude sub-scale towards profession, a pool of statements each expressing one opinion are prepared in Telugu the mother tongue of the students, after a careful study of the relevant literature and in consultation with the experts in the field. Observing the criteria laid down by different authors like Likert (1932), Edwards and Kilpatricks (1948) and Guildford (1954), the statement is refined and prepared. The list of statements is supplemented by informal interviews with teachers and student teachers. At this stage there were nearly 40 items for this scale.

These statements are typed and presented to a panel of experts for methodological criticism. They are requested: (i) to classify the statements expressing favourable attitude and unfavourable attitude; (ii) to delete redundant statements; (iii) to point out ambiguous words or items; and (iv) to suggest any modifications in the statements that they deemed necessary.

In the light of the criticism and comments of these experts, 25 items are retained and some of the terms were modified and rephrased. After editing the items carefully, the draft version of the attitude scale on profession is prepared. The response categories are Strongly Agree (SA), Agree (A), Doubtful (D), Disagree (DA) and Strongly Disagree (SDA). In this draft attitude scale the positive items are 14 in number and negative items are 11 in number.

ATTITUDE TOWARDS TRAINING

The second part of the attitude inventory is the attitude of student teachers towards training. While preparing the statements in the sub scale the same procedure was followed as above.

Today, in our training programmes the content of the course is fixed mostly with an idealistic view and some practical difficulties regarding the suitability of the training to the individual as a preparation for future teaching situations arise. This can be said as a mismatch and it may produce a negative effect upon training as well as teaching.

Secondly, the forms of training intervention should be modulated according to the trainee's accessibility characteristics such as cognitive orientation, motivational orientation, value orientation, sensory orientation and teaching orientation.

The model based attitude scale is constructed to measure the attitude of the student teachers towards training. The satisfaction or dissatisfaction, less stress or more stress in an area may be known through the favourable or unfavourable attitude of the individual in that particular area and thus predicting his high and low performance on the criterion.

While selecting the items to the attitude scale the following areas are taken into consideration:

1. Need for content—Skill Level;
2. High and Low conceptual level—Cognitive orientation;
3. High social approval and High intrinsic motivation-Motivation orientation;
4. Attitude of acceptance of values—Value orientation;
5. Preference for visual and auditory presentation and feedback—Sensory orientation;
6. Attitude towards practice teaching; and
7. Class room practice—Teaching orientation

This draft attitude scale contain 101 items viz., the 25 items in the first sub scale (14 are Positive and 11 are Negative), the 76 items in the second sub scale (38 positive and 38 negative).

A separate answer sheet for the entire 101 items is also prepared to record the responses of the DIET students.

PILOT STUDY

The pilot study was conducted after obtaining permission from the concerned Heads of the Institutions during the academic year 1999-2000. The Pilot study was conducted on 200 DIET students with a stratified random sample of 3 DIETs in 3 regions, which represent the three geographical regions viz., Andhra (Guntur), Telangana (Mahaboob Nagar) and Rayalaseema (Kurnool) within the state of A.P.

While administering the inventory, the students are instructed and motivated not to leave any item without answering and not to go for the doubtful category (D) as far as possible. The purpose of the test is explained and sufficient time was given to them and they are assured that their responses would be kept confidential.

SCORING

For the purpose of scoring numerical values were assigned to each of the five categories of responses—Strongly Agree (SA),

Agree (A), Doubtful (D), Disagree (DA) and Strongly Disagree (SDA). The numerical values for positive and negative items are shown in Table 4.1.

Table 4.1: Numerical Values (Weights) for Positive and Negative items to Different Alternatives

Nature of the Statement	*SA*	*A*	*D*	*DA*	*SDA*
Favourable or Positive (+)	5	4	3	2	1
Unfavourable or Negative (-)	1	2	3	4	5

The score of an individual on each sub scale is computed by summing up the weights of responses of the individual for each item.

SELECTION OF THE ITEMS

The selection of the items was based on the results of item analysis, which provides an index of item difficulty. Since, the discrimination of each item was to be determined; the student teachers were classified into top (high) group and bottom (low) group.

First the total answer scripts (200) were arranged in an ascending order on the basis of the total score obtained by the student teachers. The top 27 per cent of the papers (i.e., 54 papers) were placed in the top group and the bottom 27 per cent of the papers (i.e., 54 papers) were placed in the bottom group. The rest were excluded from the analysis. These two groups provide criterion groups to evaluate the individual items.

The calculation of 't' value for the item number 97 of the pilot study inventory is shown in Table 4.2.

Table 4.2: The Calculation of 't' Value for Evaluating the Difference in the Mean Response to the Item No. 97 of the Pilot Study of Teacher Attitude Inventory for the Top and Bottom Groups

Response Categories	*Top Group*				*Bottom Group*			
	x	*f*	*f(x)*	*fx*²	*x*	*f*	*f(x)*	*Fx*²
Strongly Agree	5	30	150	750	5	3	15	75
Agree	4	12	48	192	4	11	44	176
Doubtful	3	1	3	9	3	6	18	54
Disagree	2	9	18	36	2	28	56	112
Strongly Disagree	1	2	2	2	1	6	6	6
Sum		54	221	989		54	139	423

$$\bar{x}_H = \frac{\Sigma fx}{\Sigma f} = \frac{221}{54} = 4.09 \qquad \bar{x}_L = \frac{\Sigma fx}{\Sigma f} = \frac{139}{54} = 2.57$$

$$\Sigma(x_H - \bar{x}_H)^2 = \Sigma fx^2 - \frac{(\Sigma fx)^2}{\Sigma f} \qquad \Sigma(x_L - \bar{x}_L)^2 = \Sigma fx^2 - \frac{(\Sigma fx)^2}{\Sigma f}$$

$$= 989 - \frac{(221)^2}{54} = 84.53 \qquad = 423 - \frac{(139)^2}{54} = 65.20$$

$$t = \frac{(\bar{x}_H - \bar{x}_L)}{\sqrt{\dfrac{\Sigma(x_H - \bar{x}_H)^2 + \Sigma(x_L - \bar{x}_L)^2}{n(n-1)}}} \qquad t = \frac{(4.09 - 2.57)}{\sqrt{\dfrac{(84.53 + 65.20)}{54 \times 53}}} = 6.64$$

For the calculation of the 't' values the procedure suggested by Edwards (1957) was followed.

The 't' values of the items of the pilot study are presented in Table 4.3.

Table 4.3: The 't' Values for All the Items of Teacher Attitude Inventory of the Pilot Study

Item No.	*'t' Value*	*Remarks*
1	2	3
1.	1.06	Detained
2.	5.0	Retained
3.	2.14	Retained
4.	3.78	Retained
5.	4.72	Retained
6.	2.49	Retained
7.	3.42	Retained
8.	0.28	Detained
9.	4.95	Retained
10.	2.77	Retained
11.	3.36	Retained
12.	2.13	Retained
13.	4.88	Retained
14.	0.76	Detained
15.	3.96	Retained
16.	3.33	Retained
17.	2.36	Retained
18.	3.89	Retained
19.	-0.26	Detained
20.	3.15	Retained
21.	2.29	Retained
22.	3.78	Retained
23.	0.94	Detained
24.	2.9	Retained
25.	-1.6	Detained
26.	4.36	Retained
27.	6.89	Retained
28.	5.58	Retained
29.	2.03	Retained

(Contd...)

1	*2*	*3*
30.	-5.89	Detained
31.	3.99	Retained
32.	3.32	Retained
33.	4.54	Retained
34.	7.83	Retained
35.	2.4	Retained
36.	3.22	Retained
37.	2.31	Retained
38.	6.47	Retained
39.	2.49	Retained
40.	1.44	Detained
41.	3.99	Retained
42.	2.96	Retained
43.	2.5	Retained
44.	4.72	Retained
45.	2.32	Retained
46.	5.29	Retained
47.	3.67	Retained
48.	4.15	Retained
49.	3.71	Retained
50.	3.99	Retained
51.	5.44	Retained
52.	1.35	Detained
53.	3.09	Retained
54.	4.12	Retained
55.	2.87	Retained
56.	2.18	Retained
57.	0.45	Detained
58.	2.03	Retained
59.	3.01	Retained
60.	2.47	Retained
61.	12.99	Retained

(Contd...)

1	2	3
62.	-3.57	Detained
63.	2.45	Retained
64.	3.44	Retained
65.	3.97	Retained
66.	4.4	Retained
67.	3.79	Retained
68.	2.45	Retained
69.	2.17	Retained
70.	3.74	Retained
71.	2.82	Retained
72.	4.78	Retained
73.	4.99	Retained
74.	3.43	Retained
75.	2.07	Retained
76.	2.51	Retained
77.	5.02	Retained
78.	2.23	Retained
79.	2.34	Retained
80.	2.19	Retained
81.	0.37	Detained
82.	3.08	Retained
83.	0.53	Detained
84.	0.32	Detained
85.	0.59	Detained
86.	2.76	Retained
87.	4.68	Retained
88.	0.1	Detained
89.	2.78	Retained
90.	5.14	Retained
91.	2.29	Retained
92.	3.61	Retained
93.	3.03	Retained

(Contd...)

1	2	3
94.	4.25	Retained
95.	0.98	Detained
96.	5.41	Retained
97.	6.64	Retained
98.	3.19	Retained
99.	8.24	Retained
100.	3.88	Retained
101.	-0.53	Detained

Note: 't' Value less than 1.98 (0.05 level of significance) are deleted.

The items with 't' values less than 1.98 (0.05 level of significance) were deleted. In this investigation 18 items were deleted and 83 items were retained for the final study.

Out of 83 items in the final study, there are 52 positive items. The item numbers 1, 2, 3, 4, 10, 11, 12, 16, 18, 19, 20, 21, 22, 23, 26, 27, 28, 30, 33, 35, 36, 37, 9, 42, 44, 50, 54, 55, 56, 58, 61, 63, 64, 65, 67, 71, 73, 74, 75, 77, 79, 80, 81, 85, 86, 88, 89, 90, 91, 95, 100 and 101 are positive. The remaining items (49 items) are negative.

A copy of English version of Teacher Attitude inventory (final study) is given in Appendix-A.

RELIABILITY OF THE TEACHER ATTITUDE INVENTORY (TAI)

An attitude scale has been developed to measure the attitude of a specific group of individuals representing a specific category. In order to find out effectiveness of the attitude scale developed, its test-retest reliability has been examined by obtaining scores for the tool with an interval of three weeks between the first and the second administration of the scale to the same set of teacher trainees. The correlation co-efficient between the two sets of scores is 0.845, which is significant at 0.01 level. Hence the scale may be considered as having high reliability.

VALIDITY OF THE SCALE

Validity is another criteria considered to estimate the appropriateness of any tool developed to examine a particular aspect of an individual's attitude. The attitude scale of the present study, developed on the lines described above, indicates satisfying content validity, item validity and intrinsic validity. The details relating to them are described below.

(i) Content Validity

Content validity refers to the establishment and evaluation of the significance of the test items individually and as a whole. Every item should be a sampling of that aspect which the test purports to measure. In addition, items should collectively constitute a representative sample of the variable that is measured.

The items have been collected from different sources viz., review of literature, principals of colleges, lecturers, senior lecturers, student teachers and university teachers. In addition, it has also been supplemented by interviewing selected learners and experts to make sure that all the possible items are covered. Thus, it can be reasonably assumed that the attitude scale developed possesses satisfactory content validity.

(ii) Item Validity

Item validity stresses the number of discriminations of the desired sort that the item is capable of making. It stresses the extent to which the item predicts segregation of respondents into those with high versus those with low criterion scores. The discriminative power of each item of the present scale has been established as explained earlier. Thus the items chosen for the scale have been found to be satisfactorily valid.

(iii) Criterion Validity

On the basis of the responses obtained for the 97th item in the pilot form the entire group of 200 subjects has been divided into two groups (Top and Bottom groups). The mean scores obtained by these two groups and the respective standard deviations have been calculated. Critical ratio ('t'-test) has been employed to see whether the two groups differ significantly from each other. The obtained critical ratio value 6.64 is far greater than the table value at 0.05 level of probability for 198 df (degrees of freedom). Similarly 't' values were computed for all the items and 't' values of those items less than the table value at 0.05 level were deleted. Thus, the instrument to measure the attitude of teacher trainees has Criterion Validity.

(iv) Intrinsic Validity

According to Guilford (1954), intrinsic validity indicates the degree to which the test measures what it purports to measure. In other words, this means verification of how well the obtained scores measure the test true score component. Intrinsic validity of a test is expressed in terms of square root of its reliability value. Thus the intrinsic validity of the attitude scale is $\sqrt{0.845}$ 0.919 and it can be assumed as a highly satisfactory intrinsic validity.

CONSTRUCTION OF THE STUDY HABITS INVENTORY (SHI)

The first study habits inventory has constructed by Wrenn (SHI) in 1933 with a view to survey this feature among students. Mary Esther St. did an analysis of study habits in 1945. Jammur's (1958) study habits inventory aims at measuring students' habits of concentration, note taking, time budgeting and social relationship. Patel (1976) also constructed and standardized the study habits inventory with 45 statements, and these statements are classified into seven areas.

They are:

1. Their home environment and planning of work
2. Their planning of subject
3. Their habit of concentration
4. Their preparation for examination
5. Their reading and note taking habit
6. Their school environment
7. Their general habits and attitude towards work

Besides seven areas of Patel's inventory, the investigator has changed with some added two more areas in the constructed inventory and the items are arranged as follows. Finally the two items were added on the basis of theoretical findings concerning conditions of efficient learning. The inventory was set with nine sub areas:

1. Home environment
2. Reading, Listening and note taking techniques
3. Planning of work and subject
4. Habits of concentration
5. Preparation for examination
6. Social relationship in study
7. Audio-visual programmes
8. General habits and attitude towards work
9. College environment

Thus, on the basis of the sources mentioned above, a list of 150 items was prepared. These items were given to some experts. On the views of the experts 105 items were retained and 45 items were deleted. The experts had checked the vocabulary used in the items. All the items retained were suitable to the study practices of DIET students. Each item of the inventory was arranged on a uni polar 5-point scale with responses–Always, Often, Sometime, Seldom and Never. A separate answer sheet for the entire 105 items is also prepared to record the responses of the DIET students.

It was translated into Telugu version, the regional language of the subjects on whom it had to be used. Five judges who were well versed with psychological testing checked the translation. Terms, which were ambiguous, were discussed and resolved.

PILOT STUDY

The Telugu version of the inventory was administered on a representative sample of 200. The Pilot study was conducted on 200 DIET students with a stratified random sample of 3 DIETs in 3 regions, which represent the three geographical regions viz., Andhra (Guntur), Telangana (Mahaboob Nagar) and Rayalaseema (Kurnool).

While administering the inventory, they are instructed and motivated not to leave any item without answering. The purpose of the test is explained and sufficient time was given to them and they are assured that their responses would be kept under confidential.

SCORING

For the purpose of scoring, numerical values were assigned to each of the five categories of responses—Always, Often, Sometime, Seldom and Never. The numerical values for positive and negative items are shown in Table 4.4. The score of an individual is computed by summing up the weights of each item responses of the individual.

Table 4.4: Numerical Values for Different Alternatives of the Positive and Negative Items

Nature of the Statement	*Alternatives*				
	Always	*Often*	*Sometime*	*Seldom*	*Never*
Positive (+)	5	4	3	2	1
Negative (-)	1	2	3	4	5

The total score of the each student on study habits inventory was indicated on the top of the answer sheet.

SELECTION OF THE ITEMS

First the total answer scripts (200) were arranged in an ascending order on the basis of the total score obtained by the pupils. The top 27 per cent of the papers (i.e., 54 papers) were placed in the Top group and the bottom 27 per cent of the papers (i.e., 54 papers) were placed in the Bottom group. The rest were excluded from the analysis. These two groups provide criterion groups to evaluate the individual items. For the calculation of the 't' values the procedure suggested by Edwards (1957) was followed. The 't' values of the items of the Pilot Study are presented in Table 4.5.

Table 4.5: The 't' Values for All the Items of the Pilot Study of Study Habits Inventory

Item No.	*'t' Value*	*Remarks*
1	2	3
1.	2.72	Retained
2.	6.22	Retained
3.	2.64	Retained
4.	6.09	Retained
5.	2.71	Retained
6.	1.29	Detained
7.	6.48	Retained
8.	9.12	Detained
9.	3.61	Detained
10.	3.48	Retained
11.	1.10	Detained
12.	3.88	Retained
13.	3.40	Retained
14.	3.23	Retained
15.	5.1	Retained
16.	5.98	Retained
17.	3.44	Retained
18.	5.51	Retained
19.	2.06	Retained
20.	5.08	Retained
21.	-0.20	Detained
22.	4.24	Retained
23.	3.04	Retained
24.	2.12	Retained
25.	3.64	Retained
26.	5.74	Retained
27.	2.05	Retained
28.	6.98	Retained
29.	9.16	Retained
30.	5.59	Retained
31.	7.07	Retained

(Contd...)

1	2	3
32.	3.33	Retained
33.	4.75	Retained
34.	4.09	Retained
35.	4.43	Retained
36.	2.02	Retained
37.	4.98	Retained
38.	3.18	Retained
39.	4.19	Retained
40.	3.71	Retained
41.	7.46	Retained
42.	3.82	Retained
43.	12.73	Retained
44.	1.52	Detained
45.	4.16	Retained
46.	5.34	Retained
47.	2.49	Retained
48.	3.97	Retained
49.	2.49	Retained
50.	6.04	Retained
51.	6.44	Retained
52.	6.47	Retained
53.	1.52	Detained
54.	5.34	Retained
55.	14.14	Retained
56.	4.29	Retained
57.	2.95	Retained
58.	4.72	Retained
59.	5.85	Retained
60.	2.25	Retained
61.	2.23	Retained
62.	8.89	Retained
63.	1.23	Detained
64.	4.92	Retained
65.	4.48	Retained
66.	3.93	Retained
67.	4.88	Retained
68.	2.81	Retained
69.	2.81	Retained

(Contd...)

1	2	3
70.	1.18	Detained
71.	6.27	Retained
72.	4.02	Retained
73.	4.58	Retained
74.	5.27	Retained
75.	8.37	Retained
76.	4.28	Retained
77.	5.21	Retained
78.	6.21	Retained
79.	5.58	Retained
80.	1.44	Detained
81.	2.73	Retained
82.	3.53	Retained
83.	2.75	Retained
84.	4.57	Retained
85.	2.84	Retained
86.	2.57	Retained
87.	4.18	Retained
88.	3.99	Retained
89.	3.71	Retained
90.	1.43	Detained
91.	3.55	Retained
92.	3.13	Retained
93.	5.92	Retained
94.	1.21	Detained
95.	4.24	Retained
96.	3.82	Retained
97.	5.62	Retained
98.	4.77	Retained
99.	4.28	Retained
100.	6.34	Retained
101.	3.18	Retained
102.	3.29	Retained
103.	6.96	Retained
104.	4.95	Retained
105.	5.11	Retained

Note: 't' Value less than 1.98 (0.05 level of significance) is deleted.

The items with 't' values less than 1.98 (0.05 level of significance) were deleted. In this investigation 10 items were deleted and 95 items were retained for the final study. Among 95 items in the Study Habits Inventory, items 1 to 13 come under the study habits area 'Home environment'; items 14 to 22 come under 'Reading, listening and note taking technique'; items 23 to 38 come under 'Planning of work and subject'; items 39 to 52 come under 'Habits of concentration'; items 53 to 65 come under 'Preparation for examinations'; items 66 to 72 come under 'Social relationship in study'; items 73 to 80 come under 'Audio-Visual programmes'; items 81 to 87 come under 'General habits and attitude of work' and the items 88 to 95 come under 'College environment'.

Out of 95 items in the final study, there are 52 positive items and 43 items are negative.

A copy of English version of study habits inventory (Final Study) is given in Appendix-B.

The main aim of the Pilot Study was to establish the validity and reliability of the inventory prepared.

RELIABILITY

Next to validity, reliability is the most indispensable characteristic of any measuring instrument. A test is reliable if it measures efficiently what it proposes to measure (or) what it does measure. It refers to the consistency of scores obtained by the same individuals at different occasions (or) with different sets of equivalent items.

A tool is said to be reliable if it reveals similar results in various situations. The test-retest and parallel form methods of estimating reliability may be common and legitimate for both power and speed tests. In the power test, each pupil has enough time to write what he knows. The Split-Half method is not proper for speed test in which he doesn't have time to respond to some questions for which he knows the correct answer. Speed test usually yields spuriously high reliability co-efficient when split-half and internal consistency methods are employed (Stanley, 1958).

Split-Half Reliability

It is some time called co-efficient of equivalence. The test is split into two equivalent halves usually by pooling the odd numbered items for one half where as, the even numbered items are forming the second half of the test. This usually makes the two scores obtained from a single test reasonably equivalent. By applying the Spearman–Brown prophecy formula the calculated correlation co-efficient for the half test is 0.887. The correlation co-efficient for the full test is also calculated and it is equal to 0.942. It shows that the reliability of the instrument is very high.

VALIDITY OF THE INVENTORY

The definition suggest that to determine how valid the test is, one must compare the reality of what it does measure with some ideal construction what it ought to measure. The validity of the test is an estimate of the correlation between the raw test scores and true criterion scores. Although a test is developed to serve a defined purpose, it is often used for other purposes also. For example, a test of intelligence developed to measure the mental ability of children can serve other useful purposes; predict school performance, serve as a basis of classification in vocational selection, identify study habits and learning difficulties, etc.

Content Validity

This form of validity is estimated by evaluating the relevance of the test items, individually and as a whole. Validity of content should not depend upon the subjective judgment of only one specialist. In the construction of the inventory, therefore, several specialists, of related literature and empirical findings and actual subject matter based on the selection of items upon careful analysis. Thus, content validation rested first upon the expert analysis of the materials to be sampled and second upon the use of available statistical procedures to refine the original selection of items. Thus, it can be reasonably assumed that the SHI has content validity.

Intrinsic Validity

Guilford (1954) defined intrinsic validity as "the degree to which a test measures what it measures". This can also be stated in terms of how well the obtained scores measure the test true scores component. The square root of reliability gives this validity. Hence, the intrinsic validity of the SHI is $\sqrt{0.889} = 0.943$.

Face Validity

If a common thread of study habits runs through all the items of the test, the resultant test has 'face validity'. All the items in the SHI have a common thread for measuring study habits. So there is face validity in SHI.

The inventory was constructed on the lines of their characteristics and their study behaviour.

CONSTRUCTION OF OBJECTIVE ACHIEVEMENT TEST

An achievement test is essentially a tool or device of measurement that helps in ascertaining quantity and quality of learning at the end in a subject of study or group of subjects after a period of instructions by measuring the present ability of the individual concerned. In the College situation, an achievement test is used as a tool for measuring the nature and extent of students learning in a particular subject or a group of subjects.

Achievement is defined as the specified level of attainment of proficiency in academic work designed by test scores. Both physical maturation and mental readiness facilitate academic achievement. Other things being equal, more intelligent the student, the greater will be his achievement in College (Kennedy, 1975).

There are many achievement tests to study the achievement of the DIET students. But the investigator thought of conducting an objective achievement test on their curriculum before going to take the annual examination. For this purpose the investigator prepared 200 multiple choice questions based on their first year general subjects.

While administering the Test, they are instructed and motivated not to leave any item without answering. The purpose of the test is explained and sufficient time was given to them. A separate answer sheet for the entire 200 items is prepared to record the responses of the DIET students.

SCORING

The achievement test had awarded one mark for every correct answer. The score of an individual on each sub-scale is computed by summing up the weight of each item responses of the individual.

ITEM ANALYSIS

The major objective of item analysis is to obtain objective information concerning the items written for the test. This information is valuable for several reasons. It provides the opportunity to check-up on the test writer's subjective judgments in selecting the items to compose the test. It enables the investigator to know-how tests read to items of the test. Item analysis is useful to find the difficulty level and discrimination power and ultimately for the selection of the best items to compose the final test form.

In the preceding sections, the investigator has considered reliability and validity of test scores as being two aspects of a common attribute—namely, test efficiency, the adequacy of the test. These aspects depend upon the care with which the items of the test have been chosen. There are many approaches to the study of item analysis desired in textbooks on test construction. The researcher is concerned here, therefore, only with those features of item analysis, which are primarily dependent upon statistical method. Item analysis will be treated under three heads: (1) Item selection; (2) Item difficulty; and (3) Item validity.

After preparing the test items, the investigator must make some judgments regarding the difficulty level, discrimination power and content validity of the items. Some quantitative evidence to support the difficulty and discrimination indices of test-items must be obtained. Item analysis is the process of examining the response to each item. Specifically, what one looks for is the difficulty and discriminating ability of the item as well as the effectiveness of each alternative.

Item Difficulty Index

The difficulty values of the items were calculated using the formula.

D = R X 100/T

where D = Item difficulty

R = Number of students who answered item correctly

T = Total number of students who tried the item 200.

Preparing Data for Use of Chart

The test papers were divided into three groups: high, middle and low groups following the procedure suggested by Kelley (1939).

Kelley (1939) showed that the Product–Moment correlation between a test item score and the total score on the test could be estimated by using only the tails of the distribution and also showed that the most efficient division to use was the top and bottom 27 per cent tails. The answer scripts were arranged from the highest score to the lowest score. Following Kelley's suggestion, the best 27 percent of the answer scripts were kept in one group. This was the Top group. The poorest 27 per cent of the answer scripts were kept on the other group. This was the Bottom group. The middle group consisting of 46 per cent of the papers was kept aside since the two extreme groups, high and low, were needed for item analysis.

"Item validity and the validity index chart showing difficulty and discrimination indices for item analysis" (Garrett, 1958) was used to find the difficulty and discrimination indices.

Item Selection

The choice of an item depends, in the first instance, upon the judgement of competent persons as to its suitability for the purposes of the test. This is the 'Content validity'. Certain types of items have proved to be generally useful in intelligence examination. The validity of the items in most tests of educational achievement depends, as a first step, upon the consensus of teachers and educators as to the adequacy of the material included. Courses of study, grade requirements, and curricula from various parts of the country are carefully selected over by test makers in order to determine what content should be included in the various subject fields. In its preliminary form, the educational achievement test represents items carefully selected from all sources of information judged to be suitable.

The final selection of the items was made on the basis of: (1) Item discrimination and (2) Item difficulty.

Item Discrimination

This was the main technique used in eliminating the weak and defective items. The question arises as to what should be the minimum internal consistency discrimination index of an item for its being selected in the final form of the test. According to Garrett (1958) "as a general rule, items with validity indices of 0.2 or more are regarded as satisfactory". But according to Lindquist (1959) in the case of a predictor test, if item analysis data are available with the total on all the items, some preference should be given to items that have the lowest internal consistency discrimination indices. Keeping these suggestions in view, the investigator decided to retain the items having internal consistency discrimination indices of 0.20 or more. The items with internal consistency indices less than 0.20 were rejected altogether.

Difficulty Value

The difficulty of an item may be determined in several ways. By the judgments of competent people who rank the items in order of difficulty, (2) by how quickly the item can be solved, and (3) by the number of examinees in the group who get the item right. But the number right, or the proportion of the group which an item passed by 0 per cent or 100 per cent has no differentiating value, of course, but such items may be included in a test solely for the psychological effect. Difficulty indices within more narrow ranges may, of course, be taken from the normal curve can solve an item correctly, is the 'standard' method for determining difficulty in objective examinations.

Garrett (1958) says, "The larger the variance of item, therefore, the greater the number of separations among individuals, the test item is able to make. Other things being equal, items of moderate difficulty 40-50-60 per cent passing—are to be preferred to those which are much easier or much harder". The same author again suggests, "The normal curve can be taken as a guide in the selection of difficulty indices. Thus, 50 per cent of the items might have difficulty indices between 0.2 and 0.375, 25 percent indices larger than 0.375 and 25 per cent smaller than 0.2. The results were presented in Table 4.6.

Table 4.6: The Discriminative Indices for All the Items of the Pilot Study of Objective Achievement Test

Item No.	*No. of correct responses in top group 27%*	*No. of correct responses in bottom group 27%*	*Percentage of correct responses in top group 27%*	*Percentage of correct responses in bottom group 27%*	*Difficulty Index*	*Validity Index (Discriminating power)*
1	2	3	4	5	6	7
1.	30	15	55.5	27.7	46.6	0.2925
2.	19	15	35.1	27.7	31.4	0.0725 *
3.	20	15	37	27.7	32.35	0.0925 *
4.	45	28	83.3	51.8	67.55	0.335
5.	29	12	53.7	22.2	37.95	0.34
6.	35	23	64.8	42.5	53.65	0.2375
7.	12	5	22.2	9.25	15.72	0.235
8.	38	27	70.4	50	60.2	0.21
9.	24	10	44.4	18.5	31.45	0.30
10.	02	02	3.70	3.70	3.7	00 *
11.	36	24	66.6	44.4	55.5	0.24
12.	46	27	85.1	50	67.55	0.405
13.	37	21	68.5	38.8	53.65	0.30
14.	24	14	44.4	25.9	35.15	0.2
15.	27	15	50	27.7	38.85	0.23
16.	44	39	81.4	72.2	76.8	0.1175*
17.	42	31	77.7	57.4	67.55	0.22
18.	20	16	37	29.6	33.3	0.0775 *
19.	47	35	87	64.8	76.4	0.2925

(Contd...)

1	*2*	*3*	*4*	*5*	*6*	*7*
20.	15	11	27.7	20.3	24	0.11 *
21.	23	11	42.5	20.3	31.4	0.255
22.	31	18	57.4	33.3	43.85	0.235
23.	23	18	42.5	33.3	37.9	0.10 *
24.	36	29	66.6	53.7	60.15	0.14 *
25.	37	31	68.5	57.4	62.95	0.12 *
26.	15	7	27.7	12.9	20.3	0.22
27.	22	12	40.7	22.2	31.45	0.22
28.	52	42	96.29	77.7	86.99	0.385
29.	47	24	87.03	44.4	65.71	0.48
30.	52	38	96.29	70.3	83.14	0.475
31.	06	02	11.1	3.70	7.4	0.2237
32.	29	19	53.7	35.1	44.4	0.2
33.	33	17	61.1	61.4	46.25	0.31
34.	23	17	42.5	31.4	36.95	0.12 *
35.	54	48	100	88.88	94.44	0.2825
36.	47	35	87.03	64.8	75.91	0.2975
37.	13	6	24.0	11.11	17.55	0.2137
38.	29	16	53.7	29.6	41.65	0.25
39.	22	13	40.74	24.0	32.37	0.2
40.	46	23	85.1	42.5	63.8	0.4594
41.	25	14	46.29	25.9	36.09	0.22
42.	29	25	53.7	46.29	49.99	0.08 *
43.	38	35	70.3	64.8	67.55	0.0525 *
44.	14	11	25.9	20.3	23.1	0.085 *
45.	37	29	68.5	53.7	61.1	0.14 *
46.	23	10	42.5	18.5	30.5	0.28
47.	24	14	44.4	25.9	35.15	0.2
48.	31	19	57.4	35.18	46.29	0.2275
49.	37	20	68.5	37	52.75	0.33
50.	19	7	35.18	12.96	24.07	0.27
51.	30	17	55.5	31.48	44.42	0.26
52.	42	37	77.7	68.5	73.1	0.125 *

(Contd...)

1	2	3	4	5	6	7
53.	51	29	94.44	53.7	74.1	0.53
54.	11	4	20.3	7.40	13.85	0.2587
55.	30	18	55.5	33.33	44.44	0.24
56.	15	06	27.77	11.11	19.44	0.26
57.	37	25	68.5	46.29	57.39	0.24
58.	27	24	50	44.5	47.25	0.06 *
59.	44	33	81.4	61.11	71.25	0.2319
60.	27	10	50.0	18.5	34.25	0.36
61.	23	13	42.5	24.0	33.25	0.205
62.	47	38	87.03	70.3	78.66	0.235
63.	46	31	85.1	57.4	71.25	0.335
64.	21	11	38.88	20.3	29.59	0.2287
65.	16	8	29.6	14.8	22.2	0.205
66.	40	29	74.07	53.70	63.88	0.22
67.	36	34	66.6	62.9	64.75	0.09 *
68.	29	8	53.7	14.81	34.25	0.435
69.	53	41	98.14	75.9	87.02	0.48
70.	29	26	53.7	48.1	50.9	0.06 *
71.	19	17	35.1	31.4	33.25	0.042 *
72.	26	19	53.7	35.1	44.4	0.2
73.	32	14	59.2	25.9	42.55	0.34
74.	33	15	61.1	27.7	44.4	0.34
75.	40	28	74	51.8	62.9	0.24
76.	6	2	11.11	3.70	7.40	0.2237
77.	29	11	53.7	20.3	37	0.365
78.	25	21	46.29	38.8	42.54	0.07 *
79.	36	25	66.6	46.29	56.44	0.22
80.	52	38	96.29	70.3	83.29	0.475
81.	33	22	61.1	40.7	50.9	0.214
82.	24	10	44.4	18.5	31.45	0.3175
83.	40	19	74	35.1	54.55	0.40
84.	41	25	75.9	46.29	61.09	0.32

(Contd...)

1	2	3	4	5	6	7
85.	11	8	20.3	14.81	17.55	0.0787 *
86.	52	51	96.29	94.44	95.36	0.095 *
87.	41	20	75.9	37	56.45	0.3962
88.	29	18	53.7	33.3	43.5	0.22
89.	40	26	74	48.1	61.05	0.28
90.	26	14	48.14	25.9	37.02	0.24
91.	19	5	35.18	9.25	22.21	0.35
92.	4	4	7.40	7.40	7.40	00 *
93.	50	41	92.59	75.9	84.24	0.285
94.	29	18	53.7	33.33	43.51	0.12 *
95.	51	43	94.44	79.62	87.03	0.285
96.	24	12	44.4	22.2	33.3	0.25
97.	13	10	24	18.5	21.25	0.09 *
98.	21	13	53.7	54.0	38.85	0.32
99.	30	18	55.55	33.3	44.44	0.24
100.	45	32	83.3	59.2	71.25	0.2875
101.	50	37	92.59	68.5	80.54	0.395
102.	31	19	57.4	35.1	46.25	0.2275
103.	21	11	38.88	20.37	29.625	0.2265
104.	22	11	40.74	20.3	32.52	0.24625
105.	53	47	98.14	87.03	92.58	0.3525
106.	36	21	66.6	53.7	60.15	0.14 *
107.	33	18	61.1	33.3	47.2	0.29
108.	44	29	81.4	53.7	67.55	0.3075
109.	39	33	72.2	61.1	66.65	0.125 *
110.	40	18	74	33.3	53.65	0.4175
111.	47	38	87.03	70.3	78.66	0.24
112.	47	30	87.03	55.55	71.29	0.3775
113.	20	18	37	33.3	35.15	0.0365 *
114.	28	14	51.8	25.9	38.85	0.28
115.	22	12	40.7	22.2	31.45	0.22
116.	52	43	96.29	79.62	87.95	0.37

(Contd...)

1	2	3	4	5	6	7
117.	52	44	96.29	81.4	88.84	0.3575
118.	48	36	88.88	66.6	77.7	0.3225
119.	37	31	68.5	57.4	62.95	0.12 *
120.	54	52	100	96.29	98.14	0.095 *
121.	51	33	94.44	61.1	77.77	0.4775
122.	28	16	51.85	29.6	40.72	0.23
123.	20	8	37	14.81	25.90	0.253
124.	53	50	98.14	92.59	95.365	0.2175
125.	54	45	100	83.3	91.65	0.415
126.	41	14	75.9	25.9	50.9	0.5
127.	25	12	46.29	22.2	34.245	0.27
128.	51	32	94.44	59.2	76.82	0.4925
129.	47	34	87.03	62.9	74.965	0.3175
130.	23	8	42.6	14.81	28.70	0.295
131.	42	26	77.7	48.1	62.9	0.325
132.	40	23	74	42.5	58.25	0.3225
133.	19	7	35.18	12.96	24.07	0.3325
134.	36	11	66.6	20.3	43.45	0.48
135.	30	13	55.55	24	39.775	0.3375
136.	44	30	81.4	24	52.7	0.57
137.	27	13	50	24	37	0.285
138.	25	23	46.29	42.5	44.395	0.04 *
139.	9	9	16.66	16.66	16.66	00 *
140.	52	36	96.29	66.6	81.445	0.5012
141.	51	44	94.44	81.5	87.97	0.26
142.	25	14	46.29	25.9	36.095	0.22
143.	17	16	31.4	29.6	30.5	0.01 *
144.	35	21	64.8	38.88	42.58	0.29
145.	2	8	3.70	14.8	9.25	00 *
146.	12	10	22.22	18.5	20.35	0.055 *
147.	38	23	70.3	42.5	56.4	0.29
148.	41	27	75.92	50	62.96	0.285

(Contd...)

1	2	3	4	5	6	7
149.	44	28	81.4	51.8	66.6	0.3275
150.	31	18	57.4	33.33	43.365	0.25
151.	40	21	74	38.88	56.44	0.36
152.	14	11	25.9	20.3	23.1	0.13 *
153.	23	17	42.5	31.4	36.95	0.13 *
154.	16	15	29.6	27.7	28.65	0.025 *
155.	35	18	64.8	33.3	49.05	0.3456
156.	38	32	70.3	59.2	64.75	0.12 *
157.	53	51	98.14	94.44	96.29	0.2
158.	26	16	48.1	29.16	38.63	0.2
159.	44	32	81.4	59.2	70.3	0.2594
160.	16	10	29.6	18.5	24.05	0.145 *
161.	11	8	20.3	16.66	18.48	0.046 *
162.	17	15	31.4	27.7	29.55	0.0331*
163.	34	21	62.9	38.8	50.85	0.247
164.	49	43	90.7	79.6	85.15	0.206
165.	25	12	46.29	22.2	34.24	0.27
166.	36	22	66.66	40.7	53.65	0.27
167.	35	27	64.8	50	57.4	0.16 *
168.	37	17	68.5	31.4	49.95	0.3844
169.	22	10	40.7	18.5	29.6	0.2594
170.	47	25	87.03	46.29	66.66	0.465
171.	7	5	12.9	9.2	11.05	0.0875 *
172.	49	32	90.7	59.2	74.95	0.425
173.	41	25	75.9	46.29	61.09	0.32
174.	38	33	70.3	61.1	65.7	0.10 *
175.	10	7	18.5	12.9	15.7	0.092 *
176.	35	19	64.8	35.1	49.95	0.315
177.	51	33	94.44	61.1	77.77	0.4625
178.	18	7	33.33	12.66	23.14	0.27
179.	39	16	72.2	29.66	50.93	0.42
180.	39	29	72.2	53.7	62.95	0.2

(Contd...)

1	2	3	4	5	6	7
181.	26	12	48.1	22.2	35.15	0.29
182.	18	5	33.33	9.25	21.29	0.355
183.	29	14	53.7	25.9	39.8	0.30
184.	34	23	62.9	42.5	52.7	0.2125
185.	18	13	33.3	24	28.65	0.109 *
186.	45	29	83.3	53.7	68.5	0.335
187.	49	33	90.7	61.1	75.9	0.41
188.	18	13	33.3	24	28.65	0.109 *
189.	26	20	48.1	37	42.55	0.116 *
190.	33	15	61.1	27.7	44.4	0.34
191.	26	14	48.1	25.9	37	0.24
192.	12	6	22.2	11.11	16.65	0.2
193.	23	14	42.5	25.9	34.2	0.14 *
194.	53	48	98.14	88.88	93.51	0.3175
195.	35	19	64.8	35.1	49.95	0.31
196.	49	42	90.7	77.7	84.2	0.21
197.	39	17	72.2	31.4	51.8	0.4125
198.	53	45	98.14	83.3	90.72	0.415
199.	54	46	100	85.1	92.55	0.385
200.	18	7	33.3	12.9	23.1	0.2757

* Indicates the deleted items.

A copy of Final form (Final Study) of English version of Objective Achievement Test (with 150 items) is given in Appendix-C.

RELIABILITY

A test score is called reliable when there are reasons for believing the score to be stable and trustworthy. The correlation of the test with itself is called the reliability coefficient of the test. Reliability can be defined as the degree of consistency between two measures of the same thing.

VALIDITY

The validity of a test is concerned with the question of what is measured. "When used with out qualification and when used in the practical setting, the term validity refers to the agreement to which the test scores or other measures predict some practical criterion measures. In a broad sense, validity has to do with the question of what test scores measure and what they will predict?" (Guilford,1954). There are various methods of estimating validity of a measuring instrument. For the purpose of this investigation, the following type of validity was established for the objective achievement test.

Establishment of the Validity

The validity of a test, or of any measuring instrument, depends upon the fidelity with which it measures what it purports to measure. A test is valid when the performance which it measures, corresponds to the same performances as otherwise independently measured or objectively defined. The difference between validity and reliability can be made clear.

There is a close connection between the two concepts-reliability and validity, in that both stress test efficiency. Reliability is concerned with the stability of test scores. It does not go beyond the test itself. Reliability on the other hand, implies evaluation in terms of out sided independent criteria. Perhaps the greatest difficulty encounter in test validation is the problem of finding authentic criteria. Criteria must, of necessity, often be approximate and indirect, for, if readily accessible and reliable criteria were available. These measures would be used instead of the test. The purpose of test is to find a measure, which will be an adequate, and time saving substitute for criterion measures obtainable only after long intervals of time. To be valid, a test must be reliable. A highly reliable test is always a valid measure of some function. Thus, if a test has a reliability coefficient of 0.95 its index of validity is $\sqrt{0.0.95}$ or 0.97. This means that the test correlates with the true measures of itself.

SELECTION OF THE 16 PERSONALITY FACTORS QUESTIONNAIRE (16 PF)

It is obvious that selection of a tool for measuring personality poses serious problems. In this connection it may also be noted that the problem of justification of the choice looms large. One may cut a sorry figure in explaining for choice. This situation can be solved if we study the theory behind a particular tool and the rational with which it was prepared. The selection of Catell's 16 PF test in the present research was also not arbitrary and has been made after lot of deliberations and study of theory which has been supported amply by Stern (1921) and Allport (1937) in the following works.

Stern observes as, "We have the right and obligation to develop a concept of trait as a definitive doctrine, for, in all activity of the person, there is besides a variable portion, likewise a constant purposive portion, and this later we isolate as the concept of trait".

Allport's contention is equally forceful. He asserts that, "Traits are discovered not by deductive reasoning, not by faith, not by naming, and are themselves never directly observed. They are discovered only through an inference made necessary by the demonstrable consistency of the separate observable acts of behaviour.

In view of the above theoretical as well as practical considerations Cattell's 16 PF questionnaire was selected. The 16 PF questionnaires is an objectively acceptable test devised by basic research in psychology to give the most complete coverage of personality possible in a brief time. 16 functionally independent insure coverage of personality and psychologically meaningful dimensions isolated by over twenty years of factor analytical research on normal and clinical groups. Therefore, having a certain position on one does not prevent the persons having any position whatever on any other. Thus, each of the sixteen scales brings an entirely new piece of information about the person, a condition not found in many alleged multi-dimensional scales.

Moreover, a scoring system is provided whereby, from the sixteen factors, one can extract and work with only four broader (and less specific) traits–anxiety, extraversion, alert poise and independence. Experience with 16 PF in clinical, educational and industrial psychology shows that the use of the 16 traits gives actual prediction.

The Catell's 16 Personality factors questionnaire was used to measure the personality of the student teachers, in the present investigation. The 16 personality factors are:

Factor A : Reserved Vs Outgoing

Factor B : Less intelligent Vs More intelligent

Factor C : Emotionally less stable Vs Emotionally stable

Factor E : Submissive Vs Dominance

Factor F : Desurgency Vs Surgency

Factor G : Weaker super-ego strength Vs Stronger super ego strength

Factor H : Threctia Vs Parnia

Factor I : Harria Vs Premsia

Factor L : Alaxia Vs Protension

Factor M : Praxermia Vs Autia

Factor N : Artlessness Vs Shrewdness

Factor O : Untroubled adequacy Vs Guilt proneness

Factor Q_1 : Conservatism Vs Radicalism

Factor Q_2 : Group adherence Vs Self-sufficiency

Factor Q_3 : Low integration Vs High self-concept control

Factor Q_4 : Low ergic tension Vs Ergic tension

ADOPTION OF THE INSTRUMENT

The Catell's 16 personality factor questionnaire Form-C was adopted as a tool to assess the personality of the student teachers in the present study. In terms of personality factors measured, Form-C is exactly parallel to Form-A and B. The 16 PF test leaves out no important aspects of total personality. Among personality tests, this is as pure a product of factor analysis as can be found. Each item has an appreciable saturation by one of the 16 source traits of ability, temperament and character integration as claimed by the authors. In addition, Form-C has the advantage of ease of administration and scoring. A note may be added about the motivational distortion (MD) scores. In the opinion of Catell, most questions are designed to be as free as possible of value implications so that the persons will not be tempted to answer on any particular dimension for the sake of social approval. Still the likelihood of distortion in factor H and Q_2 is recognised and a correction for these factors is suggested. The correction is done by taking away one point from factor H and to add one to factor Q_2 if MD score exceeds twelve points (Catell and Eber, 1962).

16 PF Form-C, being shorter in length than A and B Forms, is as effective as Forms A or B. It has an elementary vocabulary, which most subjects would follow. The inclusion of index to guard against attempts at distortions of self-picture is an additional advantage. The growing evidence from a number of studies in various fields suggest that the taking into account of all the 16 dimensions of personality gives a better prediction than what may be obtained by a single scale test. In this sense, the 16 personality factor questionnaire is that to be the most suitable for the present investigation.

Moreover, in the 16 PF questionnaire, we do not interpret the factors from the nature of the subject's statements about himself, but from the known correlation between 'mental interiors' as found in questionnaire factors and the factors established in behaviour. In other words, the question responses are treated as behaviour, not as valid self-ratings.

Thus, the 16 Personality factor test Form-C of 1969 was adopted for the present investigation to assess the personality of the student teachers.

A copy of English version 16 PF Form-C is presented in Appendix-D.

SCORING PROCEDURE FOR 16 PF FORM-C

In the 16 personality factors questionnaire, three alternative answers are given to each question. The subjects are motivated to give only one answer for each question. A preliminary instruction was made to know whether there is more than one answer or not to each question in the answer sheet. Then the answers are scored according to the weightages given by the author. The scoring was done for each individual student teacher and for each factor.

RELIABILITY AND VALIDITY OF THE FORM

For calculating reliability and validity, the procedure suggested by Garrett (1973) was followed. Reliability of the sub-tests of each factor (based on raw scores) as obtained by split-half technique and validity which is the square root of reliability, are presented in Table 4.7. The split-half reliability was calculated on a sample of 200.

Table 4.7: Reliability and Validity of 16 PF Form–C using Split-Half Technique

Factor	*A*	*B*	*C*	*E*	*F*	*G*	*H*	*I*
Reliability	0.593	0.623	0.537	0.669	0.657	0.756	0.679	0.696
Validity	0.770	0.789	0.733	0.818	0.811	0.869	0.824	0.834
Factor	*L*	*M*	*N*	*O*	Q_1	Q_2	Q_3	Q_4
Reliability	0.562	0.578	0.603	0.717	0.706	0.767	0.560	0.692
Validity	0.750	0.760	0.776	0.847	0.840	0.876	0.748	0.832

Retest was also conducted on a sample of 100 with a gap of 21 days. The test-retest reliability and validity for each factor are given in Table 4.8.

Table 4.8: Reliability and Validity of 16 PF Form–C using Test-retest Technique

Factor	*A*	*B*	*C*	*E*	*F*	*G*	*H*	*I*
Reliability	0.561	0.638	0.564	0.645	0.629	0.763	0.649	0.683
Validity	0.749	0.799	0.751	0.803	0.793	0.873	0.806	0.826
Factor	*L*	*M*	*N*	*O*	Q_1	Q_2	Q_3	Q_4
Reliability	0.539	0.589	0.616	0.702	0.722	0.776	0.538	0.676
Validity	0.734	0.767	0.785	0.838	0.850	0.881	0.733	0.822

DEMOGRAPHIC AND SOCIO-ECONOMIC SCALE (DSES)

Demographic and Socio-Economic scale is defined as the ranking of an individual in terms of his/her material belongings and cultural possessions along with the degree of respect, power and influence she/he derives.

The investigator prepared the Demographic and Socio-Economic scale and used in the present study.

ORGANISATION OF ITEMS

The number of items was collected and selected to obtain information regarding the Demographic and Socio-Economic variables selected for this study. A panel of judges consisting of experienced teachers and experts perused all the items. They were requested to examine the items carefully and to comment on clarity of expression and adequacy of information to be collected for the study. The comments and suggestions were carefully examined and the scale is accordingly modified and improved.

Some items were provided with a number of alternative responses to restrict the responses strictly to the point required. In this scale: (1) Education, Employment and Income of the parents, brothers and sisters of the student teacher; (2) Caste; (3) Place of birth; (4) Order of birth; (5) Size of the family etc., are covered. Adequate number of copies were printed and used in the study.

The final form of the DSES (English version) is presented in Appendix-E.

The investigator used the Telugu version of DSES to draw out the Demographic and Socio-Economic factors of the students in the study.

ACADEMIC ACHIEVEMENT

An achievement test is essentially a tool or device of measurement that helps in ascertaining quantity and quality of learning at the end in a subject of study or group of subjects after a period of instructions by measuring the present ability of the individual concerned. In the college situation, an achievement test is used as a tool for measuring the nature and extent of students learning in a particular subject or a group of subjects.

Academic achievement is defined as the specified level of attainment of proficiency in academic work designed by test scores. Both physical maturation and mental readiness facilitate academic achievement.

DIETs SCHEME OF EXAMINATION

A. THEORY

There shall be 10 Subject areas viz., basic subjects and strategic (Methodologies related). There shall be an external board of examination 70 marks in each paper. At the end of first year, external examination shall be conducted for the five basic subjects. As regards strategic subjects, even though teaching commences in the first year external examination shall be conducted at the end of second year. In each subject there shall be two terminal examinations, which are internal and 20 marks are allotted for each. Further in each paper there shall be one assignment for 10 marks.

B. TEACHING PRACTICE

This is the most important part of the course and needs careful planning and organization. Trainees will be required to teach a particular class only after they have observed demonstration lessons they have participated in workshops on teaching-learning strategies they have acquired grasp on the subject based on teaching materials prescribed for that class.

For teaching practice 7 periods are prescribed for each strategic subjects. Every trainee shall necessarily observe 5 periods of peer trainees in each of the strategic subjects. The trainee is also expected to teach minimum of 7 periods in each subject during internship, which will be assessed by the school teachers. There shall be one final lesson in each subject, which will be assessed by the external board constituted for this purpose. The minimum pass marks both for theory and practical is 40 per cent i.e., both in external and internal assessment.

There will be automatic promotion from first year to second year. However the trainee is expected to put in 80 per cent of attendance and should have appeared for at least one paper in Basic subject in the first year.

C. DEMONSTRATION LESSONS

This forms an important part of the course and should not on any account be neglected. In every method the master is expected to give a minimum of 5 demonstration lessons. Trainees should have exposure to demonstration lessons on pre-primary, primary and multi-grade classes.

Demonstrations should have brief outline of the lesson by a brief discussion during which useful points should be suggested and trainees doubts – if-any need to be clarified.

Both practical and Theory results will be decided as follows:

I Division : 60% and above

II Division : 50% and above but less than 60%

III Division : 40% and above but less than 50%

Results will be declared separately for theory and practical. The split for allocation of marks area wise is as follows:

Area	*Theory (external) + internal assessment*	*Assessment in Practical*
1. Basic Subject	350 + 150	–
2. Strategies	350 + 150	–
3. Teaching practice (Strategies)		500
4. Field experience		500
Total Marks	1000	1000

The practical and internal assessment records, which are internally evaluated by DIET faculty shall be assessed by an external board nominated by the Director, State Council of Educational Research and Training (SCERT).

FINAL STUDY

Tools Used

For the purpose of gathering data, the following tolls are employed in the present investigation:

1. Teachers Attitude Inventory (TAI) with 83 items.
2. Study Habits Inventory (SHI) with 95 items.
3. The 16 Personality Factor Questionnaire (16 PF) of Cattell Form-C of 1969.
4. Objective Achievement Test (OAT) with 150 items.
5. Demographic and Socio-Economic Status Scale (DSES).
6. Marks secured by the student teachers in the Annual Examination are taken into consideration for their Academic Achievement.

SAMPLE FRAME

Geographically Andhra Pradesh State is divided into three regions i.e. Andhra (9 Districts), Telangana (10 Districts) and Rayalaseema (4 Districts). In every district one DIET is established. Besides these 23 DIETs, two additional sub-DIETs are established for the sake of Tribal in-service teachers in Adilabad (Utnur) and Visakhapatnam (Araku Valley) districts. Based on the population the investigator selected 4 DIETS from Andhra, 4 DIETs from Telangana and 2 DIETs from Rayalaseema region; 60 students were selected at randomly in each DIET. The sample frame for the study consists of 244 Girls and 356 Boys (N = 600) are presented in Table 4.9.

Table 4.9: The Sample Frame for the Present Study

Region/ Sex	*TELANGANA*				*RAYALASEEMA*		*ANDHRA*				*Total*
	Karim nagar	*Medak*	*Nal-gonda*	*Ranga Reddy*	*Anantapur*	*Cuddapah*	*East Godavari*	*Krishna*	*Visakhapatnam*	*Vizianagaram*	
Boys	40	36	32	33	43	34	34	34	33	37	356
Girls	20	24	28	27	17	26	26	26	27	23	244
Total	**60**	**60**	**60**	**60**	**60**	**60**	**60**	**60**	**60**	**60**	**600**

DATA COLLECTION

The heads of the selected DIETs in the sample frame were requested to permit the investigator for collection of data in their DIETs. The programme and the time schedule were communicated to the heads of the Institutions well in advance. The required number of student teachers was selected and they were properly motivated to respond genuinely to all the items in the data gathering tools. The test booklets and the answer sheets were distributed to them and instructions were read out. Sufficient time was given to them in the forenoon, to handle the TAI, SHI, and 16 PF tests. First the investigator distributed the TAI, SHI to student teachers and gave them the instructions on how to take the test. They were assured that the information given by them would be kept under confidential. After the completion of the test, the booklets were collected. After giving a reasonable time of rest, 16 PF was administered for the same group of pupils in the similar manner.

After the lunch break, student teachers are seated before administering the OAT and DSES. In the afternoon, the investigator supplied the OAT and DSES Booklets and Answer sheets and instructed them about the test. Sufficient time was given to them. The investigator examined the pupils, whether they have taken it properly or not. After sufficient time is given, the booklets and answer sheets are collected from the student teachers.

After getting permission from the heads of departments the investigator collected the DIET public examination marks of the sample subjects, which were taken as the indices of the levels of their academic achievement.

STATISTICAL TECHNIQUES EMPLOYED

Frequency distribution tables were prepared for Sex, Region and College, Measures of central tendency, measures of dispersion, skeweness, kurtosis, co-efficient of variance and standard error of mean were calculated wherever necessary. The significance tests like 't' and 'F' were employed to test different hypotheses. Multiple 'R' was calculated by carry out the stepwise regression analysis to find out whether it was possible to estimate the Academic

Achievement score of the student teachers. The obtained numerical results were adumbrated by graphical representations.

The significance levels employed with respective symbols are given below:

** Indicates significant at 0.01 level.

* Indicates significant at 0.05 level.

@ Indicates not significant at 0.05 level.

A MODEL OF RELATIONSHIPS BETWEEN INDEPENDENT VARIABLES AND DEPENDENT VARIABLES

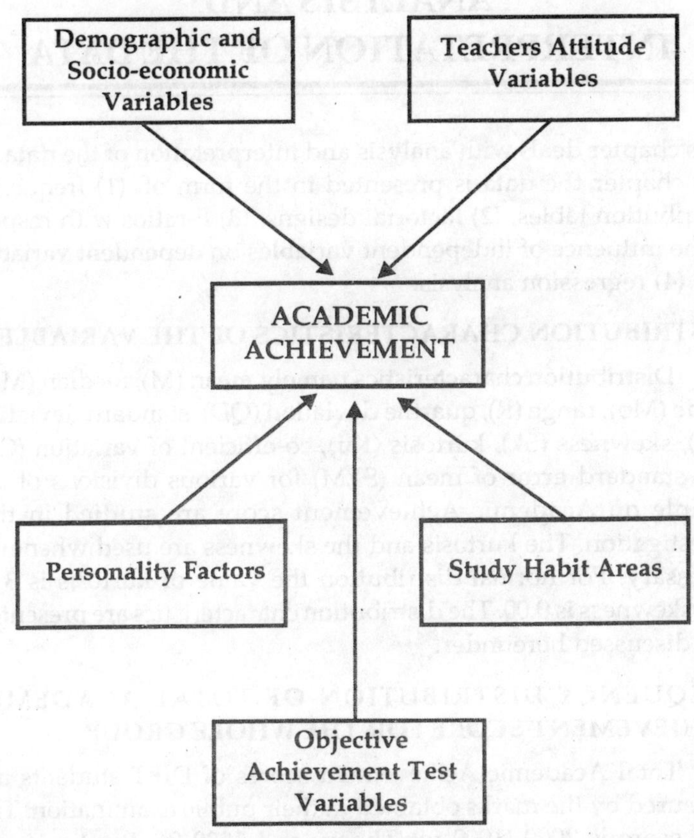

5

ANALYSIS AND INTERPRETATION OF THE DATA

This chapter deals with analysis and interpretation of the data. In this chapter the data is presented in the form of: (1) frequency distribution tables; (2) factorial designs; (3) F-ratios with respect to the influence of independent variables on dependent variable; and (4) regression analysis.

DISTRIBUTION CHARACTERISTICS OF THE VARIABLES

Distribution characteristics namely mean (M), median (Md), mode (Mo), range (R), quartile deviation (QD), standard deviation (SD), skewness (Sk), kurtosis (Ku), co-efficient of variation (CV) and standard error of mean (SEM) for various divisions of the sample on Academic Achievement score are studied in this investigation. The kurtosis and the skewness are used whenever necessary. For normal distribution the value of kurtosis is 3.00 and skewness is 0.00. The distribution characteristics are presented and discussed hereunder.

FREQUENCY DISTRIBUTION OF TOTAL ACADEMIC ACHIEVEMENT SCORE FOR THE WHOLE GROUP

Total Academic Achievement scores of DIET students are measured by the marks obtained in their public examination. The total score is 2000 (1000 for Theory and 1000 for Practical) and minimum passing score is 720.

The frequency distribution of total academic achievement score for the whole group (N=600) is presented in Table 5.1.

Table 5.1 Frequency Distribution of Total Academic Achievement Score for the Whole Group

S. No.	*Class Interval*	*Frequency*	*Mid-point*	*Cum. Freq*	*CPF*
1.	1235-1285	6	1260	6	1.00
2.	1285-1335	37	1310	43	7.16
3.	1335-1385	74	1360	117	19.5
4.	1385-1435	83	1410	200	33.33
5.	1435-1485	95	1460	295	49.16
6.	1485-1535	110	1510	405	67.50
7.	1535-1585	102	1560	507	84.50
8.	1585-1635	54	1610	561	93.50
9.	1635-1685	31	1660	592	98.66
10.	1685-1735	8	1710	600	100.00
		600			

M: 1481.86 Md: 1490.00 Mo: 1506.28 R: 497 Q D: 74.50

S D: 98.61 Sk: 0.0001 Ku: 2.363 Cv: 6.655 SEM: 4.026

It is observed from Table 5.1 that the Mean Academic Achievement score is 1481.86 and Median is 1490.00, the gap between the Mean and Median is negligible. Hence, the distribution is very nearly normal.

The values of Skewness and Kurtosis are 0.0001 and 2.363 respectively. It is slightly positively skewed and Platy Kurtic. Hence the Total Academic Achievement score for the total sample is nearer to the normal distribution.

The Histogram for the distribution of Total Academic Achievement score for the whole group is presented in Fig. 5.1.

The Frequency Polygon for the distribution of Total Academic Achievement score for the whole group is shown in Fig. 5.2.

The Ogive for the distribution of Total Academic Achievement score for the whole group is given in Fig. 5.3.

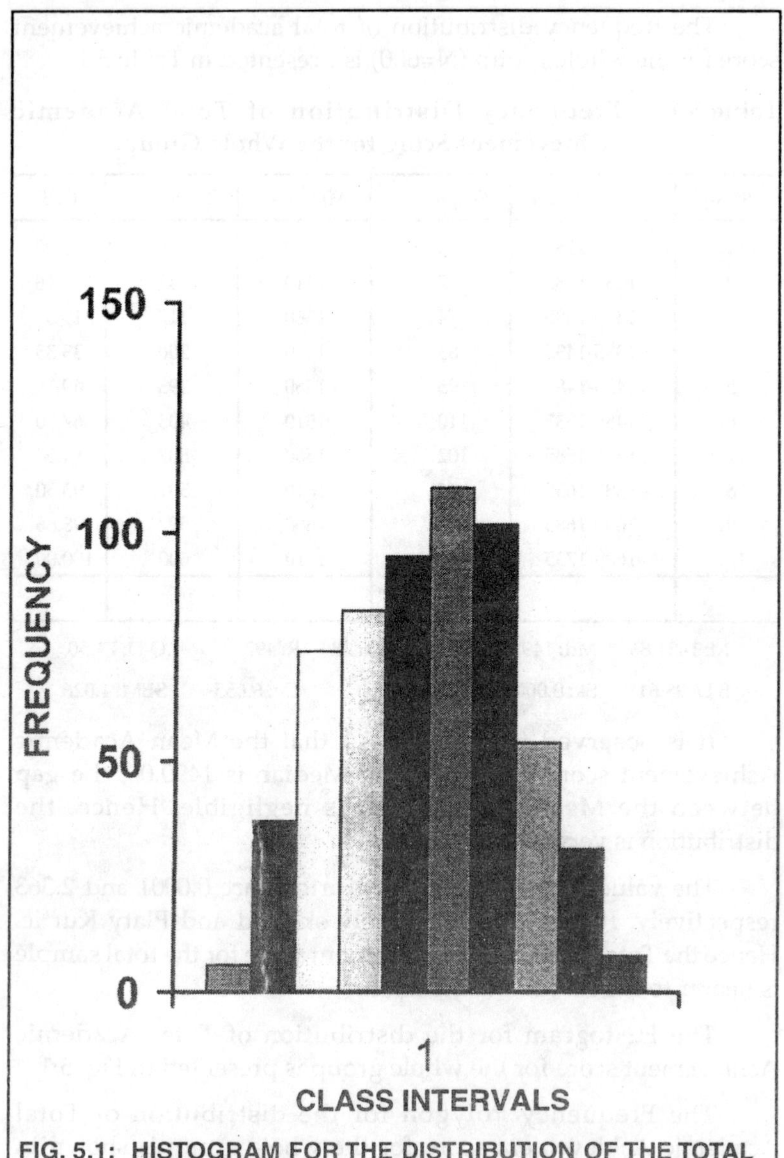

FIG. 5.1: HISTOGRAM FOR THE DISTRIBUTION OF THE TOTAL ACADEMIC ACHIEVEMENT SCORE FOR THE WHOLE GROUP

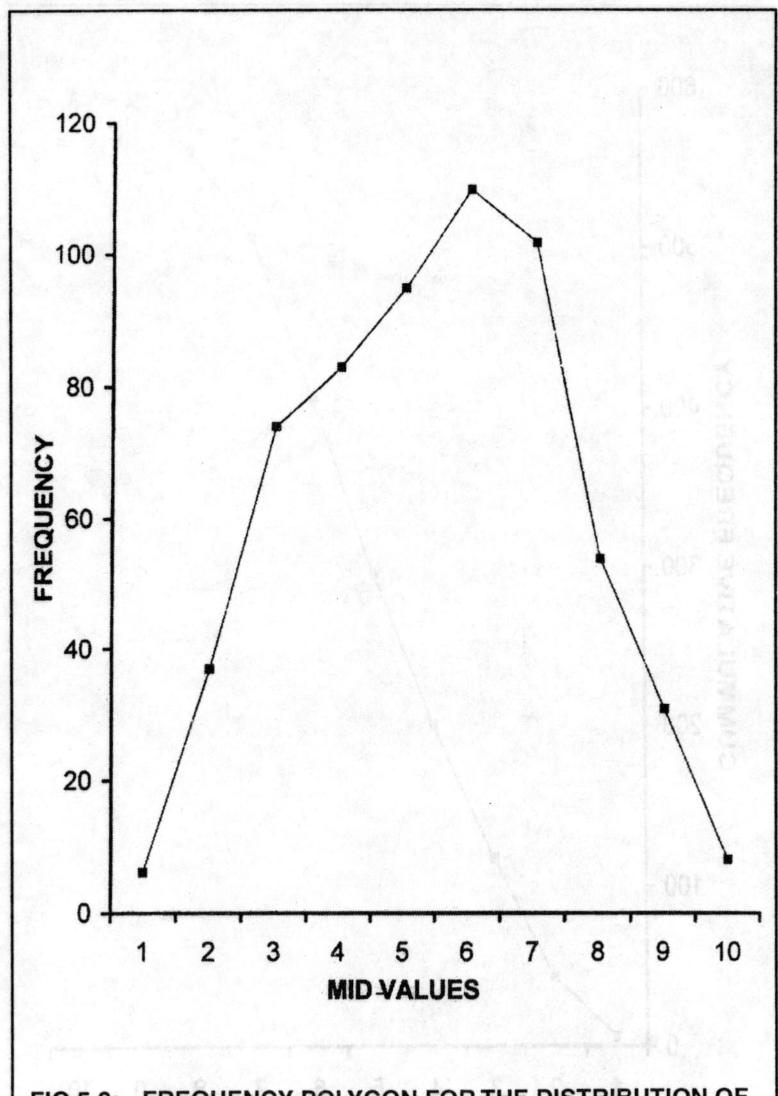

FIG 5.2: FREQUENCY POLYGON FOR THE DISTRIBUTION OF TOTAL ACADEMIC ACHIEVEMENT FOR THE WHOLE GROUP

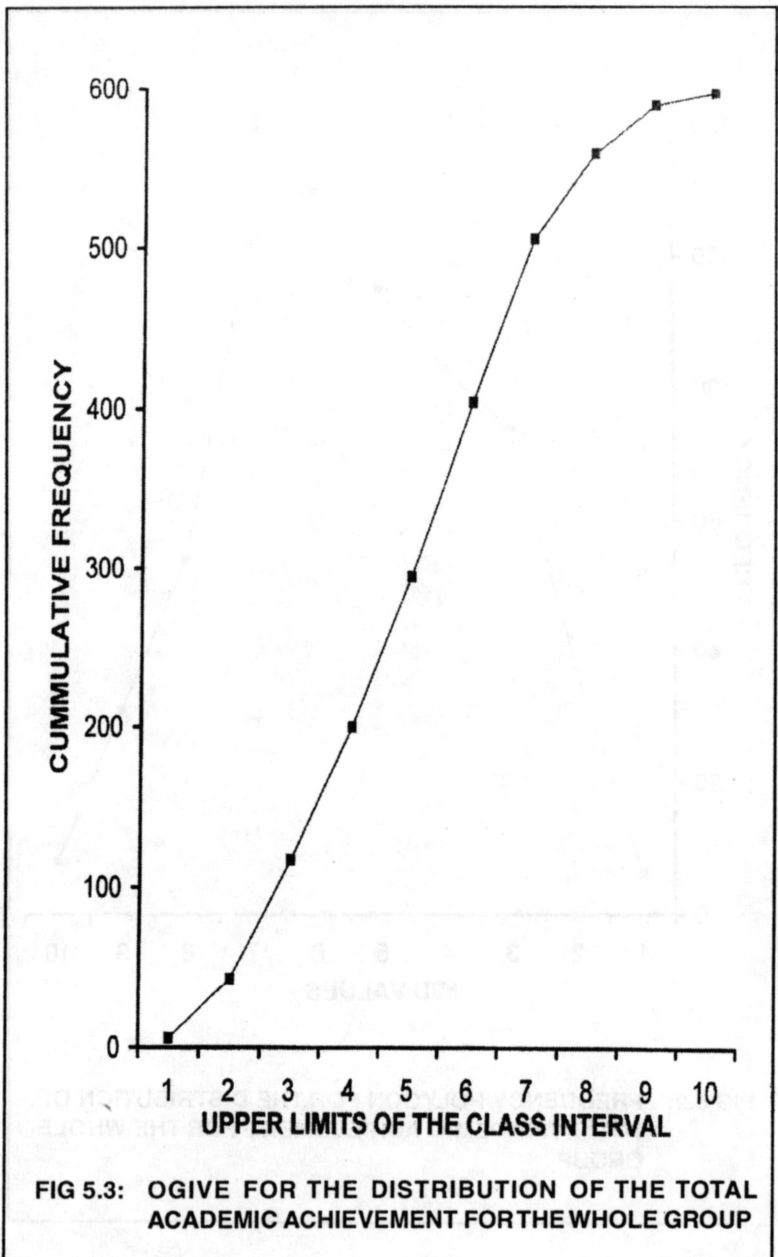

FIG 5.3: OGIVE FOR THE DISTRIBUTION OF THE TOTAL ACADEMIC ACHIEVEMENT FOR THE WHOLE GROUP

FREQUENCY DISTRIBUTION OF ACHIEVEMENT SCORE IN THEORY FOR THE WHOLE GROUP

Academic Achievement scores of DIET students in Theory were measured by the marks obtained in their theory examination.

The frequency distribution of achievement score in theory for the whole group is presented in Table 5.2.

Table 5.2: Frequency Distribution of Achievement Score in Theory for the Whole Group

S. No.	*Class Interval*	*Frequency*	*Mid-point*	*Cum. FREQ*	*CPF*
1.	575-625	20	600	20	3.33
2.	625-675	129	650	149	24.83
3.	675-725	262	700	411	68.50
4.	725-775	158	750	569	94.83
5.	775-825	29	800	598	99.66
6.	825-875	2	850	600	100.00
		600			

M: 703.622 Md: 704.00 Mo: 704.76 R: 251 Q D : 28.5
S D: 43.23 Sk: 0.0028 Ku: 2.98 Cv: 6.144 SEM: 1.765

It is observed from Table 5.2 the Mean Achievement score in Theory is 703.622 and Median is 704.00, the gap between the Mean and Median is negligible. Hence the distribution is normal.

The values of Skewness and Kurtosis are 0.0028 and 2.98 respectively. It is slightly positively skewed and Platy Kurtic. These values indicate that the distribution is normal. Hence, the Achievement score in Theory for the total sample follows the normal distribution.

The Histogram for the distribution of Achievement score in Theory for the whole group is presented in Fig. 5.4.

The frequency polygon for the distribution of Achievement score in Theory for whole group is shown in Fig. 5.5.

The Ogive for the distribution of Achievement score in Theory for the whole group is given in Fig. 5.6.

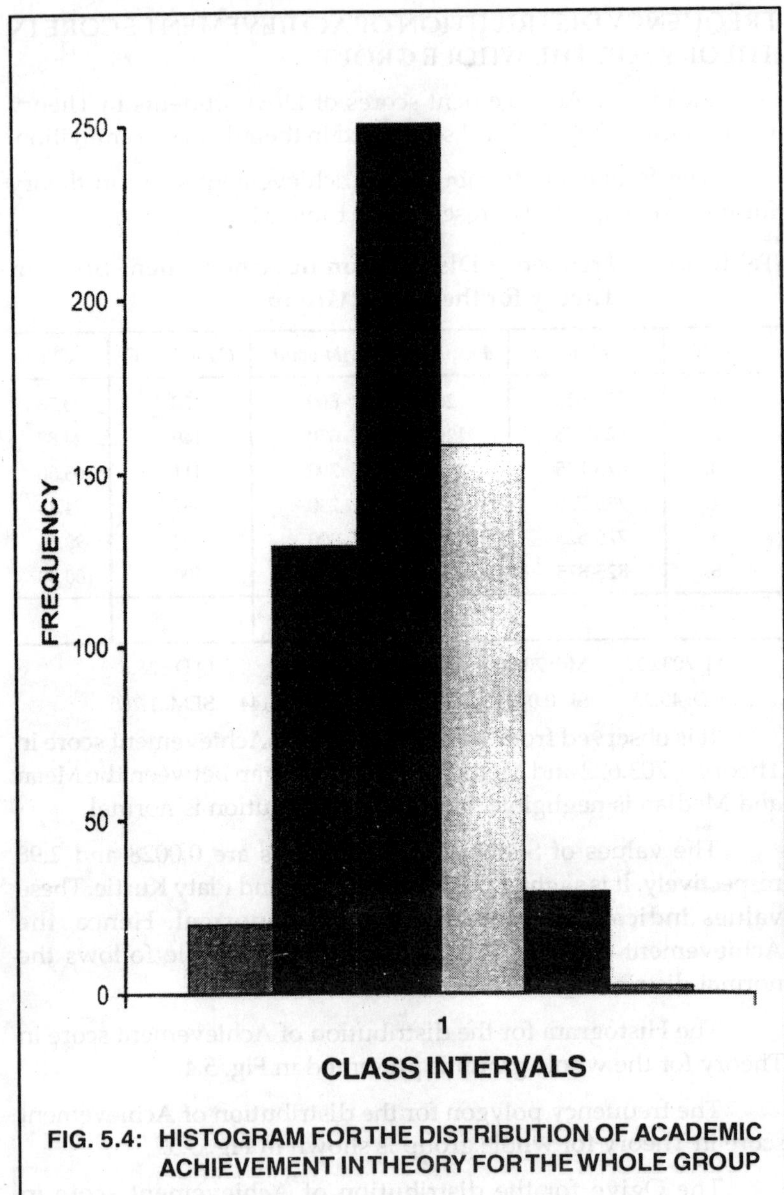

FIG. 5.4: HISTOGRAM FOR THE DISTRIBUTION OF ACADEMIC ACHIEVEMENT IN THEORY FOR THE WHOLE GROUP

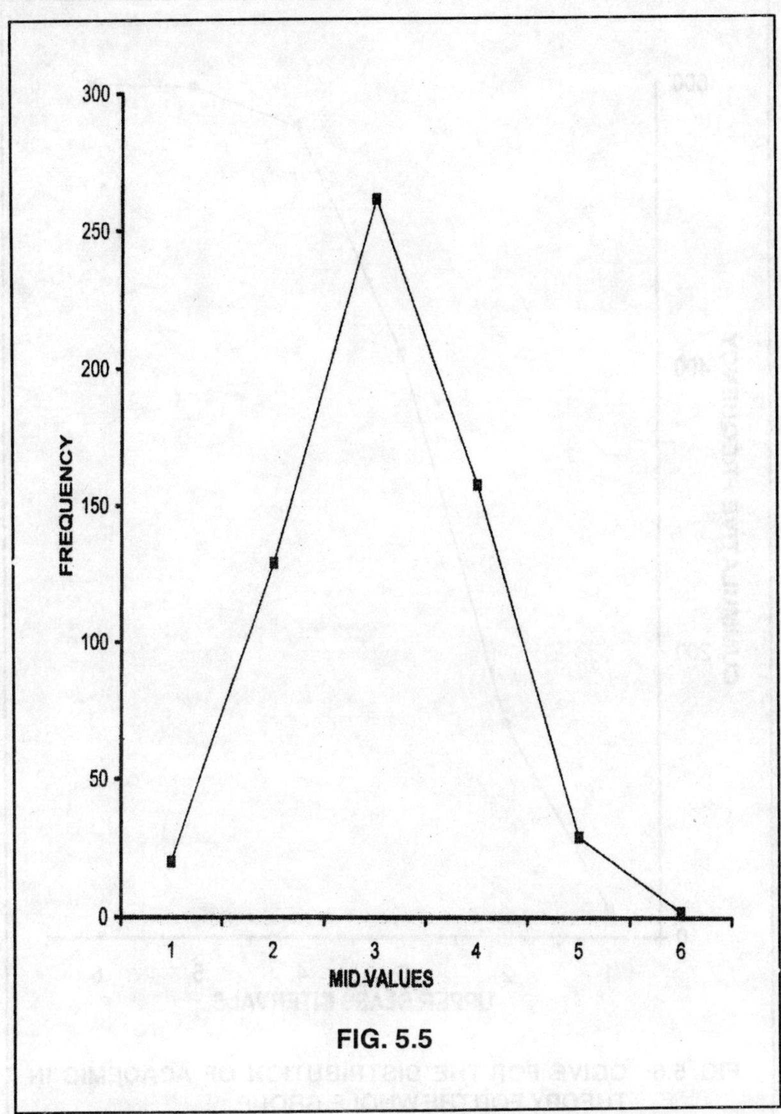

FIG. 5.5

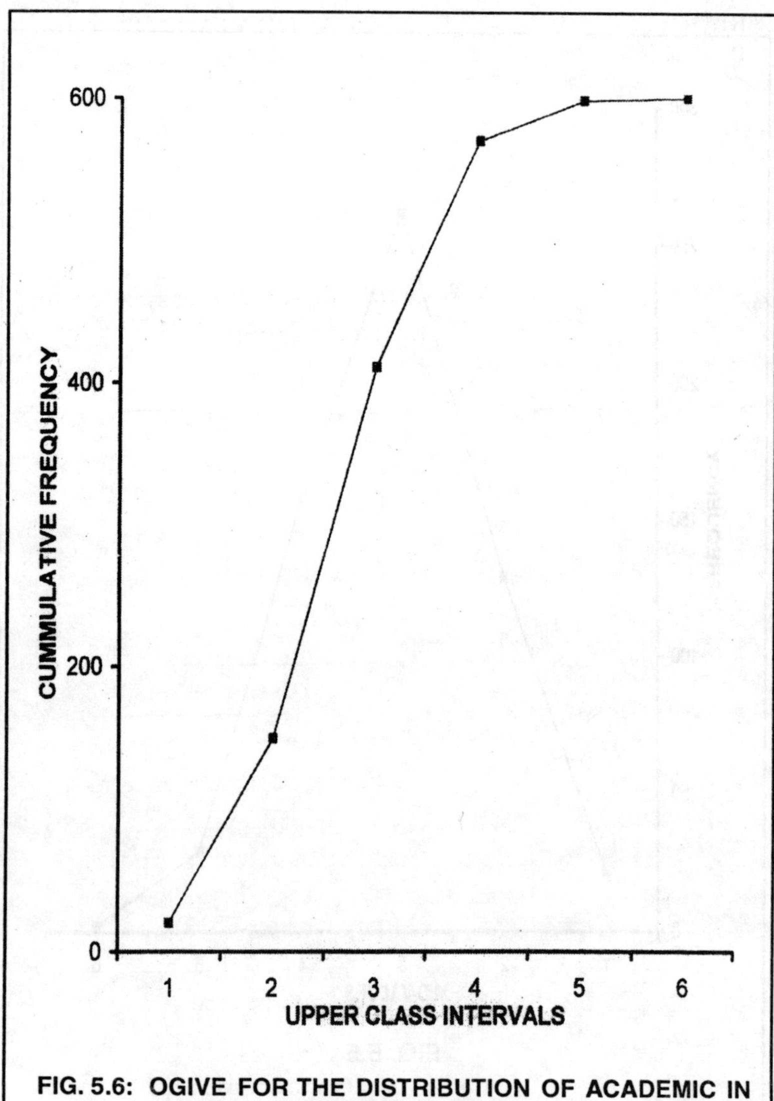

FIG. 5.6: OGIVE FOR THE DISTRIBUTION OF ACADEMIC IN THEORY FOR THE WHOLE GROUP

FREQUENCY DISTRIBUTION OF ACHIEVEMENT SCORE IN PRACTICALS FOR THE WHOLE GROUP

Academic Achievement scores of DIET students in Practicals were measured by the marks obtained in their Practical examination.

The frequency distribution of Achievement score in Practicals for the whole group is presented in Table 5.3.

Table 5.3: Frequency Distribution of Achievement Score in Practicals for the Whole Group

S. No.	Class Interval	Frequency	Mid-point	CUM.FREQ	CPF
1.	575-625	4	600	4	0.6
2.	625-675	75	650	79	13.16
3.	675-725	103	700	182	30.33
4.	725-775	87	750	269	44.83
5.	775-825	123	800	392	65.33
6.	825-875	161	850	553	92.16
7.	875-925	47	900	600	100.00
		600			

M: 778.24 Md: 800.00 Mo: 843.52 R: 317 Q D: 69.00

S D: 77.31 Sk: 0.091 Ku: 1.814 Cv: 9.934 SEM: 3.156

It is observed from Table 5.3 that the Mean Achievement score in Practicals is 778.24 and Median is 800.00. The values of Skewness and Kurtosis are 0.091 and 1.814 respectively. It is slightly positively skewed and Platy Kurtic.

The Histogram for the distribution of Achievement score in Practicals for the whole group is presented in Fig. 5.7.

The Frequency Polygon for the distribution of Achievement score in Practicals for whole group is shown in Fig. 5.8.

The Ogive for the distribution of Achievement score in Practicals for the whole group is given in Fig. 5.9.

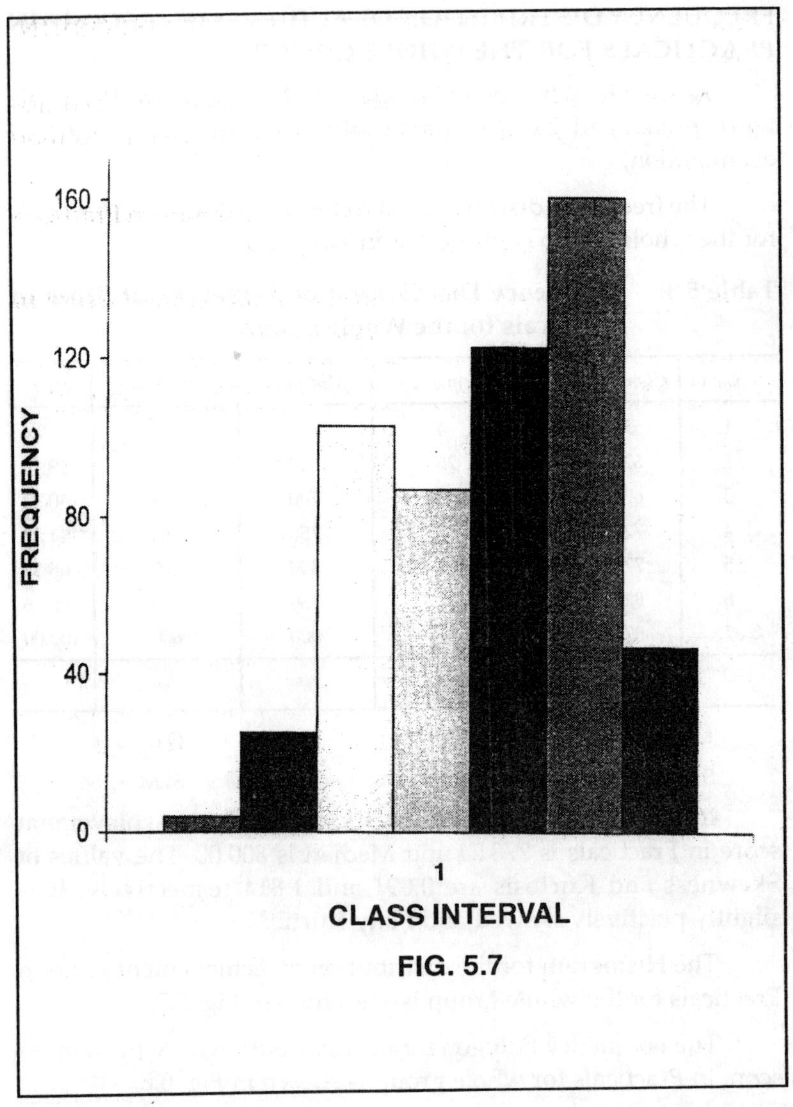

FIG. 5.7

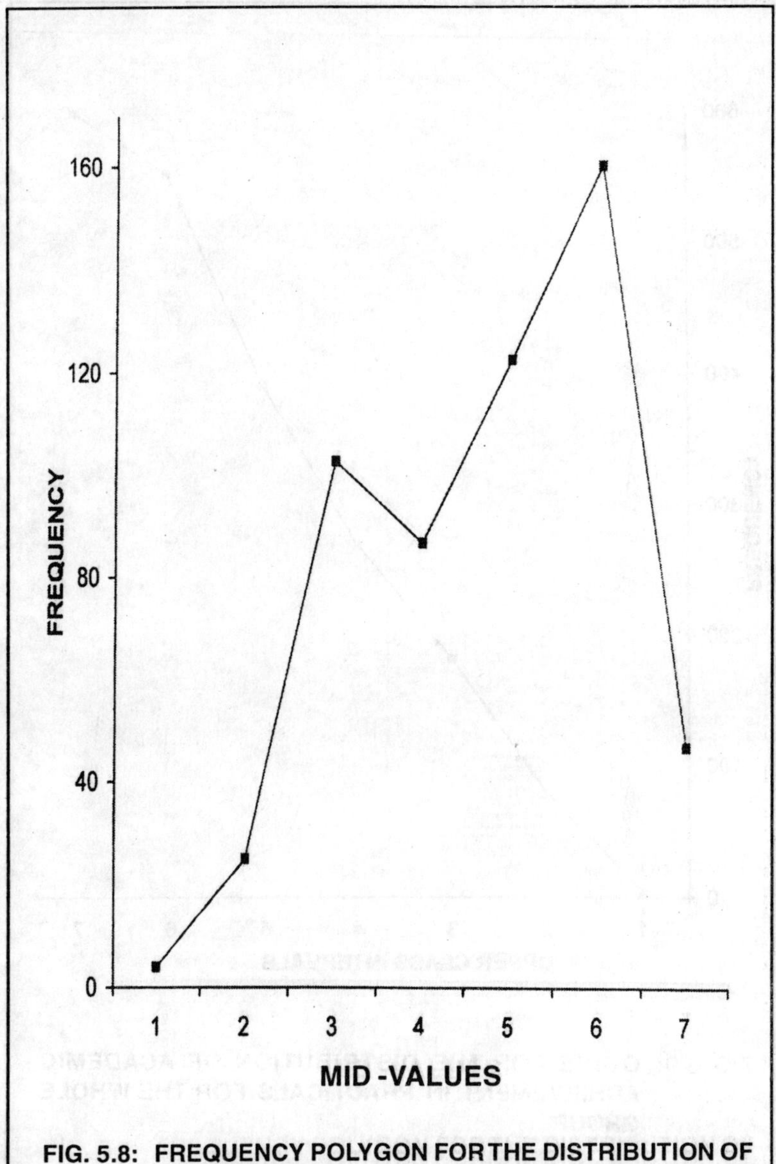

FIG. 5.8: FREQUENCY POLYGON FOR THE DISTRIBUTION OF ACADEMIC ACHIEVEMENT IN PRACTICALS FOR THE WHOLE GROUP

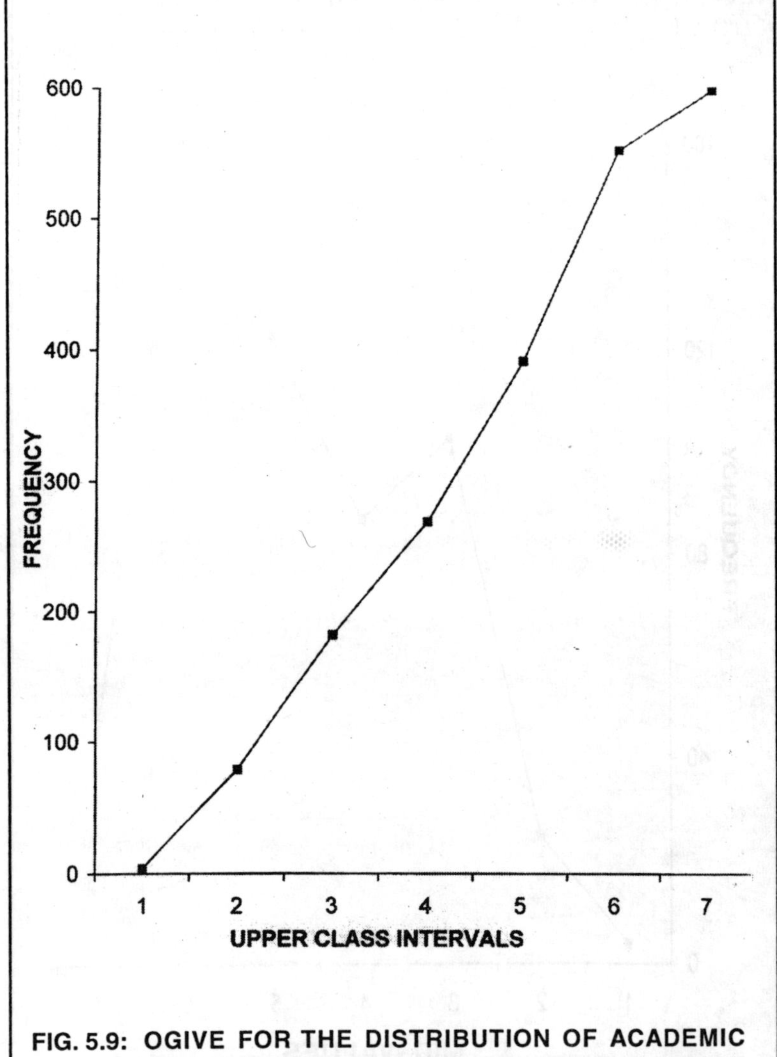

FIG. 5.9: OGIVE FOR THE DISTRIBUTION OF ACADEMIC ACHIEVEMENT IN PRACTICALS FOR THE WHOLE GROUP

FREQUENCY DISTRIBUTION OF TOTAL ACADEMIC ACHIEVEMENT SCORES FOR BOYS AND GIRLS

Academic Achievement scores of DIET students with respect to their sex in their theory examination.

A. FREQUENCY DISTRIBUTION OF TOTAL ACADEMIC ACHIEVEMENT SCORES FOR BOYS

Frequency distribution of Total Academic Achievement score for boys (N=356) is presented in Table 5.4.

Table 5.4: Frequency Distribution of Total Academic Achievement Score for Boys

S. No.	*Class Interval*	*Frequency*	*Mid-point*	*CUM. FREQ*	*CPF*
1.	1235-1285	4	1260	4	1.12
2.	1285-1335	23	1310	27	7.58
3.	1335-1385	50	1360	77	21.62
4.	1385-1435	51	1410	128	35.95
5.	1435-1485	51	1460	179	50.28
6.	1485-1535	64	1510	243	68.25
7.	1535-1585	57	1560	300	84.26
8.	1585-1635	26	1610	326	91.57
9.	1635-1685	23	1660	349	98.03
10.	1685-1735	7	1710	356	100.00
		600			

M: 1480.27 Md: 1484.00 Mo: 1491.46 R: 497 Q D: 78.00

S D: 102.87 Sk: 0.012 Ku: 2.35 Cv: 6.95 SEM: 5.45

It is revealed from Table 5.4 that the mean Total Academic Achievement score for Boys is 1480.27 and median value is 1484.00, the difference between these two is negligible. The magnitudes of Sk and Ku are 0.012 and 2.35 respectively. It is slightly Platy Kurtic. Hence, the distribution of total academic achievement score for boys is very close to normal distribution.

B. FREQUENCY DISTRIBUTION OF TOTAL ACADEMIC ACHIEVEMENT SCORES FOR GIRLS

Frequency distribution of Total Academic Achievement scores for girls (N = 244) is shown in Table 5.5.

Table 5.5: Frequency Distribution of Total Academic Achievement Score for Girls

S. No.	*Class Interval*	*Frequency*	*Mid-point*	*CUM. FREQ*	*CPF*
1.	1250-1300	4	1275	4	1.63
2.	1350-1400	17	1325	21	8.60
3.	1400-1450	29	1375	50	20.49
4.	1450-1500	36	1425	86	35.24
5.	1500-1550	42	1475	128	52.45
6.	1550-1600	50	1525	178	72.95
7.	1600-1650	43	1575	221	90.57
8.	1650-1700	20	1625	241	98.77
		244	1675	244	100.00

M: 1484.176 Md: 1493.00 Mo: 1510.47 R: 440 Q D: 70.00

S D: 91.987 Sk: 0.052 Ku: 2.349 Cv: 6.198 SEM: 5.89

It is observed from Table 5.5 that the mean and median scores are 1484.176 and 1493.00 respectively. The variation between the mean and median of the distribution is negligible. The value of Skewness is 0.052 and Ku is 2.349. Hence, the distribution of total academic achievement scores for girls is very close to normal distribution. It is slightly positively skewed and Platy Kurtic.

From the above tables it is evident that the mean value of total academic achievement score of girls is more than that of boys. Hence, the performance of girls is better than that of boys.

FREQUENCY DISTRIBUTION OF ACHIEVEMENT SCORES IN THEORY FOR BOYS AND GIRLS

Academic Achievement scores of DIET students with respect to their sex in their theory examination.

A. FREQUENCY DISTRIBUTION OF ACADEMIC ACHIEVEMENT SCORES IN THEORY FOR BOYS

Frequency distribution of Achievement score in Theory for Boys (N=356) is presented in Table 5.6.

Table 5.6: Frequency Distribution of Achievement Score in Theory for Boys

S. No.	Class Interval	Frequency	Mid-point	CUM. FREQ	CPF
1.	575-625	11	600	11	3.08
2.	625-675	78	650	89	25.00
3.	675-725	155	700	244	68.53
4.	725-775	90	750	334	93.82
5.	775-825	21	800	355	99.71
6.	825-875	1	850	356	100.00
		600			

M: 704.07 Md: 701.00 Mo: 614.85 R: 245 Q D: 29.0

S D: 44.84 Sk: 0.082 Ku: 2.99 Cv: 6.37 SEM: 2.38

It is revealed from the Table 5.6 that the mean score for boys is 704.07 and median value is 701.00, the difference between these two is negligible. The magnitudes of Sk and Ku are 0.082 and 2.99 respectively. It is slightly Platy Kurtic. Hence, the distribution of achievement score in theory for boys is very close to normal distribution.

B. FREQUENCY DISTRIBUTION OF ACADEMIC ACHIEVEMENT SCORES IN THEORY FOR GIRLS

Frequency distribution of achievement scores in theory for girls (N=244) is shown in Table 5.7.

Table 5.7: Frequency Distribution of Achievement Score in Theory for Girls

S. No.	Class Interval	Frequency	Mid-point	CUM. FREQ	CPF
1.	600-650	25	625	25	10324
2.	650-700	82	675	107	43.85
3.	700-750	107	725	214	87.70
4.	750-800	28	775	242	99.18
5.	800-850	2	825	244	100.00
		244			

M: 702.96 Md: 705.00 Mo: 709.074 R: 226 Q D: 27.5

S D: 40.76 Sk: 0.006 Ku: 2.853 Cv: 5.798 SEM: 2.61

It is observed from Table 5.7 that the mean and median scores are 702.96 and 705.00 respectively. The variation between the mean and median of the distribution is negligible. The value of Sk is 0.006 and Ku is 2.853. Hence, the distribution of achievement scores in theory for girls is very close to normal distribution. It is slightly positively skewed and Platy Kurtic.

From the above tables it is evident that the mean value of academic achievement score in theory for boys is more than that of girls. Hence, the performance of boys is better than that of girls.

FREQUENCY DISTRIBUTION OF ACHIEVEMENT SCORE IN PRACTICALS FOR BOYS AND GIRLS

Academic Achievement scores of DIET students with respect to their sex in their practical examination.

A. FREQUENCY DISTRIBUTION OF ACADEMIC ACHIEVEMENT SCORES IN PRACTICALS FOR BOYS

Frequency distribution of Achievement score in Practicals for Boys (N=356) is presented in Table 5.8.

Table 5.8: Frequency Distribution of Achievement Score in Practicals for Boys

S. No.	*Class Interval*	*Frequency*	*Mid-point*	*CUM. FREQ*	*CPF*
1.	575-625	3	600	3	0.84
2.	625-675	44	650	47	13.20
3.	675-725	67	700	114	32.02
4.	725-775	45	750	159	44.66
5.	775-825	78	800	237	66.57
6.	825-875	91	850	328	92.13
7.	875-925	28	900	356	100.00
		356			

M: 776.20 Md: 801.00 Mo: 850.60 R: 317 Q D: 70.5

S D: 77.98 Sk: 0.066 Ku: 1.80 Cv: 10.046 SEM: 4.13

It is revealed from the Table 5.8 that the mean score for boys is 776.20 and median value is 801.00. The magnitudes of Sk and Ku are 0.066 and 1.80 respectively. Hence, the distribution is Platy Kurtic.

B. FREQUENCY DISTRIBUTION OF ACADEMIC ACHIEVEMENT SCORES IN PRACTICALS FOR GIRLS

Frequency distribution of Achievement score in Practicals for Girls (N = 244) is shown in Table 5.9.

Table 5.9: Frequency Distribution of Achievement Score in Practicals for Girls

S. No.	*Class Interval*	*Frequency*	*Mid-point*	*CUM. FREQ*	*CPF*
1.	575-625	1	600	1	0.40
2.	625-675	31	650	32	13.11
3.	675-725	36	700	68	27.86
4.	725-775	42	750	110	45.08
5.	775-825	45	800	155	63.52
6.	825-875	70	850	225	92.21
7.	875-925	19	900	244	100.00
		244			

M: 781.213 Md: 800.00 Mo: 837.55 R: 280 Q D: 67.5

S D: 76.22 Sk: 0.134 Ku: 1.841 Cv: 9.756 SEM: 4.879

It is observed from Table 5.9 that the mean and median scores are 781.213 and 800.00 respectively. The value of Sk is 0.134 and Ku is 1.841. Hence, the distribution of achievement score in practicals for girls is slightly positively skewed and Platy Kurtic.

From the above tables it is evident that the mean value of achievement score in practicals for boys is less than that of girls. Hence, the performance of girls is better than that of boys.

FREQUENCY DISTRIBUTION OF TOTAL ACADEMIC ACHIEVEMENT SCORE FOR THE STUDENTS OF THREE REGIONS

The distribution of Total Academic Achievement score for the students of different regions namely Andhra, Rayalaseema and Telangana are prepared.

A. FREQUENCY DISTRIBUTION OF TOTAL ACADEMIC ACHIEVEMENT SCORE FOR THE STUDENTS OF ANDHRA REGION

Frequency distribution of Total Academic Achievement score for the students of Andhra region (N=240) is presented in Table 5.10.

Table 5.10: Frequency Distribution of Total Academic Achievement Score for the Students of Andhra Region

S.No.	*Class Interval*	*Frequency*	*Mid-point*	*CUM. FREQ*	*CPF*
1.	1335-1385	2	1360	2	0.83
2.	1385-1435	18	1410	20	8.33
3.	1435-1485	41	1460	61	25.41
4.	1485-1535	64	1510	125	52.68
5.	1535-1585	51	1560	176	73.33
6.	1585-1635	33	1610	209	87.08
7.	1635-1685	23	1660	232	96.66
8.	1685-1735	8	1710	240	100.00
		240			

M: 1536.88 Md: 1527.00 Mo: 1507.23 R: 375 Q D: 55.0

S D: 75.706 Sk: 0.076 Ku: 2.57 Cv: 4.926 SEM: 4.887

It is observed from Table 5.10 that the mean and median values of the distribution are 1536.88 and 1527.00 respectively. The values of Sk and Ku are 0.076 and 2.57 respectively. Hence the distribution is positively skewed and Platy Kurtic.

B. FREQUENCY DISTRIBUTION OF TOTAL ACADEMIC ACHIEVEMENT SCORE FOR THE STUDENTS OF RAYALASEEMA REGION

The Frequency distribution of Total Academic Achievement score for the students of Rayalaseema region (N=120) is shown in Table 5.11.

Table 5.11: Frequency Distribution of Total Academic Achievement Score for the Students of Rayalaseema Region

S. No.	Class Interval	Frequency	Mid-point	CUM. FREQ	CPF
1.	1225-1275	2	1250	2	1.66
2.	1275-1325	6	1300	8	6.66
3.	1325-1375	28	1350	36	30.00
4.	1375-1425	34	1400	70	58.33
5.	1425-1475	26	1450	96	80.00
6.	1475-1525	17	1500	113	94.16
7.	1525-1575	6	1550	119	99.66
8.	1575-1625	1	1600	120	100.00
		120			

M: 1413.72 Md: 1410.00 Mo: 1402.59 R: 365 Q D: 42.5

S D: 66.84 Sk: 0.118 Ku: 3.26 Cv: 4.73 SEM: 6.102

It is observed from Table 5.11 that the mean and median values of the distribution are 1413.72 and 1410.00 respectively. There is negligible difference between the above values. Hence, the distribution is very close to normal. The values of Sk and Ku are 0.118 and 3.26 respectively.

C. FREQUENCY DISTRIBUTION OF TOTAL ACADEMIC ACHIEVEMENT SCORE FOR THE STUDENTS OF TELANGANA REGIONS

Frequency distribution of Total Academic Achievement score for the students of Telangana region (N=240) is presented in Table 5.12.

It is observed from Table 5.12 that the mean and median values of the distribution are 1460.91 and 1472.00 respectively. The values of Sk and Ku are 0.003 and 1.917 respectively.

From the above tables it is observed that the mean values of Andhra region students are more than that of the students of Telangana and Rayalaseema region. Hence, it is concluded that the total academic achievement score for the students of Rayalaseema region is less than the other regions.

Table 5.12: Frequency Distribution of Total Academic Achievement Score for the Students of Telangana Region

S. No.	*Class Interval*	*Frequency*	*Mid-point*	*CUM. FREQ*	*CPF*
1.	1225-1275	4	1250	4	1.66
2.	1275-1325	22	1300	26	10.83
3.	1325-1375	38	1350	62	25.83
4.	1375-1425	36	1400	98	40.83
5.	1425-1475	25	1450	123	51.25
6.	1475-1525	37	1500	160	66.66
7.	1525-1575	41	1550	201	83.75
8.	1575-1625	31	1600	232	96.66
9.	1625-1675	8	1650	240	100.00
		240			

M: 1460.91 Md: 1472 Mo: 1494.18 R: 433 Q D: 89.5

S D: 102.74 Sk: 0.003 Ku: 1.917 Cv: 7.003 SEM: 6.632

FREQUENCY DISTRIBUTION OF ACHIEVEMENT SCORES IN THEORY FOR THE STUDENTS OF THREE REGIONS

The distribution of Academic Achievement score in theory for the students of different regions namely Andhra, Rayalaseema and Telangana are prepared.

A. FREQUENCY DISTRIBUTION OF ACADEMIC ACHIEVEMENT SCORE IN THEORY FOR THE STUDENTS OF ANDHRA REGION

Frequency distribution of Achievement score in Theory for the students of Andhra region (N=240) is presented in Table 5.13.

It is observed from Table 5.13 that the mean and median values of the distribution are 710.475 and 708.00 respectively. There is negligible difference between the above values. Hence, the distribution is very close to normal. The values of Sk and Ku are 0.09 and 2.96 respectively.

Table 5.13: Frequency Distribution of Achievement Score in Theory for the Students of Andhra Region

S. No.	Class Interval	Frequency	Mid-point	CUM. FREQ	CPF
1.	575-625	4	600	4	1.66
2.	625-675	40	650	44	18.33
3.	675-725	116	700	160	66.66
4.	725-775	57	750	217	90.41
5.	775-825	22	800	239	99.58
6.	825-875	1	850	240	100.00
		240			

M: 710.475 Md: 708.00 Mo: 703.05 R: 242 Q D: 29.0
S D: 46.042 Sk: 0.09 Ku: 2.96 Cv: 6.48 SEM: 2.972

B. FREQUENCY DISTRIBUTION OF ACHIEVEMENT SCORE IN THEORY FOR THE STUDENTS OF RAYALASEEMA REGION

The Frequency distribution of Achievement score in Theory for the students of Rayalaseema region (N=120) is shown in Table 5.14.

Table 5.14: Frequency Distribution of Achievement Score in Theory for the Students of Rayalaseema Region

S. No.	Class Interval	Frequency	Mid-point	CUM. FREQ	CPF
1.	575-625	8	600	8	6.66
2.	625-675	31	650	39	32.50
3.	675-725	48	700	87	72.50
4.	725-775	32	750	119	99.16
5.	775-825	1	800	120	100.00
		120			

M: 693.325 Md: 691.00 Mo: 686.35 R: 209 Q D: 29.0
S D: 39.81 Sk: 0.0104 Ku: 2.826 Cv: 5.742 SEM: 3.634

It is observed from Table 5.14 that the mean and median values of the distribution are 693.325 and 691.00 respectively. There is negligible difference between the above values. Hence, the distribution is very close to normal. The values of Sk and Ku are 0.0104 and 2.826 respectively.

C. FREQUENCY DISTRIBUTION OF ACHIEVEMENT SCORE IN THEORY FOR THE STUDENTS OF TELANGANA REGION

The Frequency distribution of Achievement score in Theory for the students of Telangana region (N=240) is shown in Table 5.15.

Table 5.15: Frequency Distribution of Achievement Score in Theory for the Students of Telengana Region

S. No.	*Class Interval*	*Frequency*	*Mid-point*	*CUM. FREQ*	*CPF*
1.	600-650	27	625	29	12.08
2.	650-700	86	675	115	47.91
3.	700-750	90	725	205	85.41
4.	750-800	34	775	239	99.58
5.	800-850	1	825	240	100.00
		240			

M: 701.93 Md: 703.00 Mo: 705.16 R: 224 Q D: 30.5
S D: 40.70 Sk: 0.002 Ku: 2.58 Cv: 5.80 SEM: 2.63

it is observed from Table 5.15 that the mean and median values of the distribution are 701.93 and 703.00 respectively. There is negligible difference between the above values. Hence, the distribution is very close to normal. The values of Sk and Ku are 0.002 and 2.58 respectively.

From the above tables it is observed that the mean achievement values of Andhra and Telangana region students in theory are more than that of the students of Rayalaseema regions. Hence, it is concluded that the academic achievement score in theory for the students of Rayalaseema region is less than that of the other regions.

FREQUENCY DISTRIBUTION OF ACHIEVEMENT SCORE IN PRACTICALS FOR THE STUDENTS OF THREE REGIONS

The distribution of Achievement score in Practicals for the students of different regions namely Andhra, Rayalaseema and Telangana are prepared.

A. FREQUENCY DISTRIBUTION OF ACHIEVEMENT SCORE IN PRACTICALS FOR THE STUDENTS OF ANDHRA REGION

Frequency distribution of Achievement score in Practicals for the students of Andhra region (N=240) is presented in Table 5.16.

Table 5.16: Frequency Distribution of Achievement Score in Practicals for the Students of Andhra Region

S. No.	*Class Interval*	*Frequency*	*Mid-point*	*CUM. FREQ*	*CPF*
1.	725-775	42	750	42	17.50
2.	775-825	75	800	117	48.75
3.	825-875	92	850	209	87.08
4.	875-925	31	900	240	100.00
		240			

M: 826.41 Md: 826.00 Mo: 825.18 R: 189 Q D: 28.0
S D: 41.58 Sk: 0.01 Ku: 2.243 Cv: 5.031 SEM: 2.684

It is observed from Table 5.16 that the mean and median values of the distribution are 826.41 and 826.00 respectively. There is negligible difference between the above values. Hence, the distribution is normal. The values of Sk and Ku are 0.01 and 2.243 respectively.

B. FREQUENCY DISTRIBUTION OF ACHIEVEMENT SCORE IN PRACTICALS FOR THE STUDENTS OF RAYALASEEMA REGION

The Frequency distribution of Academic Achievement score in Practicals for the students of Rayalaseema region (N=120) is shown in Table 5.17.

It is observed from Table 5.17 that the mean and median values of the distribution are 720.392 and 715.00 respectively. The values of Sk and Ku are 0.356 and 3.512 respectively. Hence the distribution is positively skewed and platy kurtic.

Table 5.17: Frequency Distribution of Achievement Score in Practicals for the Students of Rayalaseema Region

S. No.	Class Interval	Frequency	Mid-point	CUM. FREQ	CPF
1.	600-650	1	625	1	0.8
2.	650-700	39	675	40	33.33
3.	700-750	55	725	95	79.16
4.	750-800	20	775	115	95.83
5.	800-850	5	825	120	100.00
		120			

M: 720.392 Md: 715.00 Mo: 704.217 R: 227 Q D: 26.5

S D: 40.16 Sk: 0.356 Ku: 3.512 Cv: 5.575 SEM: 3.666

C. FREQUENCY DISTRIBUTION OF ACHIEVEMENT SCORE IN PRACTICALS FOR THE STUDENTS OF TELANGANA REGION

The Frequency distribution of Achievement score in Practicals for the students of Telangana region (N=240) is shown in Table 5.18.

Table 5.18: Frequency Distribution of Achievement Score in Practicals for the Students of Telangana Region

S. No.	Class Interval	Frequency	Mid-Point	CUM. FREQ	CPF
1	575-625	3	600	3	1.25
2	625-675	65	650	68	28.33
3	675-725	45	700	113	47.08
4	725-775	6	750	119	49.58
5	775-825	38	800	157	65.54
6	825-875	67	850	224	93.33
7	875-925	16	900	240	100.00
		240			

M: 758.99 Md: 789.00 Mo: 849.02 R: 304 Q D: 86.0

S D: 89.68 Sk: 0.0003 Ku: 1.332 Cv: 11.851 SEM: 5.789

It is observed from Table 5.18 that the mean and median values of the distribution are 758.99 and 789.00 respectively. The values of Sk and Ku are 0.0003 and 1.332 respectively. Hence the distribution is slightly positively skewed and Platy Kurtic.

From the above tables it is observed that the mean achievement values of Andhra and Telangana region students are more than that of the students of Rayalaseema region.

THE VALUES OF N, M, R, QD, SD, SK, KU, CV AND SEM FOR THE TOTAL ACHIEVEMENT SCORE FOR ALL THE GROUPS

The values of N, M, R, QD, SD, Sk, Ku, CV and SEM for Total Achievement score for all the groups were presented in Table 5.19.

Table 5.19: The Value of N, M, R, Q.D., S.D., SK, KU, CV and SEM for the Total Achievement Score for all the Groups

Sl.No.	*Group*	*N*	*M*	*R*	*Q.D.*	*S.D.*	*Sk*	*Ku*	*Cv*	*SEM*
1.	Whole Group	600	1481.86	497	74.5	98.61	0.0001	2.363	6.66	4.03
2.	Boys	356	1480.27	497	78.0	102.87	0.012	2.347	6.95	4.45
3.	Girls	244	1484.18	440	70.0	91.99	0.052	2.349	6.20	5.89
4.	Andhra Region	240	1536.68	375	55.0	75.71	0.076	2.57	4.93	4.89
5.	Telangana Region	240	1460.91	433	89.5	102.74	0.0003	1.917	7.03	6.63
6.	Rayalaseema Region	120	1413.72	365	42.5	66.84	0.118	3.26	4.73	6.10
7.	East Godavari DIET	60	1369.52	209	37.5	46.39	0.086	2.334	3.39	5.99
8.	Krishna DIET	60	1378.40	381	41.5	66.77	0.534	4.467	4.84	8.62
9.	Visakhapatnam DIET	60	1545.80	226	35.0	52.00	0.022	2.543	3.36	6.71
10.	Vizainagaram DIET	60	1549.92	212	43.5	51.22	0.058	2.379	3.31	6.61
11.	Anantapur DIET	60	1432.08	314	43.0	68.45	0.0023	2.699	4.78	8.84
12.	Cuddapah DIET	60	1395.35	365	36.5	59.79	0.558	5.217	4.29	7.72
13.	Karimnagar DIET	60	1591.07	278	47.5	69.31	0.024	2.336	4.36	8.95
14.	Medak DIET	60	1508.55	345	45.5	73.31	0.202	3.001	4.86	9.47
15.	Nalgonda DIET	60	1529.53	308	51.0	69.89	0.357	3.065	4.57	9.02
16.	Ranga Reddy DIET	60	1518.38	243	45.5	61.05	0.002	2.359	4.02	7.88

From Table 5.19, it is clearly observed that the mean value of total achievement score for the students of Karimnagar DIET is 1591.07, which is the highest mean among all the groups. The lowest mean value is 1369.52, corresponding to East Godavari DIET students.

The S.D. of the Boys is the highest i.e., 102.87 among all the groups. It is inferred that the dispersion of total achievement score is more in boys. The values of kurtosis for all the groups are positive. The magnitudes of kurtosis for most of the groups are less than the normal distribution value.

THE VALUES OF N, M, R, QD, SD, SK, KU, CV AND SEM FOR ACHIEVEMENT SCORE IN THEORY FOR ALL THE GROUPS

The values of N, M, R, QD, SD, Sk, Ku, CV and SEM for achievement score in theory for all the groups are presented in Table 5.20.

From Table 5.20, it is clearly observed that the mean value of achievement score in theory for the students of Karimnagar DIET is 736.50, which is maximum score among all the groups. The lowest value is 689.77. Vizainagaram DIET students scored the lowest mean values in the theory out of all the groups.

The S.D. of the Karimnagar DIET students is the highest i.e., 48.39 among all the groups. It is inferred that the dispersion of achievement score in theory is more in the students of Karimnagar DIET. The Sk values for all the groups are positive. The magnitudes of kurtosis for most of the groups are less than the normal distribution value.

THE VALUES OF N, M, R, QD, SD, SK, KU, CV AND SEM FOR ACHIEVEMENT SCORE IN PRACTICALS FOR ALL THE GROUPS

The values of N, M, R, QD, SD, Sk, Ku, CV and SEM for achievement score in practicals for all the groups are presented in Table 5.21.

Table 5.20: The Values of N, M, R, Q.D., S.D., SK, KU, CV and SEM for the Achievement Score in Theory for all the Groups

Sl. No.	*Group*	*N*	*M*	*R*	*Q.D.*	*S.D.*	*Sk*	*Ku*	*Cv*	*SEM*
1.	Whole Group	600	703.62	251	28.5	43.23	0.028	2.98	6.14	1.77
2.	Boys	356	704.07	245	29.0	44.84	0.082	2.99	6.37	2.38
3.	Girls	244	702.96	226	27.5	40.76	0.006	2.85	5.80	2.61
4.	Andhra Region	240	710.48	242	29.0	46.04	0.09	2.96	6.48	2.97
5.	Telangana Region	240	701.92	224	30.5	40.70	0.002	2.58	5.80	2.63
6.	Rayalaseema Region	120	693.33	209	29.0	39.81	0.010	2.83	5.74	3.63
7.	East Godavari DIET	60	701.50	155	26.0	36.00	0.408	2.937	5.13	4.65
8.	Krishna DIET	60	698.63	219	27.0	41.89	0.143	3.326	5.99	5.41
9.	Visakhapatnam DIET	60	717.77	147	33.0	39.18	0.014	1.910	5.46	5.06
10.	Vizainagaram DIET	60	689.77	153	31.0	40.37	0.0004	2.067	5.85	5.21
11.	Anantapur DIET	60	691.90	170	29.5	40.13	0.107	2.429	5.80	5.18
12.	Cuddapah DIET	60	694.75	208	27.0	39.44	0.019	3.179	5.68	5.09
13.	Karimnagar DIET	60	736.50	209	31.0	48.39	0.0003	2.538	6.57	6.25
14.	Medak DIET	60	700.72	198	30.0	46.68	0.0094	2.579	6.66	6.03
15.	Nalgonda DIET	60	706.50	195	23.0	42.00	0.353	3.285	5.94	5.42
16.	Ranga Reddy DIET	60	698.18	175	18.5	35.43	0.012	3.085	5.07	4.57

Table 5.21: The values of N, M, R, Q.D., S.D., SK, KU, CV and SEM for Achievement Score in Practicals for All the Groups

Sl. No.	*Group*	*N*	*M*	*R*	*Q.D.*	*S.D.*	*Sk*	*Ku*	*Cv*	*SEM*
1.	Whole Group	600	778.24	317	69.00	77.31	0.091	1.81	9.93	3.16
2.	Boys	356	776.20	317	70.5	77.98	0.066	1.80	10.05	4.13
3.	Girls	244	781.22	280	67.5	76.22	0.134	1.84	9.76	4.88
4.	Andhra Region	240	826.41	189	28.00	41.58	0.01	2.24	5.03	2.68
5.	Telangana Region	240	758.99	304	86.00	89.68	0.0003	1.33	11.82	5.79
6.	Rayalaseema Region	120	720.39	227	26.5	40.16	0.356	3.51	5.58	3.67
7.	East Godavari DIET	60	668.02	110	14.0	20.94	0.0004	3.42	3.13	3.70
8.	Krishna DIET	60	679.77	191	23.0	35.95	0.395	3.55	5.29	4.64
9.	Visakhapatnam DIET	60	823.03	107	13.0	22.58	0.97	3.89	2.73	2.92
10.	Vizainagaram DIET	60	860.15	87	14.0	19.34	0.022	2.62	2.25	2.50
11.	Anantapur DIET	60	740.18	191	24.5	38.97	0.149	3.22	5.27	5.03
12.	Cuddapah DIET	60	700.60	194	19.0	30.39	0.463	5.26	4.34	3.92
13.	Karimnagar DIET	60	854.57	150	26.5	31.95	0.112	2.58	3.74	4.13
14.	Medak DIET	60	807.83	167	29.5	42.63	0.229	2.31	5.28	5.50
15.	Nalgonda DIET	60	823.03	178	26.0	39.26	0.002	2.50	4.77	5.07
16.	Ranga Reddy DIET	60	820.20	159	24.5	36.70	0.046	2.47	4.48	4.74

From Table 5.21, it is clearly observed that the mean value of achievement score in practicals for the students of Vizainagaram DIET is 860.15, which is maximum score among all the groups. The lowest value is 679.77. It is evident that the Krishna DIET students scored the lowest mean value in Practicals among all the other groups.

The S.D. of the Telegana Region students is the highest i.e., 89.68 among all the groups. It is inferred that the dispersion of achievement score in practicals is more in Telegana Region. The Sk values for all the groups are positive. The magnitudes of kurtosis for most of the groups are less than the normal distribution value.

THE RESULTS OF ANOVA OF 3 x 2 FACTORIAL DESIGN FOR TOTAL ACHIEVEMENT SCORE

To examine whether sex and region have any significant influence on total achievement score of the DIET students and probe into the effect of interaction between the variables, ANOVA technique using 3 × 2 factorial design is employed. The following hypotheses are formulated.

Hypothesis-1:

There would be no significant influence of the variables sex and region on total achievement score of the DIET students.

Hypothesis-2:

There would be no significant interaction effect of the variables sex and region on total achievement score of the DIET students.

To test the above hypotheses, ANOVA technique is applied using 3 × 2 factorial design and the results are presented in Table 5.22.

It is evident from Table 5.22 that the variable region, the calculated 'F' value for 2 and 594 df is 84.61, which is significant at 0.01 level of confidence. Therefore hypothesis-1 for the variable region is rejected and concluded that region has significant influence on total achievement score of the DIET students.

Table 5.22: Results of ANOVA of 3 × 2 Factorial Design for the Variables Region and Sex on Total Achievement scores

Factor A = Region (3 Levels) Factor B = Sex (2 Levels)

Sl. No.	*Source of Variance*	*Sum of Squares*	*Degree of Freedom*	*Mean Squares*	*F-Value*	*Level of Significance*
1.	A	1263990.00	2	631994.80	84.61	**
2.	B	1957.83	1	1957.83	0.26	@
3.	AB	9789.13	2	4894.57	0.66	@
4.	Error	4436912.00	594	7469.55		

The calculated value of 'F' for 1 and 594 df for the variable sex is 0.26 and not significant at 0.05 level of confidence. Hence, hypothesis-1 is accepted and concluded that the variable sex has no significant influence on total achievement score of DIET students.

For the two factor interaction effects namely region × sex, the calculated 'F' ratio is not significant at 0.05 level of confidence. Hence, the hypothesis-2 is accepted. Therefore the two factor interaction region × sex has no significant influence on total achievement of the DIET students.

THE RESULTS OF ANOVA OF 3 × 2 FACTORIAL DESIGN FOR ACHIEVEMENT SCORE IN THEORY

To examine whether sex and region have any significant difference on achievement score in theory for the DIET students and probe into the effect of interaction between the variables, ANOVA technique using 3 × 2 factorial design is employed. The following hypotheses are formulated.

Hypothesis-3:

There would be no significant influence of the variable sex and region on achievement score in theory of the DIET students.

Hypothesis-4:

There would be no significant interaction effect of the variable sex and region on achievement score in theory of the DIET students.

To test the above hypotheses, ANOVA technique is applied using 3 × 2 factorial design and the results are presented in Table 5.23.

Table 5.23: Results of ANOVA of 3 × 2 Factorial Design for the Variables Region and Sex on Achievement Score in Theory

Factor A = Region (3 Levels) Factor B = Sex (2 Levels)

Sl. No.	*Source of Variance*	*Sum of Squares*	*Degree of Freedom*	*Mean Squares*	*F-Value*	*Level of Significance*
1.	A	21876.58	2	40938.29	5.95	**
2.	B	85.12	1	85.12	0.05	@
3.	AB	2596.25	2	1298.12	0.71	@
4.	Error	1093082.00	594	1840.21		

It is evident from Table 5.23 that for the variable region, the calculated F value for 2 and 594 df is 5.95, which is significant at 0.01 level of confidence. Therefore hypothesis-3 for the variable region is rejected and concluded that region has its own influence on achievement score in theory of the DIET students.

The calculated value of 'F' for 1 and 594 df for the variable sex is 0.05, which is not significant at 0.05 level of confidence. Hence, hypothesis -3 is accepted and concluded that the variable sex has no significant influence on achievement score in theory.

For the two factor interaction effects namely region x sex, the calculated 'F' ratio is 0.71. It is not significant at 0.05 level of confidence. Hence, the hypothesis-4 is accepted. Therefore the two factor interaction region x sex has no significant influence on achievement score in theory of the DIET students.

THE RESULTS OF ANOVA OF 3 × 2 FACTORIAL DESIGN FOR ACHIEVEMENT SCORE IN PRACTICALS

To examine whether sex and region have any significant influence on achievement score in practicals of the DIET students and to probe into the effect of interaction between the variables, ANOVA technique using 3 × 2 factorial design is employed. The following hypotheses are formulated.

Hypothesis-5:

There would be no significant influence of the variable sex and region on achievement score in practicals of the DIET students.

Hypothesis-6:

There would be no significant interaction effect of the variable sex and region on achievement score in practicals of the DIET students.

To test the above hypotheses, ANOVA technique is applied using 3×2 factorial design and the results are given in Table 5.24.

Table 5.24: Results of ANOVA of 3×2 Factorial Design for the Variables Region and Sex on Achievement Score in Practicals

Factor A = Region (3 Levels) **Factor B = Sex (2 Levels)**

S. No.	*Source of Variance*	*Sum of Squares*	*Degree of Freedom*	*Mean Squares*	*F-Value*	*Level of Significance*
1.	A	957355.80	2	478677.90	112.26	**
2.	B	2702.65	1	2702.65	0.63	@
3.	AB	4724.32	2	2362.16	0.55	@
4.	Error	2532934.00	594	4264.20		

It is evident from Table 5.24 that for the variable region, the calculated 'F' value for 2 and 594 df is 112.26, which is significant at 0.01 level of confidence. Therefore, hypothesis-5 is rejected and concluded that region has its own influence on achievement score in practicals of the DIET students.

The calculated value of 'F' for 1 and 594 df for the variable sex is 0.63, which is not significant at 0.05 level of confidence. Hence, hypothesis-5 is accepted and concluded that the variable sex has no significant influence on achievement score in practicals. of DIETS students.

For the two factor interaction effects namely region x sex, the calculated 'F' ratio is 0.55. It is not significant at 0.05 level of confidence. Hence, the hypothesis-6 is accepted. Therefore the two factor interaction region x sex has no significant influence on achievement score in practical of the DIET students.

The variables used in the study representative symbols and codes are presented in Table 5.25.

Table 5.25: Variables used in the Study Represantative Symbols and Codes

Variable code No.	*Description of the variable*	*Symbol used*	*Variable code No.*	*Description of the variable*	*Symbol used*
1	*2*	*3*	*4*	*5*	*6*
	DSES SCALE	DSES	38	Audio Visual Programmes	S_7
1.	Region	R	39	General Habits and Attitude of work	S_8
2.	College	C	40	College Environment	S_9
3.	Sex	S	41	Total Score of the Study Habits Inventory	ST
4.	Age	A		**16 PERSONALITY FACTORS**	16 PF
5.	Marital Status	Ms	42	FACTOR A	PFA
6.	Father's Education	FE	43	FACTOR B	PFB
7.	Mother's Education	ME	44	FACTOR C	PFC
8.	Brother's Education	BE	45	FACTOR E	PFE
9.	Sister's Education	SE	46	FACTOR F	PFF
10.	Father's Employment	FEM	47	FACTOR G	PFG
11.	Mother's Employment	MEM	48	FACTOR H	PFH
12.	Brother's Employment	BEM	49	FACTOR I	PFI
13.	Sister's Employment	SEM	50	FACTOR L	PFL

(Contd...)

1	*2*	*3*	*4*	*5*	*6*
14.	Annual Family Income	AFI	51	FACTOR M	PFM
15.	Caste	CA	52	FACTOR N	PFN
16.	Group Subjects in Intermediate	G	53	FACTOR O	PFO
17.	Place of Birth	PB	54	FACTOR Q_1	PFQ1
18.	Order of Birth	OB	55	FACTOR Q_2	PFQ2
19.	Economic Status of the Family	ES	56	FACTOR Q_3	PFQ3
	TEACHER ATTITUDE INVENTORY	**TAI**	57	FACTOR Q_4	PFQ4
20.	Attitude towards Profession	TA_1	58	Teacher Education in Emerging India	A_1
21.	Training: Need for Content	TA_2	59	Educational Psychology, Measurement & Evaluation	A_2
22.	High Conceptual Level	TA_3	60	Elementary Education, Educational Planning and Management	A_3
23.	Low Conceptual Level	TA_4	61	Perspectives in Primary Education	A_4
24.	High Social Approach	TA_5	62	Art, Health, Physical and Computer Education	A_5
25.	High Intrinsic Motivation	TA_6	63	Total Score in the Achievement Test	A_6
26.	Acceptance of Values	TA_7	65	II Year Theory Total Score	AT_2
27.	Preference for visual and auditory presentation	TA_8	66	I & II Year Theory Total Score	AT

(Contd...)

1	2	3	4	5	6
28.	Attitudes towards pupils during practice teaching	TA_9		**ACHIEVEMENT SCORE IN PRACTICALS**	
29.	Classroom Practice	TA_{10}	67	I Year Practical Total Score	AP_2
30.	Total Score for attitude towards training	TA_{11}	68	II Year Practical Total Score	AP_1
31.	Total Score for attitude towards Profession and training	TA_{12}	69	I & II Year Practical Total Score	AP
	STUDY HABITS INVENTORY	**SHI**	70	Grand Total for Theory & Practicals	GT
32.	Home Environment	S_1			
33.	Reading, Listening and Note taking techniques	S_2			
34.	Planning of work and Subject	S_3			
35.	Habits of Concentration	S_4			
36.	Preparation for Examinations	S_5			
37.	Social Relationships in Study	S_6			

IMPACT OF THEORY AND PRACTICAL SCORES ON TOTAL ACHIEVEMENT SCORE

The total achievement score means the sum of the scores of theory and practicals of the DIET students. The influence of the first and second year theory and practicals on total achievement is investigated.

The students are divided into three groups using quartiles on the basis of scores in the respective variables. The students upto first Quartile (Q1) form group I, the students above the first Quartile (Q1) and upto the third Quartile (Q3) form group II and the students above the third Quartile (Q3) form group III.

The influence of these groups for the variables (1) AT1, (2) AT2, (3) AT, (4) AP!, (5) AP2 and (6) AP on the total achievement scores i.e. Grand Total for Theory and Practicals (GT) is studied by employing one way analysis of variance technique. The following hypothesis is formulated.

Hypothesis-7:

There would be no significant influence of the various groups, formed on the basis of theory and practical scores of students on total achievement.

For testing the above hypothesis one way analysis of variance is used. The respective means, S.Ds. and F values are given in Table 5.26.

It is observed from Table 5.26 that the computed 'F' values for all the theory and practicals scores are significant beyond 0.01 level of confidence. Hence, hypothesis-7 is rejected. It is observed from Table 5.26 that the mean values of total achievement score in Group I in all the theory and practical scores are less than those in Group II and the respective mean values of Group II are less than those in Group III. It is inferred that the students who secured less score in theory and practicals also secured less score in total achievement score. Hence, there is perfect positive correlation between each theory and practical score and the total achievement score. Therefore, it is concluded that theory and practical scores have their own influence on total achievement of the DIET students.

Table 5.26: Influence of Theory and Practical Scores of the Students on Total Academic Achievement Score

S. No.	*No. of Observations*			*Mean Value*			*Standard Deviation*			*F Value*	*Level of Significance*
	I	*II*	*III*	*I*	*II*	*III*	*I*	*II*	*III*		
1.	155	297	148	1439.28	1473.57	1543.10	87.02	87.88	101.88	51.37	*
2.	151	303	146	1404.57	1479.04	1567.64	80.25	76.89	87.26	153.19	*
3.	153	279	148	1404.41	1478.20	1569.32	77.03	77.60	85.87	162.17	*
4.	154	299	147	1365.56	1489.61	1587.95	47.49	63.50	60.40	539.16	*
5.	155	300	145	1367.32	1492.17	1582.97	50.70	67.43	60.75	462.94	*
6.	151	301	148	1361.85	1488.22	1591.38	45.84	59.87	57.25	631.61	*

* Significant at 0.01 level.

IMPACT OF TEACHER ATTITUDE ON TOTAL ACHIEVEMENT SCORE

The constructed Teacher Attitude Inventory is prepared and administered to assess the attitudes of the DIET students in the present study. The Teacher Attitude Inventory consists of two main parts covering 12 areas. The groups are formed on the basis of Quartiles.

To identify the impact of Teacher Attitude score on Total Achievement of DIET students, one way ANOVA technique is employed. The following hypothesis is formulated.

Hypothesis-8:

There is no significant influence of Teacher Attitude score on Total Achievement of DIET students.

The respective means, S.Ds. and 'F' values are presented in Table 5.27.

It is observed from Table 5.27 that the computed 'F' ratios for the attitude areas, high conceptual level (TA3), low conceptual level (TA4), High Social Approach (TA), total attitude score for training (TA11) and the total Attitude score (TA12) are significant at 0.01 level. Hence, hypothesis-8 is rejected for the above variables. Therefore, the above variables have significant influence on the total achievement of the DIET students.

It is cleared from Table 5.27, the calculated 'F' values for the variable Attitude towards profession (TA1) and Classroom practice (TA10) are 3.48 and 15.16 respectively, which are above the table value at 0.05 level of significance. Therefore hypothesis-8 is rejected. Hence, the attitudes like attitude towards profession (TA1) and Classroom practice (TA10) of the DIET students have their own influence on Total Achievement. The students who have better attitude towards profession and Classroom practice also have good Achievement.

Table 5.27: Influence of Student Teachers Attitude Score on Total Academic Achievement Score

S. No.	*No. of Observations*			*Mean Value*			*Standard Deviation*			*F Value*	*Level of Significance*
	I	*II*	*III*	*I*	*II*	*III*	*I*	*II*	*III*		
1.	165	291	144	1498.14	1478.82	1469.35	100.43	96.36	99.61	3.57	*
2.	151	339	110	1497.44	1476.49	1477.02	96.01	100.14	96.43	2.53	@
3.	198	256	146	1504.81	1471.65	1468.65	98.25	98.15	95.40	8.22	**
4.	179	272	149	1508.62	1472.10	1467.54	98.25	95.39	95.44	9.75	**
5.	169	325	106	1492.70	1484.48	1456.53	101.56	95.40	93.15	4.68	**
6.	221	314	65	1483.24	1484.29	1465.45	97.39	101.58	88.22	1.02	@
7.	151	373	76	1492.52	1479.78	1470.92	104.36	95.51	101.95	1.43	@
8.	169	296	135	1494.46	1476.68	1477.45	99.61	99.16	95.78	1.92	@
9.	182	319	99	1466.66	1473.82	1476.99	110.27	111.67	99.15	0.36	@
10.	179	290	131	1494.72	1481.60	1464.87	96.33	102.37	91.41	3.48	*
11.	151	309	140	1518.96	1467.30	1473.99	93.76	98.32	95.07	15.16	**
12.	152	303	145	1515.56	1470.65	1469.95	98.92	96.59	95.32	12.32	**

* Significant at 0.05 level.

** Significant at 0.01 level.

@ Not Significant at 0.05 level.

It is evident from Table 5.27 that the computed 'F' values for the Need for content (TA2), High intrinsic motivation (TA6), Acceptance of values (TA7), Preference for visual and auditory presentation (TA8) and Attitude towards pupils during practice teaching (TA9) are less than the table value at 0.05 level. Hence, hypothesis-8 is accepted. It is concluded that the above attitudes do not show any significant influence on Total Achievement.

IMPACT OF STUDY HABITS ON TOTAL ACHIEVEMENT

The Study Habits Inventory developed by the investigator consists of 9 areas. The groups in each study habit areas are formed on the basis of quartiles as is done earlier. The impact of the study habits on Total Achievement of DIET students is investigated by employing one way ANOVA technique. The following hypothesis is formulated.

Hypothesis-9:

There is no significant influence of students study habits on Total Achievement of the DIET students.

For testing the above hypothesis, one way ANOVA technique is used. The respective Means, S.Ds. and 'F' Values are given in Table 5.28.

It is observed from Table 5.28 that the computed 'F' values for the study habit areas namely S_1, S_2 and S_8 are significant beyond 0.01 level of confidence. Hence, hypothesis-9 is rejected. Therefore, it is concluded that the above study habit areas have its own influence on Total Achievement of DIET students.

From Table 5.28, the 'F' values of the study habit areas namely S3, S4, S5 and ST are significant at 0.05 level of significant. Hence, hypothesis-9 is rejected. Therefore the study habit areas S3, S4, S5 and ST have significant impact on Total Achievement score.

From Table 5.28 that the 'F' values for the study habit areas namely S6, S7, and S9 are not significant at 0.05 level. Hence, hypothesis-9 is accepted. Therefore the study habit areas S6, S7, and S9 have no significant impact on Total Achievement score.

Table 5.28: Influence of Study Habits Score of the Students on Total Academic Achievement Score

Sl. No.	*Area*	*No. of Observations*			*Mean Value*			*Standard Deviation*			*F Value*	*Level of Significance*
		I	*II*	*III*	*I*	*II*	*III*	*I*	*II*	*III*		
1.	S1	160	304	136	1463.43	1483.21	1500.52	105.87	96.27	91.96	5.32	**
2.	S2	167	313	120	1464.48	1494.89	1472.07	92.93	97.39	105.56	6.01	**
3.	S3	151	314	135	1465.91	1490.97	1478.51	92.48	103.90	90.87	3.42	*
4.	S4	175	305	120	1467.25	1484.08	1497.53	97.05	98.44	99.64	3.53	*
5.	S5	158	293	149	1466.44	1491.38	1479.49	97.61	98.60	98.46	3.36	*
6.	S6	161	312	127	1477.44	1483.12	1484.38	100.98	94.76	105.63	0.22	@
7.	S7	164	299	137	1481.93	1480.56	1484.61	98.09	97.69	102.19	0.07	@
8.	S8	172	293	135	1464.31	1483.93	1499.73	99.13	99.97	92.15	5.06	**
9.	S9	159	318	123	1479.81	1485.13	1476.07	103.85	100.41	87.11	0.42	@
10.	ST	160	291	149	1463.78	1488.50	1488.32	95.10	100.72	96.66	3.69	*

* Significant at 0.05 level.

** Significant at 0.01 level.

@ Not Significant at 0.05 level.

IMPACT OF 16 PERSONALITY FACTORS (16 PF) ON TOTAL ACHIEVEMENT

The Cattell's 16 Personality Factors (16 PF) Form–C was adopted as a tool to assess the personality of the DIET students for the purpose of present study. It consists of 16 Personality Factors.

To identify the impact of 16 Personality Factors on Total Achievement Score of DIET students, one way ANOVA technique is employed. The students are divided into 3 groups on each factor of 16 PF, based on sten values. The sten values 1 to 4 are grouped as low scorers (group I), 5 and 6 as average scorers (group II), and 7 to 10 as high scorers (group III). The Mean values of Total Achievement score for the three groups of each personality factor are tested for significance by employing one way Analysis of Variance Technique. The following hypothesis is formulated to see the influence of the 16 personality factors on Total Achievement score of DIET students.

Hypothesis-10:

There would be no significant influence of 16 PF on Total Achievement score of the DIET students.

To test the above hypothesis one way ANOVA technique is employed. A comparison of Means, S.Ds. and 'F' values are presented in Table 5.29.

It is evident from Table 5.29 that the computed 'F' values for the personality factors B, E, F, M, Q2, and Q4 are significant at 0.05 level of significance. Hence hypothesis-10 is rejected. It is concluded that the factors B, E, F, M, Q2, and Q4 of 16 PF have shown influence on Total Achievement score of the DIET students.

It is clear from Table 5.29 that the calculated value of 'F' for Factors A, C, G, H, I, L, N, O, Q1 and Q3 are below the table value at 0.05 level of significance. Therefore, hypothesis-10 is accepted. Hence the Factors A, C, G, H, I, L, N, O, Q1 and Q3 of 16 PF have no significant influence on Total Achievement score of the DIET students.

Table 5.29: Influence of 16 Personality Factors of the Student Teachers on Total Academic Achievement Score

Sl. No.	16 PFs	No. of Observation			Mean values			S.D.			F Value	Level of Significance
		I	II	III	I	II	III	I	II	III		
1.	PFA	211	195	194	1489.37	1484.07	1471.46	90.72	101.89	103.26	1.74	@
2.	PFB	250	122	228	1493.77	1473.93	1473.04	99.58	96.31	98.05	3.14	*
3.	PFC	155	261	184	1480.80	1474.56	1493.11	95.36	96.97	103.28	1.92	@
4.	PFE	164	245	191	1488.39	1489.50	1466.45	98.70	98.67	97.45	3.45	*
5.	PFF	225	227	148	1485.21	1468.26	1497.62	110.35	84.27	98.30	4.22	*
6.	PFH	219	232	149	1490.54	1476.33	1477.72	97.59	104.12	91.08	1.34	@
7.	PFI	189	249	162	1477.38	1479.94	1490.05	98.38	102.23	93.50	0.80	@
8.	PFJ	133	335	132	1483.50	1481.07	1482.21	90.49	99.87	104.16	0.03	@
9.	PFL	245	225	130	1477.04	1482.30	1490.19	94.17	103.46	98.75	0.75	@
10.	PFM	159	226	215	1496.79	1482.20	1470.46	91.48	100.63	100.70	3.28	*
11.	PFN	218	185	197	1489.80	1473.40	1481.03	102.96	96.32	95.83	1.39	@
12.	PFO	152	275	173	1488.61	1481.76	1476.09	101.53	99.66	94.73	0.64	@
13.	PFQ1	171	295	134	1476.66	1479.46	1493.46	89.42	103.69	98.48	1.24	@
14.	PFQ2	135	285	180	1501.66	1473.96	1479.52	104.05	95.64	97.85	3.71	*
15.	PFQ3	212	195	193	1469.82	1491.10	1485.75	97.09	99.83	98.48	2.59	@
16.	PFQ4	207	188	205	1468.33	1483.39	1494.11	96.28	101.34	97.40	3.58	*

* Significant at 0.05 level.

@ Not Significant at 0.05 level.

IMPACT OF OBJECTIVE ACHIEVEMENT TEST SCORE ON TOTAL ACHIEVEMENT SCORE

The objective Achievement test constructed by the investigator consists of 5 areas namely 1. Teacher Education in emerging India (A1), 2. Educational Psychology, Measurement and Evaluation (A2), 3. Elementary Education, Educational Planning and Management (A3), 4. Perspectives in Primary Education (A4), and 5. Art, Health, Physical education and Computer education (A5) based on the syllabus.

The influence of these 5 areas of Objective Achievement Test scores and total score in Objective Achievement test on Total Achievement score are studied by employing one way ANOVA technique. The following hypothesis is formulated.

Hypothesis-11:

There would be no significant influence of Objective Achievement test score on Total Achievement score of the DIET students.

For testing the above hypothesis, one way ANOVA is used. The respective means, S.Ds. and 'F' values are given in Table 5.30.

It is observed from Table 5.30 that the computed 'F' value for the area Elementary Education, Educational planning and Management (A3) and Perspectives in Primary Education (A4) are 5.73 and 5.28, which are significant at 0.01 level of confidence. Hence hypothesis-11 is rejected. It is observed from the Table 5.30, the 'F' values for Total objective achievement score is 3.43, which is significant at 0.05 level. Hence, hypothesis-11 is rejected. Therefore the achievement areas Elementary Education, Educational planning and Management (A1) and Perspectives in Primary Education (A4) and Total achievement score (A6) have significant influence on Total Achievement score of the DIET students.

It is clear from Table 5.30 that the calculated 'F' values for achievement areas namely Teacher Education in Emerging India (A1), Educational Psychology, Measurement and Evaluation (A2), Art, Health, Physical and Computer education (A5) are less than the table value at 0.05 level of confidence. Hence, hypothesis-11 is accepted. Therefore, the above areas have no significant influence on Total Achievement score of the DIET students.

Table 5.30: Influence of Objective Achievement Test Scores of the Students on Total Achievement Score

Sl. No.	*Area*	*No. of Observations*			*Mean Value*			*Standard Deviation*			*F Value*	*Level of Significance*
		I	*II*	*III*	*I*	*II*	*III*	*I*	*II*	*III*		
•1.	A1	172	318	110	1480.26	1478.43	1494.29	91.10	101.44	101.90	1.08	@
2.	A2	207	287	106	1483.45	1485.64	1468.53	100.03	97.01	100.38	1.20	@
3.	A3	195	298	107	1501.15	1474.07	1468.41	96.38	97.66	101.40	5.73	**
4.	A4	158	338	104	1492.85	1470.68	1501.50	99.41	97.83	96.33	5.28	**
5.	A5	189	286	125	1495.80	1476.24	1473.65	99.95	94.14	105.36	2.79	@
6.	A6	153	311	136	1499.52	1474.32	1479.24	95.66	99.17	99.18	3.43	*

* Significant at 0.05 level.

** Significant at 0.01 level.

@ Not Significant at 0.05 level.

IMPACT OF ACHIEVEMENT SCORES IN THEORY, PRACTICALS AND TOTAL SCORE ON ACHIEVEMENT IN THEORY

The achievement score in theory means the total marks in theory in first and second year. The influence of achievement scores in theory and practicals, Total practicals score and Total score on achievement score in Theory is investigated.

On the basis of the achievement scores of the respective variables the total sample (N=600) is divided into 3 groups using quartiles as is done earlier.

The influence of these groups in each theory and practical scores of first and second year, Total practical score and Total Achievement score of the students on achievement score in theory is studied by employing one way ANOVA technique. The following hypothesis is formulated.

Hypothesis-12:

There would be no significant influence of theory and practical scores of first and second year, practicals total score and Total achievement score of students on achievement score in theory.

For testing the above hypothesis one way analysis of variance is used. The respective means, S.D s and F values are given in Table 5.31.

It is observed from Table 5.31 that the computed 'F' values for all the theory and practicals scores of first and second year, practicals total score and total achievement score are significant beyond 0.01 level of confidence. Hence, hypothesis-12 is rejected. It is observed from Table 5.31 that the mean value of achievement score in Theory, Group I in all the theory and practical scores and Total Achievement score are less than the mean value of Group II and the respective mean values of Group II are less than that of Group III. Hence, there is perfect positive correlation between each theory score, practicals score, practical Total score and the total achievement score with total academic achievement scores in theory. Therefore, it is concluded that theory and practical scores have their own influence on achievement scores in theory of the DIET students.

Table 5.31: Impact of Achievement Test Score in Theory, Practicals and Total on Achievement Score in Theory

Sl. No.	*Area*	*No. of Observations*			*Mean Value*			*Standard Deviation*			*F Value*	*Level of Significance*
		I	*II*	*III*	*I*	*II*	*III*	*I*	*II*	*III*		
1.	AT1	155	297	148	656.88	704.45	750.92	27.59	24.66	32.33	443.20	*
2.	AT2	151	303	146	658.74	702.57	752.23	28.44	26.00	31.73	411.21	*
3.	AP1	154	299	147	692.82	700.02	722.26	37.90	40.60	48.04	20.76	*
4.	AP2	155	300	145	689.61	701.94	722.08	38.45	41.79	44.91	23.15	*
5.	AP	151	301	148	691.13	700.61	722.49	38.67	39.66	48.49	22.62	*
6.	GT	151	302	147	675.24	696.56	747.29	32.89	35.64	33.02	176.82	*

* Significant at 0.01 level.

IMPACT OF THE STUDENT TEACHERS ATTITUDE ON ACHIEVEMENT SCORE IN THEORY

The constructed Student Teachers Attitude inventory is prepared and administered to assess the attitudes of the DIET students in the present study. The Teacher Attitude Inventory consists of two main parts with covering 12 areas. Groups are formed in these 12 areas on the basis of Quartiles.

To identify the impact of Teacher Attitude score on Achievement score in Theory of the DIET students, one way ANOVA technique is employed. The following hypothesis is formulated.

Hypothesis-13:

There would be no significant influence of Teacher Attitude scores on Achievement score in Theory of DIET students.

For testing the above hypothesis one way ANOVA is used. The respective means, S.Ds. and 'F' values are given in Table 5.32.

It is cleared from Table 5.32 that the calculated 'F' values for the attitude area high intrinsic motivation (TA6) is 3.14, which is above the table value at 0.05 level of significant. Therefore hypothesis-13 is rejected. Hence, the attitude area high intrinsic motivation of the DIET students has its own influence on Achievement score in theory.

It is evident from Table 5.32, the computed 'F' values for all the other remaining 11 variables in Table 5.32 are not significant at 0.05 level. Hence, hypothesis-13 is accepted. It is concluded that the above 11 areas of attitude towards profession and training do not have significant influence on Achievement score in Theory.

IMPACT OF STUDY HABITS ON ACHIEVEMENT SCORE IN THEORY

The Study Habits inventory developed by the investigator consists of 9 areas. The impact of the study habits on Achievement score in theory of the DIET students is investigated by employing one way ANOVA technique. The following Hypothesis is formulated.

Table 5.32: Impact of Student Teachers Attitude Score on Achievement Score in Theory

Sl. No.	Area	No. of Observations			Mean Value			Standard Deviation			F Value	Level of Significance
		I	II	III	I	II	III	I	II	III		
1.	TA1	165	291	144	706.39	701.99	701.99	47.35	42.80	39.24	0.50	@
2.	TA2	151	339	110	703.81	702.47	701.92	43.61	45.10	36.67	0.44	@
3.	TA3	198	256	146	706.22	704.04	699.37	46.21	44.08	37.20	1.08	@
4.	TA4	179	272	149	707.85	701.11	703.13	48.00	41.39	40.40	1.34	@
5.	TA5	169	325	106	705.34	705.53	695.05	43.90	42.98	42.43	2.55	@
6.	TA6	221	314	65	707.38	703.35	692.17	43.28	43.71	39.37	3.14	*
7.	TA7	151	373	76	703.46	703.64	703.87	46.13	42.60	41.11	0.01	@
8.	TA8	169	296	135	706.32	703.92	699.59	44.58	44.37	38.89	0.93	@
9.	TA9	182	319	99	694.13	695.01	699.03	53.06	52.02	42.53	0.33	@
10.	TA10	179	290	131	702.76	706.94	697.45	42.92	46.36	35.47	2.24	@
11.	T11	151	309	140	709.58	701.42	702.06	44.29	45.68	35.64	1.94	@
12.	TA12	152	303	145	709.48	702.35	700.14	47.08	44.30	35.94	2.01	@

* Significant at 0.05 level.

@ Not Significant at 0.05 level.

Hypothesis-14:

There is no significant influence of study habits on Achievement score in theory of the DIET students.

To test the above hypothesis, one way ANOVA technique is used. The respective Means, S.Ds. and 'F' Values are given in Table 5.33.

It is observed from Table 5.33 that the computed 'F' values for the study habit area—Planning of work and subject is significant beyond 0.01 level of confidence. Hence, hypothesis-14 is rejected. Therefore, it is concluded that the above study habits area has its own influence on Achievement score in Theory of the DIET students.

From Table 5.33, the 'F' values of study habit areas namely S1, S5, S8 and ST are significant at 0.05 level of confidence. Hence, hypothesis-14 is rejected. Therefore the study habit areas S1, S5 S8 and ST have significant impact on Achievement score in theory.

From Table 5.33 the 'F' values of study habit areas S2, S4, S6, S7 and S9 are not significant at 0.05 level. Hence, hypothesis 14 is accepted. Therefore the study habit areas S2, S4, S6, S7 and S9 have no significant impact on Achievement score in Theory.

IMPACT OF 16 PERSONALITY FACTORS (16 PF) ON ACHIEVEMENT SCORE IN THEORY

To identify the impact of 16 Personality Factors on Achievement score in theory of the DIET students, one way ANOVA technique is employed. The students are divided into 3 groups on each factor of 16 PF, based on sten values as mentioned earlier. The Mean values of Achievement score in Theory for these groups of each personality factor are tested for significance by employing one way Analysis of Variance Technique. The following hypothesis is formulated to test the influence of the 16 personality factors on Achievement score in Theory of the DIET students.

Hypothesis-15:

There would not significant influence of 16 PF on Achievement score in Theory of the DIET students.

Table 5.33: Impact of Study Habits Score on Achievement Score in Theory

Sl. No.	*Area*	*No. of Observations*			*Mean Value*			*Standard Deviation*			*F Value*	*Level of Significance*
		I	*II*	*III*	*I*	*II*	*III*	*I*	*II*	*III*		
1.	S1	160	304	136	695.58	705.32	709.30	49.48	39.73	41.97	4.23	*
2.	S2	167	313	120	698.34	705.89	705.08	42.03	44.89	40.22	1.75	@
3.	S3	151	314	135	693.99	707.42	705.56	43.66	44.47	38.33	5.17	**
4.	S4	175	305	120	703.38	701.02	710.58	46.90	41.63	41.36	2.12	@
5.	S5	158	293	149	695.16	706.75	706.43	46.37	42.63	40.05	4.15	*
6.	S6	161	312	127	703.94	702.25	706.58	44.92	42.81	42.38	0.46	@
7.	S7	164	299	137	702.29	701.78	709.24	46.63	42.32	40.87	1.52	@
8.	S8	172	293	135	697.23	704.90	708.99	44.09	42.63	42.88	3.07	*
9.	S9	159	318	123	705.36	704.68	698.63	46.83	43.02	38.83	1.05	@
10.	ST	160	291	149	696.58	703.80	710.52	46.08	42.27	42.15	3.88	*

* Significant at 0.05 level.

** Significant at 0.01 level.

@ Not Significant at 0.05 level.

To test the above hypothesis one way ANOVA technique is employed. Comparisons of the 'F' values are presented in Table 5.34.

It is evident from Table 5.34, the computed 'F' values for the factor F is significant at 0.01 level. Hence, hypothesis -15 is rejected. It is concluded that the factor F of 16 PF has its own influence on Achievement score in Theory of the DIET students.

It is clear from Table 5.34, the calculated values of 'F' ratios for Factors M and Q4 are significant at 0.05 level of confidence. Therefore, hypothesis-15 is rejected. Hence the Factors M and Q4 of 16 PF have significant influence on Achievement score in Theory of the DIET students.

The other factors of the 16 Personality Factors do not have any significant influence on Achievement score in Theory of the DIET students.

IMPACT OF OBJECTIVE ACHIEVEMENT TEST SCORE ON ACHIEVEMENT SCORE IN THEORY

The objective Achievement test constructed by the investigator consists of 5 areas as mentioned earlier. The influence of these 5 areas and their total score of the Objective test on achievement score in theory is studied by employing one way ANOVA technique. The following hypothesis is formulated.

Hypothesis-16:

There is no significant influence of Objective Achievement test score on achievement score in Theory of the DIET students.

To test the above hypothesis, one way ANOVA is used. The respective means, S.Ds. and 'F' values are given in Table 5.35.

It is observed from Table 5.35 that the computed 'F' value for the area Perspectives in Primary Education (A4) is 6.39, which is significant at 0.01 level of confidence. Hence hypothesis-16 is rejected. It is observed from Table 5.35 the 'F' ratios for the area Educational Psychology, Measurement and Evaluation (TA1) is 4.26, which is significant at 0.05 level of confidence. Hence, Hypothesis-16 is rejected. Therefore the achievement areas Perspectives in Primary Education and Educational Psychology, Measurement and Evaluation have significant influence on Achievement score in Theory of the DIET students.

Table 5.34: Influence of 16 Personality Factors of the Student Teachers on Achievement Score in Theory

Sl. No.	Area	No. of Observation			Mean values			S.D.			F Value	Level of Significance
		I	II	III	I	II	III	I	II	III		
1.	PFA	211	195	194	704.43	705.84	700.52	42.66	44.56	42.62	0.80	@
2.	PFB	250	122	228	705.00	702.26	702.84	47.09	40.04	40.59	0.22	@
3.	PFC	155	261	184	702.83	702.38	706.04	46.82	42.64	42.78	1.33	@
4.	PFE	164	245	191	706.52	704.86	699.53	42.93	43.78	42.78	1.33	@
5.	PFF	225	227	148	709.94	695.70	707.26	45.68	39.25	43.80	6.33	**
6.	PFG	219	232	149	704.94	704.28	700.67	47.10	42.40	38.57	0.48	@
7.	PFH	189	249	162	704.07	703.19	703.76	43.27	45.28	40.22	0.03	@
8.	PFI	133	335	132	699.05	703.66	708.12	37.98	45.32	42.70	1.46	@
9.	PFL	245	225	130	701.40	701.99	710.63	39.53	45.53	45.51	2.21	@
10.	PFM	159	226	215	711.08	699.48	702.46	39.89	44.68	43.63	3.52	*
11.	PFN	218	185	197	706.33	700.56	703.49	44.50	41.54	43.47	0.91	@
12.	PFO	152	275	173	704.05	703.39	703.62	45.72	42.60	42.30	0.02	@
13.	PFQ1	171	295	134	703.23	702.67	706.21	39.92	46.54	39.92	0.32	@
14.	PFQ2	135	285	180	708.76	701.39	703.29	45.74	41.61	43.83	1.34	@
15.	PFQ3	212	195	193	702.64	703.03	705.30	42.82	45.89	41.12	0.22	@
16.	PFQ4	207	188	205	698.77	702.51	709.54	41.37	43.96	44.00	3.32	*

* Significant at 0.05 level.

** Significant at 0.01 level.

@ Not Significant at 0.05 level.

Table 5.35: Impact of Objective Achievement Test Score on Achievement Score in Theory

Sl. No.	*Area*	*No. of Observations*			*Mean Value*			*Standard Deviation*			*F Value*	*Level of Significance*
		I	*II*	*III*	*I*	*II*	*III*	*I*	*II*	*III*		
1.	A1	172	318	110	699.49	703.42	710.67	42.27	42.93	45.19	2.27	@
2.	A2	207	287	106	698.60	708.97	698.93	44.43	41.46	44.42	4.26	*
3.	A3	195	298	107	704.25	701.28	709.02	45.88	42.01	41.60	1.30	@
4.	A4	158	338	104	698.12	702.15	716.76	46.38	41.36	42.20	6.39	**
5.	A5	189	246	125	702.48	701.53	710.14	43.98	41.18	46.41	1.83	@
6.	A6	153	311	136	700.13	702.12	710.98	44.89	41.85	44.04	2.67	@

* Significant at 0.05 level.

** Significant at 0.01 level.

@ Not Significant at 0.05 level.

It is clear from Table 5.35 the calculated 'F' values for achievement areas Teacher Education in Emerging India, Educational Planning and Management, Art, Health, Physical and Computer Education and Total achievement score are less than the table values at 0.05 level of confidence. Hence hypothesis-16 is accepted. Therefore, the above areas have no significant influence on Achievement score in Theory of the DIET students.

IMPACT OF THEORY, PRACTICALS AND TOTAL SCORES ON ACHIEVEMENT SCORE IN PRACTICALS

The influence of Theory, Practicals and total scores on Total achievement score in Practicals is studied by employing one way analysis of variance technique. The groups on the variables are formed on the basis of quartiles. The following hypothesis is formulated.

Hypothesis-17:

There is no significant influence of theory, practicals and total scores of students on achievement scoresin practicals.

For testing the above hypothesis one way analysis of variance is used. The respective means, S.Ds. and F values are given in Table 5.36.

It is observed from Table 5.36 that the computed 'F' values for all the theory, practicals and total scores are significant beyond 0.01 level of confidence. Hence, hypothesis-17 is rejected. It is observed from Table 5.36 that the mean values of achievement scores in practicals in Group I in all the theory and practical scores are less than those of Group II and the respective mean values of Group II are less than those of Group III. Hence, there is perfect positive correlation between each theory, practicals and total score with the total achievement score in Practicals. Therefore, it is concluded that theory, practical scores and total scores have its own influence on Total achievement score in practicals of the DIET students.

Table 5.36: Impact of Achievement Score in Theory, Practicals and Total on Achievement in Practical

Sl. No.	Area	No. of Observations			Mean Value			Standard Deviation			F Value	Level of Significance
		I	II	III	I	II	III	I	II	III		
1.	AT1	155	297	148	782.40	769.12	792.18	73.61	75.26	83.22	4.75	*
2.	AT2	151	303	146	745.83	776.48	815.41	76.21	71.50	74.71	33.44	*
3.	AT	153	299	148	754.74	774.68	809.72	75.28	74.36	75.65	20.94	*
4.	AP1	154	299	147	672.73	789.59	865.69	23.36	43.16	21.92	1211.11	*
5.	AP2	155	300	145	677.72	790.22	860.90	31.95	48.59	29.17	787.32	*
6.	GT	151	302	147	678.69	787.87	860.70	31.30	52.14	25.67	709.64	*

* Significant at 0.01 level.

IMPACT OF TEACHERS ATTITUDE SCORES ON ACHIEVEMENT SCORE IN PRACTICALS

The constructed Teacher Attitude Inventory is prepared and administered to assess the attitudes of the DIET students in the present study. The Teacher Attitude Inventory consists of two main parts covering 12 areas as mentioned earlier

To identify the impact of Teacher Attitude scores on Total Achievement score in practicals of DIET students,. one way ANOVA technique is employed. The following hypothesis is formulated.

Hypothesis 18:

There is no significant influence of Teacher Attitude score on Total Achievement score in practicals.

For testing the above hypothesis one way ANOVA is used. The respective Means, S.Ds. and 'F' values are given in Table 5.37.

It is observed from Table 5.37 that the computed 'F' ratios for the attitude areas High conceptual level (TA3) and Low conceptual level (TA4), total score for attitudes towards training (TA11) and Total score for attitude towards profession and training (TA12) are significant at 0.01 level. Hence, hypothesis-18 is rejected for the above attitudes.

It is cleared from Table 5.37 that the calculated 'F' values for the variables Attitude towards profession (TA1), Need for content (TA2), High social approach (TA5) and Classroom practice (TA10) are above the table value at 0.05 level of significance. Therefore hypothesis-18 is rejected. Hence, the above attitude areas have its own influence on Total Achievement score in practicals.

It is evident from Table 5.37, the computed 'F' values for the attitudes like High intrinsic Motivation (TA6), Acceptance of values (TA7), Preference for visual and Auditory presentation (TA8) and attitude towards pupils during practice teaching (TA9) are less than table value at 0.05 level. Hence, hypothesis-18 is accepted. It is concluded that the above attitudes do not show any significant influence on Total Achievement score in practicals of the DIET students.

Table 5.37: Impact of Student Teachers Attitude Score on Achievement Score in Practicals

Sl. No.	*Area*	*No. of Observations*			*Mean Value*			*Standard Deviation*			*F Value*	*Level of Significance*
		I	*II*	*III*	*I*	*II*	*III*	*I*	*II*	*III*		
1.	TA1	165	291	144	791.75	775.96	767.37	76.17	75.16	81.39	4.10	*
2.	TA2	151	339	110	793.62	774.03	770.10	74.96	77.03	79.44	4.14	*
3.	TA3	198	256	146	798.59	767.61	769.28	72.54	78.04	77.60	10.57	**
4.	TA4	179	272	149	800.77	770.99	764.41	76.03	77.73	7286	11.55	**
5.	TA5	169	325	106	787.37	778.96	761.48	78.97	76.44	75.62	3.71	*
6.	TA6	221	314	65	775.86	780.94	773.28	75.52	79.95	72.33	0.43	@
7.	TA7	151	373	76	789.06	776.14	767.05	78.64	75.15	83.93	2.42	@
8.	TA8	169	296	135	788.14	772.76	777.87	75.14	78.84	76.20	2.14	@
9.	TA9	182	319	99	772.53	778.82	777.96	82.38	79.69	78.20	0.37	@
10.	TA10	179	290	131	791.96	774.66	767.42	77.42	77.29	75.43	4.46	*
11.	TA11	151	309	140	809.38	765.88	771.93	71.07	76.40	77.31	17.56	**
12.	TA12	152	303	145	806.08	768.30	769.81	73.39	76.55	76.58	13.76	**

* Significant at 0.05 level.

** Significant at 0.01 level.

@ Not Significant at 0.05 level.

IMPACT OF STUDY HABIT SCORES ON ACHIEVEMENT SCORE IN PRACTICALS

The Study Habits Inventory developed by the investigator consists of 9 areas. The impact of the study habits on Achievement score in Practicals of the DIET students is investigated by employing one way ANOVA technique. The following hypothesis is formulated.

Hypothesis-19:

There is no significant influence of study habits on Achievement score in Practicals of the DIET students.

To test the above hypothesis, one way ANOVA technique is used. The respective Means, S.Ds. and 'F' Values are given in Table 5.38.

It is observed from Table 5.38 the computed 'F' value for the study habit area S_2 is significant at 0.01 level of confidence. Hence, hypothesis 19 is rejected. Therefore, it is concluded that the above study habits area has its own influence on Achievement score in Practicals of the DIET students.

From Table 5.38 that the 'F' values of study habit areas namely S1, S4 and S8 are significant at 0.05 level of confidence. Hence, hypothesis 19 is rejected. Therefore the study habit areas S1, S4 and S8 have significant impact on Achievement score in practicals.

The other areas of the study habit inventory do not have significant influence on achievement score in practicals of the DIET students.

IMPACT OF 16 PERSONALITY FACTORS (16 PF) ON ACHIEVEMENT SCORE IN PRACTICALS

To identify the impact of 16 Personality Factors on Achievement score in practical of the DIET students. One way ANOVA technique is employed. The students are divided into 3 groups on each factor of 16 PF, based on sten values as mentioned earlier. The Mean values of Achievement score in Practicals for the three groups of each personality factor are tested for significance, by employing one way Analysis of Variance Technique. The following hypothesis is formulated to see the influence of the 16 personality factors on Achievement score in Practicals of the DIET students.

Table 5.38: Impact of Study Habits Score on Achievement Score in Practicals

Sl. No.	*Area*	*No. of Observations*			*Mean Value*			*Standard Deviation*			*F Value*	*Level of Significance*
		I	*II*	*III*	*I*	*II*	*III*	*I*	*II*	*III*		
1.	S1	160	304	136	67.86	777.90	791.21	80.47	77.94	70.71	3.38	*
2.	S2	167	313	120	766.14	789.00	766.99	78.26	74.29	80.48	6.45	**
3.	S3	151	314	135	771.92	783.55	772.96	77.72	78.63	73.59	1.56	@
4.	S4	175	305	120	763.87	783.06	786.95	78.89	76.85	74.20	4.42	*
5.	S5	158	293	149	771.28	784.62	773.06	79.33	76.39	76.65	1.98	@
6.	S6	161	312	127	773.49	780.87	777.80	79.15	75.73	79.37	0.49	@
7.	S7	164	299	137	779.64	778.78	775.37	76.50	77.35	78.93	0.13	@
8.	S8	172	293	135	767.08	779.03	790.73	79.88	78.84	68.93	3.60	*
9.	S9	159	318	123	774.45	780.45	777.43	79.97	78.55	75.01	0.33	@
10.	ST	160	291	149	766.90	784.69	777.81	79.00	77.41	74.55	2.75	@

* Significant at 0.05 level.

** Significant at 0.01 level.

@ Not Significant at 0.05 level.

Hypothesis-20:

There would be no significant influence of 16 PF on Achievement score in Practicals of the DIET students.

To test the above hypothesis one way ANOVA technique is employed. Comparisons of the 'F' values are presented in Table 5.39.

It is clear from Table 5.39, the calculated value of 'F' for Factors B, E, M, Q2 and Q3 are significant at 0.05 level of significance. Therefore, hypothesis-20 is rejected. Hence the Factors B, E, M, Q2 and Q3 of 16 PF have its own significant influence on Achievement score in practicals of the DIET students.

The other factors of the 16 PF do not have significant influence on Achievement score in Practicals of the DIET students.

IMPACT OF OBJECTIVE ACHIEVEMENT TEST SCORE ON ACHIEVEMENT SCORE IN PRACTICALS

The Objective Achievement Test constructed by the investigator consists of 5 areas as mentioned earlier. The influence of these 5 areas and their total score of the Objective test on Achievement score in Practicals is studied by employing one way ANOVA Technique. The following hypothesis is formulated.

Hypothesis 21:

There is no significant influence of Objective Achievement test score on Achievement score in Practicals of the DIET students.

To test the above hypothesis, one way ANOVA is used. The respective means, S.Ds. and 'F' values are given in Table 5.40.

It is observed from Table 5.40 that the computed 'F' values for the areas Elementary Education, Educational planning and management (A3), Perspectives in primary education (A4), Art, Health, Physical and Computer Education (A5) and the total score of objective achievement test (A6) are significant at 0.01 level of confidence. Hence hypothesis-21 is rejected. Therefore, the above achievement areas have significant influence on Achievement score in Practicals of the DIET students.

Table 5.39: Influence of 16 Personality Factors of the Student Teachers on Achievement Score in Practicals

Sl. No.	*Area*	*No. of Observation*			*Mean values*			*S.D.*			*F Value*	*Level of Significance*
		I	*II*	*III*	*I*	*II*	*III*	*I*	*II*	*III*		
1.	PFA	211	195	194	784.94	778.24	770.95	71.58	77.12	83.19	1.66	@
2.	PFB	250	122	228	788.77	771.67	770.20	74.92	77.14	79.10	4.03	*
3.	PFC	155	261	184	777.97	772.18	787.07	76.29	75.05	81.00	2.01	@
4.	PFE	164	245	191	781.87	784.64	766.92	78.94	75.67	77.32	3.09	*
5.	PFF	225	227	148	775.99	772.56	790.36	84.14	71.57	74.32	2.54	@
6.	PFG	219	232	149	785.60	772.05	777.05	73.28	82.23	74.98	1.76	@
7.	PFH	189	249	162	773.31	776.74	786.29	77.52	77.98	76.08	1.31	@
8.	PFI	133	335	132	784.45	777.41	774.08	73.75	77.95	79.63	0.64	@
9.	PFL	245	225	130	775.64	780.31	779.55	75.54	81.46	73.86	0.24	@
10.	PFM	159	226	215	785.71	782.72	768.00	73.93	77.64	78.83	3.02	*
11.	PFN	218	185	197	783.46	772.83	777.53	79.20	78.32	74.37	0.96	@
12.	PFO	152	275	173	784.56	778.37	772.47	77.75	77.54	76.76	0.99	@
13.	PFQ1	171	295	134	773.43	776.93	787.25	75.48	79.24	75.38	1.28	@
14.	PFQ2	135	285	180	792.90	772.56	776.23	77.48	76.69	77.38	3.28	*
15.	PFQ3	212	195	193	767.18	788.07	780.45	75.95	75.30	79.80	3.86	*
16.	PFQ4	207	188	205	769.56	780.56	784.57	77.50	77.88	76.34	2.11	@

* Significant at 0.05 level.

@ Not Significant at 0.05 level.

Table 5.40: Impact of Objective Achievement Test Score on Achievement Score in Practicals

Sl. No.	*Area*	*No. of Observations*			*Mean Value*			*Standard Deviation*			*F Value*	*Level of Significance*
		I	*II*	*III*	*I*	*II*	*III*	*I*	*II*	*III*		
1	A1	172	318	110	780.76	775.01	783.62	74.08	78.98	77.94	0.63	@
2	A2	207	287	106	784.85	776.67	769.59	77.99	76.29	78.70	1.48	@
3	A3	195	298	107	796.90	772.79	759.39	70.86	77.04	83.20	9.87	*
4	A4	158	338	104	794.73	768.53	784.74	73.96	78.02	76.08	6.75	*
5	A5	189	246	125	793.32	774.71	763.51	75.33	76.88	78.31	6.26	*
6	A6	153	311	136	799.39	772.20	768.26	71.58	78.41	77.34	7.98	*

* Significant at 0.01 level.

@ Not Significant at 0.05 level.

It is clear from Table 5.40 that the calculated 'F' values for achievement areas Teacher education in emerging India (A1) and Educational psychology, Measurement and evaluation (A2) are less than the table value at 0.05 level of confidence. Hence hypothesis-21 is accepted. Therefore, the above areas have not significant influence on Achievement score in Practicals of the DIET students.

IMPACT OF DEMOGRAPHIC AND SOCIO-ECONOMIC VARIABLES ON ACHIEVEMENT SCORE

The impact of Demographic and Socio-Economic variables 1. Age; 2. Marital status; 3. Education and occupation of the family members; 4. Caste; 5. Annual family income; 6. Group subjects in Intermediate etc. are studied with the help of one way ANOVA technique. The following hypothesis is formulated and tested.

Hypothesis 22:

There would be no significant influence of demographic and Socio-economic variables on achievement of the DIET students.

A. IMPACT OF AGE ON ACHIEVEMENT

The students are divided into three groups based on their age. The students with age up to 19 years are come under group-I; students with age between 20-22 years are come under group-II; and students with 23 years and above are placed in group-III. To know the impact of the students age on achievement one way ANOVA technique is employed and the results are shown in Table 5.41.

It is seen from Table 5.41 that computed 'F' ratio for achievement score in theory is above the table value at 0.05 level of confidence. Hence the hypothesis-22 is rejected. It is concluded that age of the students has significant influence on achievement score in theory. It is clear from Table 5.41 the calculated 'F' ratios for achievement in practical and total score is less than the table value at 0.05 level of confidence and the hypothesis-22 is accepted. It is concluded that age of the students doesn't have any significant influence on Achievement in Practicals and Total achievement score.

Table 5.41: Influence of Age on Achievement Score in Theory, Practicals and Total Score

Area	No. of Observations			Mean Value			Standard Deviation			F Value	Level of Significance
	I	*II*	*III*	*I*	*II*	*III*	*I*	*II*	*III*		
Theory	194	313	93	710.14	702.11	695.12	42.33	42.26	46.88	4.24	*
Practical	194	313	93	777.41	778.33	779.68	75.63	77.85	80.10	0.03	@
Total	194	313	93	1487.55	1480.43	1474.80	99.14	98.24	99.70	0.59	@

* Significant at 0.05 level.

@ Not Significant at 0.05 level.

B. IMPACT OF MARITAL STATUS ON ACHIEVEMENT

The students are categorized into two groups on the basis of their marital status i.e. unmarried and married. One way ANOVA technique is employed to study the marital status on Achievement in Theory, Practicals and total score of the DIET students and the results are presented in Table 5.42.

Table 5.42 reveals that the obtained 'F' values for the Achievement score in theory, practicals and total score are not significant at 0.05 level. Hence, hypothesis 22 is accepted. This resulted that the marital status of the students does not have any significant influence on achievement score in Theory, Practicals and Total score.

C. IMPACT OF FATHER'S EDUCATION ON ACHIEVEMENT

The students have divided into 5 groups on the basis of their Father's Education. The Group-I: Illiterates, Group-II: up to Class X, Group-III: up to graduation, Group-IV: Post Graduation/ Professionals, and Group-V: Whose Fathers are not alive. The Group-V i.e. whose fathers are not alive (23) is not taken into consideration in this analysis.

To know whether there is any impact of father's education on achievement of the DIET students, one way ANOVA technique is employed and the results are given in Table 5.43.

It is drawn from Table 5.43 that the calculated 'F' values for the achievement in practicals is 3.14 and for the total score is 3.85. The values are beyond the table values at 0.05 level of significant. Hence, hypothesis-22 is rejected. It is concluded that the father's education of the students have significant influence on achievement in practicals and total score.

It is also clear from Table 5.43 the value of 'F' for achievement in theory is 2.07, which is not significant at 0.05 level. Hence, hypothesis-22 is accepted. It is concluded that the father's education of the students has no significant influence on achievement in theory.

Table 5.42: Influence of students marital status on achievement score in theory, practicals and total score

Area	*No. of Observations*		*Mean Value*		*Standard Deviation*		*t- Value*	*Level of Significance*
	I	*II*	*I*	*II*	*I*	*II*		
Theory	544	56	704.56	694.46	43.31	42.07	1.67	@
Practical	544	56	777.99	780.70	77.32	78.54	0.25	@
Total	**544**	**56**	**1482.55**	**1475.16**	**100.08**	**84.60**	**0.53**	@

@ Not Significant at 0.05 level.

Table 5.43: Influence of Fathers Education on Achievement Score in Theory, Practicals and Total Score

Area	*No. of Observations*				*Mean Value*				*Standard Deviation*				*F Value*	*Level of Significance*
	I	*II*	*III*	*IV*	*I*	*II*	*III*	*IV*	*I*	*II*	*III*	*IV*		
Theory	117	284	127	49	696.07	704.53	701.88	712.88	42.83	41.65	43.77	42.86	2.07	@
Practical	117	284	127	49	761.60	778.94	785.21	796.67	72.59	79.30	73.99	77.78	3.14	*
Total	**117**	**284**	**127**	**49**	**1457.67**	**1483.47**	**1487.09**	**1509.55**	**90.98**	**102.00**	**92.53**	**100.23**	**3.85**	*

* Significant at 0.05 level.

@ Not Significant at 0.05 level.

D. IMPACT OF MOTHER'S EDUCATION ON ACHIEVEMENT

The students have divided into 5 groups on the basis of their Mother's Education as in the case of father's education. The Group-V i.e., whose Mothers are not alive (9) is not taken into consideration in the analysis.

To know whether there is any impact of Mother's education on achievement of the DIET students, one way ANOVA technique is employed. The results are given in Table 5.44.

The 'F' ratios from Table 5.44 reveals that the achievement in practicals and total achievement scores are beyond the table value at 0.05 level of confidence. Hence, hypothesis-22 is rejected. It is concluded that the education of the mothers has significant influence on achievement in practical and total achievement score of the DIET students. From Table 5.44, it is observed that the 'F' value for achievement score in theory is not significant at 0.05 level of confidence. Hence, hypothesis-22 is accepted. It is finalised that the Mother's education of the DIET students doesn't show any significant influence on achievement score in theory.

E. IMPACT OF BROTHER'S EDUCATION ON ACHIEVEMENT

The students have divided into 5 groups on the basis of their Brother's Education as it is in the case of mother's education. The V group i.e. those who have no Brothers (155) are not taken into considered for the analysis.

To know whether there is any impact of Brother's education on achievement of the DIET students, one way ANOVA technique is employed and the results are given in Table 5.45.

Table 5.45 reveal that the 'F' ratio for the total achievement score is significant at 0.05 level. Hence, hypothesis-22 is rejected. It is concluded that the education of the brother's education of the students has significant influence on total achievement score.

It is observed from Table 5.45 the 'F' ratios for achievement score in theory and practicals are not significant at 0.05 level of confidence. Hence, the hypothesis 22 is accepted. It is concluded that the brother's education of the DIET students doesn't show any influence on their achievement in theory and practicals.

Table 5.44: Influence of Mothers Education on Achievement Score in Theory, Practicals and Total Score

Area	*No. of Observations*				*Mean Value*				*Standard Deviation*				*F Value*	*Level of Significance*
	I	*II*	*III*	*IV*	*I*	*II*	*III*	*IV*	*I*	*II*	*III*	*IV*		
Theory	288	250	37	16	703.09	703.30	695.22	716.25	44.19	43.36	30.43	44.87	0.91	@
Practical	288	250	37	16	761.60	778.94	785.21	796.67	72.59	79.30	73.99	77.78	3.14	*
Total	**288**	**250**	**37**	**16**	**1457.67**	**1483.47**	**1487.09**	**1509.55**	**90.98**	**102.00**	**92.53**	**100.23**	**3.85**	*

* Significant at 0.05 level.

@ Not Significant at 0.05 level.

Table 5.45: Influence of Brothers Education on Achievement Score in Theory, Practicals and Total Score

Area	*No. of Observations*				*Mean Value*				*Standard Deviation*				*F Value*	*Level of Significance*
	I	*II*	*III*	*IV*	*I*	*II*	*III*	*IV*	*I*	*II*	*III*	*IV*		
Theory	13	132	244	56	723.08	703.02	700.31	703.02	60.63	44.20	42.24	37.72	1.21	@
Practical	13	132	244	56	827.38	777.33	773.05	793.04	66.55	74.65	77.88	77.95	2.85	@
Total	**13**	**132**	**244**	**56**	**1550.46**	**1480.36**	**1473.36**	**1496.05**	**113.20**	**97.40**	**95.72**	**93.47**	**3.21**	*

* Significant at 0.05 level.

@ Not Significant at 0.05 level.

F. IMPACT OF SISTER'S EDUCATION ON ACHIEVEMENT

The students were divided into 5 groups on the basis of their Sister's Education as it is in the case of mother's education. The V group i.e. those who have no Sisters (174) are not taken into considered for the analysis.

To know whether there is any impact of Sister's education on achievement of the DIET students, one way ANOVA technique is employed and the results are given in Table 5.46.

Table 5.46 reveals that the 'F' ratios for the achievement scores in theory, practicals and total achievement scores are not significant at 0.05 level. Hence, hypothesis-22 is accepted. It is concluded that the sister's education doesn't show any influence on their theory, practicals and total achievement scores.

G. IMPACT OF FATHER'S EMPLOYMENT ON ACHIEVEMENT

The students are divided into 3 groups on the basis of their father's employment, namely 1. Daily wagers/Coolies; 2. Businessmen/Cultivators; and 3. Security job-holders. Here the students whose fathers are not alive (23) are not considered for the analysis. To verify whether there is any impact of Father's employment on achievement of the DIET students. One way ANOVA technique is used. The results are presented in Table 5.47.

It is seen from Table 5.47, that the computed 'F' ratios for achievement score in practicals is 3.07, which is significant at 0.05 level. Hence, hypothesis-22 is rejected. It is concluded that the Father's employment of the DIET students has significant influence on achievement score in practicals.

From Table 5.47, it is observed that the calculated 'F' values for the achievement score in theory and total score are below the table value at 0.05 level. Hence the hypothesis-22 is accepted. It is concluded that the Father's employment doesn't show any significant influence on achievement in theory and total score.

Table 5.46: Influence of Sisters Education on Achievement Score in Theory, Practicals and Total Score

Area	*No. of Observations*				*Mean Value*				*Standard Deviation*				*F Value*	*Level of Significance*
	I	*II*	*III*	*IV*	*I*	*II*	*III*	*IV*	*I*	*II*	*III*	*IV*		
Theory	29	190	164	43	715.59	705.85	701.60	695.86	45.28	43.96	41.45	43.89	1.50	@
Practical	29	190	164	43	798.17	780.01	776.62	769.42	85.87	77.17	78.49	79.69	0.85	@
Total	**29**	**190**	**164**	**43**	**1513.76**	**1485.86**	**1478.21**	**1465.28**	**110.05**	**101.93**	**95.76**	**105.00**	**1.53**	**@**

@ Not Significant at 0.05 level.

Table 5.47: Influence of Fathers Employment on Achievement Score in Theory, Practicals and Total Score

Area	*No. of Observations*			*Mean Value*			*Standard Deviation*			*F Value*	*Level of Significance*
	I	*II*	*III*	*I*	*II*	*III*	*I*	*II*	*III*		
Theory	147	223	208	702.83	701.88	704.29	43.76	41.72	42.77	0.18	@
Practical	147	223	208	768.59	775.54	788.26	79.16	78.10	73.61	3.07	*
Total	**147**	**223**	**208**	**1471.42**	**1477.72**	**1492.56**	**102.07**	**98.69**	**94.55**	2.29	@

* Significant at 0.05 level.

@ Not Significant at 0.05 level.

H. IMPACT OF MOTHER'S EMPLOYMENT ON ACHIEVEMENT

The students are divided into 2 groups on the basis of their mother's employment, namely 1. Employed mother and 2. Non-Employed mothers. Here the students (9) whose Mothers are not alive are not taken into considered for the analysis.

To verify whether there is any impact of Mother's employment on achievement of the DIET students, one way ANOVA technique is used. The results are presented in Table 5.48.

It is seen from Table 5.48, that the computed 'F' ratios for achievement in theory, Practical and total scores are not significant at 0.05 level of confidence. Hence hypothesis 22 is accepted and concluded that the mother's employment of the DIET students have not significant influence on achievement in theory, practicals and total scores.

I. IMPACT OF BROTHER'S EMPLOYMENT ON ACHIEVEMENT

The students are divided into 3 groups on the basis of their Brother's employment, namely 1. Students, 2. Daily wagers/ Coolies and 3. Security jobholders. Here the students (155) those who have Brother's are not taken into considered for the analysis.

To verify whether there is any impact of Brother's employment on achievement of the DIET students, one way ANOVA technique is used. The results are presented in Table 5.49.

It is observed from Table 5.49 that the computed 'F' ratio for achievement score in practicals is significant at 0.05 level of confidence. Hence hypothesis-22 is rejected and it is concluded that Brother's employment of the DIET students have significant influence on achievement score in practicals.

It is evident from Table 5.49 that the calculated 'F' ratios for achievement score in theory and total achievement scores are not significant at 0.05 level. Hence, hypothesis-22 is accepted. It is resulted that the Brother's employment of the DIET students doesn't show any influence on achievement score in theory and total achievement score.

Table 5.48: Influence of Mothers Employment on Achievement Score in Theory, Practicals and Total Score

Area	*No. of Observations*		*Mean Value*		*Standard Deviation*		*t-Value*	*Level of Significance*
	I	*II*	*I*	*II*	*I*	*II*		
Theory	556	35	702.40	713.17	42.51	51.71	1.44	@
Practical	556	35	776.65	792.40	77.51	74.35	1.17	@
Total	**556**	**35**	**1479.05**	**1505.57**	**97.42**	**107.90**	**1.55**	@

@ Not Significant at 0.05 level.

Table 5.49: Influence of Brothers Employment on Achievement Score in Theory, Practicals and Total Score

Area	*No. of Observations*			*Mean Value*			*Standard Deviation*			*F Value*	*Level of Significance*
	I	*II*	*III*	*I*	*II*	*III*	*I*	*II*	*III*		
Theory	275	110	61	701.73	704.40	700.11	45.61	33.40	45.89	0.24	@
Practical	275	110	61	774.33	774.24	806.38	79.00	72.54	72.75	4.61	*
Total	**275**	**110**	**61**	**1476.06**	**1478.64**	**1506.49**	**102.58**	**84.56**	**91.61**	**2.49**	**@**

* Significant at 0.05 level.

@ Not Significant at 0.05 level.

J. IMPACT OF SISTER'S EMPLOYMENT ON ACHIEVEMENT

The students are divided into 3 groups on the basis of their Sister's employment, namely: 1. Students; 2. Daily wagers/Coolies; and 3. Security jobholders. Here the students (174), who have no sisters, are not taken into considered for the analysis

To verify whether there is any impact of Sister's employment on achievement of the DIET students, one way ANOVA technique is used. The results are presented in Table 5.50.

It is inferred from Table 5.50 that the obtained 'F' ratio for achievement score in practicals is significant at 0.05 level of confidence. Hence, the hypothesis-22 is rejected. It is evident that the sister's employment has significant influence on achievement score in practicals of the DIET students.

It is clear from Table 5.50, the 'F' ratio for achievement score in theory and total scores are not significant at 0.05 level. Hence, hypothesis-22 is accepted. It is concluded that the sister's employment doesn't have any significant influence on achievement score in theory and total score of the DIET students.

K. IMPACT OF FAMILY ANNUAL INCOME ON ACHIEVEMENT

To study whether the annual family income shows any influence on achievement of the DIET students, they are divided into 4 categories based on their family income, namely:

1. Whose annual family income is up to Rs. 20,000.
2. Whose annual family income between Rs. 20,001 to Rs. 40,000.
3. Whose annual family income between Rs. 40,001 to Rs. 60,000; and
4. Whose annual family income is above Rs. 60,000.

To investigate the impact of the annual family income on achievement of the DIET students, one way ANOVA technique is used and the obtained results are furnished in Table 5.51.

Table 5.50: Influence of Sisters Employment on Achievement Score in Theory, Practicals and Total Score

Area	*No. of Observations*			*Mean Value*			*Standard Deviation*			*F Value*	*Level of Significance*
	I	*II*	*III*	*I*	*II*	*III*	*I*	*II*	*III*		
Theory	318	66	42	703.86	702.15	705.19	43.04	44.15	44.44	0.07	@
Practical	318	66	42	772.93	799.52	791.83	78.85	71.64	80.51	3.82	*
Total	**318**	**66**	**42**	**1476.79**	**1501.67**	**1497.02**	**99.86**	**100.30**	**103.98**	**2.16**	@

* Significant at 0.05 level.

@ Not Significant at 0.05 level.

Table 5.51: Influence of Family Income on Achievement Score in Theory, Practicals and Total Score

Area	*No. of Observations*				*Mean Value*				*Standard Deviation*				*F Value*	*Level of Significance*
	I	*II*	*III*	*IV*	*I*	*II*	*III*	*IV*	*I*	*II*	*III*	*IV*		
Theory	124	219	192	65	709.53	699.34	703.11	708.26	51.19	38.24	40.42	49.66	1.76	@
Practical	124	219	192	65	787.41	774.36	768.58	802.34	82.35	76.50	75.19	71.41	3.92	*
Total	**124**	**219**	**192**	**65**	**1496.94**	**1473.70**	**1471.69**	**1510.60**	**114.04**	**92.10**	**92.49**	**99.61**	**4.04**	*

* Significant at 0.05 level.

@ Not Significant at 0.05 level.

From Table 5.51 it is revealed that the 'F' values for achievement score in practicals and total achievement scores are more than the table value at 0.05 level. Hence, the hypothesis-22 is rejected. It is confirmed that the annual family income has significant influence on achievement score in practicals and total achievement score.

The calculated 'F' ratio for achievement score in theory has not significant at 0.05 level. Hence, the hypothesis-22 is rejected. It is inferred that the annual family income doesn't show any influence on achievement score in theory of the DIET students.

L. IMPACT OF CASTE ON ACHIEVEMENT

To study whether the Caste shows any influence on achievement of the DIET students, they are divided into 4 categories on the basis of Caste, namely: 1. Scheduled Caste/ Scheduled Tribe; 2. Minorities; 3. Backward Caste; and 4. Other Caste.

To test whether the caste has any influence on achievement of DIET students, one way ANOVA technique is applied and the obtained results are presented in Table 5.52.

It is observed from Table 5.52, the 'F' values for achievement in theory and total achievement scores are significant at 0.01 level of confidence. Hence, hypothesis-22 is rejected. It is concluded that the caste of the students has significant influence on their achievement.

From Table 5.52, it is clear that the value of 'F' for the variable achievement score in practicals has not significant at 0.05 level of confidence. Hence, the hypothesis-22 is accepted. It is concluded that the caste of the students has no significant influence on achievement in practicals.

M. IMPACT OF GROUP SUBJECTS IN INTERMEDIATE ON ACHIEVEMENT

Students are divided into two categories based on group subjects studied in Intermediate level, namely Sciences and Arts. To study whether the group subjects has any impact on their achievement is tested with one way ANOVA technique. The results are furnished in Table 5.53.

Table 5.52: Influence of Caste on Achievement Score in Theory, Practicals and Total Score

Area	*No. of Observations*				*Mean Value*				*Standard Deviation*				*F Value*	*Level of Significance*
	I	*II*	*III*	*IV*	*I*	*II*	*III*	*IV*	*I*	*II*	*III*	*IV*		
Theory	105	13	303	179	686.97	699.31	707.33	707.42	43.33	55.44	42.55	41.44	6.62	*
Practical	105	13	303	179	764.08	781.77	786.06	773.04	72.47	78.42	78.16	77.74	2.50	@
Total	**105**	**13**	**303**	**179**	**1451.06**	**1481.08**	**1493.39**	**1480.46**	**88.06**	**96.38**	**100.86**	**97.83**	**4.89**	*

* Significant at 0.01 level.

@ Not Significant at 0.05 level.

Table 5.53: Influence of Student Teachers Group Subjects in Intermediate Level on Achievement Score in Theory, Practicals and Total Score

Area	*No. of Observations*		*Mean Value*		*Standard Deviation*		*t-Value*	*Level of Significance*
	I	*II*	*I*	*II*	*I*	*II*		
Theory	437	163	707.12	694.25	44.61	37.98	3.27	*
Practical	437	163	787.63	753.06	78.91	67.07	4.96	*
Total	437	163	1494.75	1447.31	101.91	80.10	5.36	*

* Significant at 0.01 level.

From Table 5.53 the calculated 'F' values for achievement score in theory, practicals and total achievement scores are significant at 0.01 level. Hence, hypothesis-22 is rejected. It is concluded that the group subjects studied in Intermediate level by the student teachers have significant influence on their achievement.

N. IMPACT OF PLACE OF BIRTH OF THE DIET STUDENTS ON ACHIEVEMENT

The students are divided into 4 groups based on place of birth, namely: 1. Village; 2. Small Town; 3. Town; and 4. City.

To study whether the place of birth of the DIET students has any impact on their achievement, one way ANOVA technique is employed and the results are given in Table 5.54.

It is clear from Table 5.54 the computed 'F' values are not significant at 0.05 level of confidence. Hence, hypothesis-22 is accepted. Therefore, the place of birth of the students doesn't have any significant impact on achievement of the DIET students.

O. IMPACT OF ORDER OF BIRTH OF THE DIET STUDENTS ON ACHIEVEMENT

The students are divided into 3 groups based on their birth order. Student's whose birth order is first or second come under group I, Third or Four come under group II and Five and above come under group III.

To study whether the order of birth of the DIET students has any impact on their achievement, one way ANOVA technique is employed and the results are given in Table 5.55.

It is cleared from Table 5.55 that the 'F' values for achievement score in practicals and total achievement score are more than the table value at 0.01 level of confidence. Hence, hypothesis-22 is rejected and concluded that the order of birth of the students has significant impact on their achievement score in practicals and total achievement.

It is also observed from Table 5.55 the computed 'F' ratio for achievement scores in theory are not significant at 0.05 level. Hence hypothesis-22 is accepted. Therefore, order of birth of the students does not have any effect on their achievement score in theory.

Table 5.54: Influence of Place of Birth on Achievement Score in Theory, Practicals and Total Score

Area	*No. of Observations*				*Mean Value*				*Standard Deviation*				*F Value*	*Level of Significance*
	I	*II*	*III*	*IV*	*I*	*II*	*III*	*IV*	*I*	*II*	*III*	*IV*		
Theory	399	68	103	30	702.47	707.69	707.05	697.93	43.11	40.12	46.52	41.11	0.68	@
Practical	399	68	103	30	777.52	768.38	778.01	810.97	78.96	81.45	72.39	54.63	2.18	@
Total	**399**	**68**	**103**	**30**	**1479.99**	**1476.07**	**1485.06**	**1508.90**	**100.92**	**96.81**	**97.08**	**75.45**	**0.91**	**@**

@ Not Significant at 0.05 level.

Table 5.55: Influence of Order of Birth on Achievement Score in Theory, Practicals and Total Score

Area	*No. of Observations*			*Mean Value*			*Standard Deviation*			*F Value*	*Level of Significance*
	I	*II*	*III*	*I*	*II*	*III*	*I*	*II*	*III*		
Theory	306	180	114	705.59	702.23	700.54	42.55	44.83	42.73	0.70	@
Practical	306	180	114	787.44	786.76	740.09	78.92	76.32	62.28	18.09	*
Total	**306**	**180**	**114**	**1493.03**	**1488.99**	**1440.63**	**100.20**	**96.17**	**88.04**	**12.86**	*

@ Not Significant at 0.05 level.

P. IMPACT OF SOCIO-ECONOMIC STATUS OF THE FAMILY ON ACHIEVEMENT

The students are divided into 3 groups on the basis of economic status. They are: 1. Poor; 2. Middle; and 3. Rich.

To study whether economic status of the family is show any effect on achievement of the DIET students, one way ANOVA is employed and the results are given in Table 5.56.

It is observed that from Table 5.56 the calculated 'F' values for total achievement score is significant at 0.01 level. Hence hypothesis-22 is rejected and concluded that the economic status of the family has its own influence on total achievement score.

The computed value of 'F' for the achievement score in theory and practicals are significant at 0.05 level. Hence the hypothesis-22 is rejected and it is concluded that the economic status of the family has shown their impact on achievement score in theory and practicals of the DIET students.

MULTIPLE STEPWISE REGRESSION ANALYSIS

This part of the chapter concerned with the analysis of the relative contribution or magnitude of the effect of each of the different independent variables to the dependent variable (Achievement in Theory, Practical and Total Score).

MEANING AND NATURE OF THE REGRESSION ANALYSIS

Regression means to estimate or predict one variable with the value of the other. According to dictionary the term "regression" means 'act of returning' or 'going back'. In 19th century, Francis Galton for the first time used the word 'regression' while studying the relationship between the height of fathers and sons. Galton found that the offspring of abnormally tall or short parents tend to "regress" are "step back" to the average population height, But the term "regression" as now used in statistics is only a convenient term without having any reference to biometry. In regression analysis there are two types of variables. The variable whose value is influenced or is to be predicted is called dependent variable and the variable which influences values or is used for prediction, is called independent variable. The independent variable is also called regression or predictor.

Table 5.56: Influence of Socio-economic Status on Achievement Score in Theory, Practicals and Total Score

Area	*No. of Observations*			*Mean Value*			*Standard Deviation*			*F Value*	*Level of Significance*
	I	*II*	*III*	*I*	*II*	*III*	*I*	*II*	*III*		
Theory	90	474	36	694.69	706.21	691.83	47.66	41.61	49.14	4.16	*
Practical	90	474	36	760.83	782.49	765.75	82.14	76.39	72.50	3.50	*
Total	**90**	**474**	**36**	**1455.52**	**1488.71**	**1457.58**	**104.84**	**96.81**	**95.21**	**5.51**	**

* Significant at 0.05 level.

Nowadays 'regression analysis' is employed widely in all scientific disciplines, such as physical, natural and social sciences.

Correlation is a tool of ascertaining the degree of relationship between two variables, the objective of regression analysis is to study the 'nature of relationship' between the variables. The cause and effect relation is clearly indicated through regression analysis than by correlation.

In the present investigation there are three dependent variables namely: Total achievement score, achievement score in Theory, Practicals and 69 independent variables out of which, there are 16 Personality factors, 10 Study habit areas, 12 Teacher attitude variables, 6 Objective achievement test areas, 19 Demographic and Socio-Economic Status variables and 6 Achievement variables.

To study the effect of each of the achievement test scores, Personality factors, Teacher Attitude, Demographic and Socio-Economic variables and Achievement on the Dependent variables i.e. Total achievement score, achievement in Theory and Practicals, "Stepwise regression analysis" is employed. The influence of each of the independent variable (69 No.) on the dependent variables is analyzed separately.

PREDICTION OF TOTAL ACHIEVEMENT SCORES WITH THE HELP OF DEMOGRAPHIC AND SOCIO-ECONOMIC VARIABLES

The relative contribution of 19 Demographic and Socio-Economic variables (Variables Nos. 1 to 19 in Table 5.25) to the dependent variable i.e. total achievement score (Variable No. 70 in Table 5.25) is studied with the help of multiple regression analysis. The results are presented in Table 5.57.

It is seen from Table 5.57 that the first variable entered into the stepwise multiple regression analysis is College (C) and the obtained multiple correlation R value for the College (C) is 0.406 indicating that the strength of the relationship between the two variables (GT and C) is about 40.6 per cent. It is found that the F value for R is 117.82, which is significant at 0.01 level for 1 and 598 df. The value of multiple R^2 is 0.165 and it is concluded that 16.46 per cent of the variance in total achievement score is accounted by College (C).

Table 5.57: Prediction of Total Achievement Score with the Help of 19 Demographic and Socio-economic Variables

Step No.	*IV (VN)*	*R*	*R^2*	*SER For R*	*F Value*	*b(VN)*	*'t' Value for b*	*Constant*	*B*	*r*	*% of Variance*
1	2	3	4	5	6	7	8	9	10	11	12
1.	C(2)	0.406	0.165	90.282	117.82** (1,598)	13.928 (2)	10.85** (598)	1405.253	0.406	0.406	16.46
2.	G(16)	0.466	0.217	87.472	82.79** (2,597)	14.221(2) -50.856(16)	11.43** 6.63** (597)	1468.314	0.414 -0.229	-0.214	16.81 4.91
3.	OB(18)	0.481	0.231	86.756	59.73** (3,596)	14.361(2) -40.137(16) -16.331(18)	11.63** 4.66** 3.30** (596)	1481.353	0.418 -0.181 -0.128	-0.177	16.97 3.87 2.27
4.	CA(15)	0.492	0.242	86.198	47.56** (4,595)	14.353(2) -41.256(16) -15.680(18) 10.337(15)	11.70** 4.82** 3.18** 2.95** (595)	1451.471	0.481 -0.186 -0.123 0.106	0.105	16.96 3.98 2.18 1.10
5.	R(1)	0.503	0.253	85.663	40.22** (5,594)	23.634(2) -41.412(16) -15.978(18) 10.392(15) 31.887(1)	6.92** 4.87** 3.26** 3.00** 2.91** (594)	1337.191	0.688 -0.187 -0.125 0.106 0.289	-0.345	27.93 4.00 2.22 1.11 -9.97

(Contd...)

1	2	3	4	5	6	7	8	9	10	11	12
6.	ME(7)	0.512	0.262	85.234	35.02**	24.601(2)	7.20**	1347.138	0.717	0.002	29.07
					(6,593)	-41.390(16)	4.89**		0.189		4.00
						-17.401(18)	3.55**		-0.136		2.42
						11.668(15)	3.34**		0.119		1.25
						33.773(1)	3.09**		0.306		-10.55
						-12.716(7)	2.65**		-0.096		-0.01
							(593)				
7.	FE(6)	0.519	0.270	84.848	31.21**	24.581(2)	7.22**	1336.049	0.716	0.099	29.05
					(7,592)	-42.249(16)	5.01**		-0.191		4.08
						-16.087(18)	3.28**		-0.126		2.24
						10.976(15)	3.15**		0.112		1.17
						34.021(1)	3.13**		0.309		-10.63
						-20.396(7)	3.60**		0.154		-0.02
						11.382(6)	2.53*		0.108		1.07
							(592)				
8.	SEM(13)	0.524	0.275	84.626	27.96**	24.581(2)	7.16**	1336.213	0.708	0.060	28.72
					(8,591)	-42.634(16)	5.07**		-0.192		4.12
						-17.455(18)	3.53**		-0.137		2.43
						10.827(15)	3.11**		0.111		1.16
						33.121(1)	3.05**		0.300		-10.35
						-20.262(7)	3.58**		-0.153		-0.02
						10.340(6)	3.29**		0.098		0.98
						8.685(13)	2.03*		0.073		0.43
							(591)				

(Contd…)

1	2	3	4	5	6	7	8	9	10	11	12
9.	SE(9)	0.530	0.281	84.346	25.57**	23.506(2)	6.90**	1342.532	0.685	-0.028	27.78
					(9,590)	-40.922(16)	4.86**		-0.185		3.95
						-17.375(18)	3.53**		-0.136		3.42
						11.473(15)	3.30**		0.117		1.22
						31.120(1)	2.86**		0.282		-9.73
						-18.943(7)	3.34**		-0.143		-0.02
						11.152(6)	2.47*		0.106		1.05
						20.488(13)	3.01**		0.171		1.02
						-9.655(9)	2.22*		-0.129		0.36
							(590)				

** Significant at 0.01 level.

* Significant at 0.05 level.

The standard multiple regression (SER) is 90.282. From this result it may be inferred that nearly 68 per cent of the actual GT value would lie within ± 90.282 points of GT value predicted with the help of variable C.

The partial regression co-efficient (b) presented in column of Table 5.57 is 13.928. Therefore the GT value would change by 13.928 units for every unit of change in College. The 't' value for b is 10.85, which is significant at 0.01 level of confidence. The constant value that could be written to predict GT at the stage is 1405.253.

The general form of the multiple regression equation may be written as

$GT = A + b_1 (X_1) + b_2 (X_2) + \text{------} bn (X_n)$

where GT is the predicted score on dependent variable,

A is constant value,

b_1, b_2 ---- b_n are partial regression co-efficients, and

X_1, X_2 ---- X_n are scores on different independent variables.

Thus the multiple regression equation at the end of this step could be written as

GT = 1405.253 + 13.928 (C).

The variable (G), group subjects studied at the Intermediate level is very significant variable in the stepwise regression analysis. The value of R between GT on one side and C and G on the other side is 0.466. The strength of the relationship between GT and 2 independent variables C and G put together is about 46.6 per cent. The 'F' ratio of R is 82.79, which is significant at 0.01 level for 2 and 597 df.

The value of R^2 is 0.217, which shows that the two variables put together could explain 21.7 per cent of variance on the dependent variable i.e. total achievement score. Out of this 16.8 per cent of variance is explained by the variable C and 4.9 per cent of variance is explained by variable G. These percentages can be obtained by multiplying the B (Beta) co-efficient or standard partial regression co-efficient with the corresponding simple correlation between the dependent variable and the respective independent variable (shown in column 12). The 't' value for b is significant beyond 0.01 level for the variables C and G. The regression equation to predict GT with these two variables C and G as predictor variables is

GT =1468.314 + 14.221 (C) – 50.856 (G).

The third predictor variable entered in this analysis is Order of Birth (OB i.e. variable No. 18 in Table 5.25). The 'F' value for R is 59.73 which is significant at 0.01 level. The regression equation at this stage is

GT =1481.353 +14.361 (C) – 40.137 (G) – 16.331 (OB).

There are 9 steps in the stepwise regression analysis. Hence the total Demographic and Socio-Economic variables predict the dependent variable GT. The last variable entered into the analysis is Sister's Education (SE i.e. variable No. 16 in Table 5.25). The regression equation at the end of this stage is

GT = 1342.532 + 23.506 (C) – 40.922 (G) – 17.375 (OB) + 11.473 (CA) + 31.120 (R) – 18.943 (ME) + 11.152 (FE) + 20.488 (SEM) – 9.051 (SE).

PREDICTION OF TOTAL ACHIEVEMENT SCORE WITH THE HELP OF TEACHER ATTITUDE VARIABLES

This section deals with the Total Achievement Score (GT) with the help of 12 Teacher Attitude variables (Variable Nos. 20 to 31 in Table 5.25). The stepwise regression analysis is carried out and the results are presented in Table 5.58.

From Table 5.58 it could be seen that the most important predictor variable that entered first in this analysis is Attitude towards high conceptual level (TA_3 i.e., variable No. 22 in Table 5.25).

The values of R and R^2 are 0.192 and 0.032 respectively. It is significant (F-value for R is 20.71) at 0.01 level for 1 and 598 df. The 't' value of b is 4.77, which is significant at 0.01 level. The constant value is 1613.156. Thus the regression equation at this stage is:

GT = 1613.156 – 5.134 (TA_3).

Table 5.58: Prediction of Total Achievement Score with the Help of 12 Teacher Attitude Variables

Step No.	*IV (VN)*	*R*	*R^2*	*SER*	*F Value For R*	*b(VN)*	*'t' Value for b*	*Constant*	*B*	*r*	*% of Variance*
1	*2*	*3*	*4*	*5*	*6*	*7*	*8*	*9*	*10*	*11*	*12*
1.	TA_3(22)	0.192	0.032	96.953	20.71** (1,598)	-5.134(22)	4.77** (598)	1613.156	-0.191	-0.191	3.66
2.	TA_9(28)	0.212	0.045	96.596	14.15** (2,597)	-3.890(22) -2.682(28)	3.24** 2.33* (597)	1640.697	-0.145 -0.104	-0.169	2.77 1.75
3.	TA_4(23)	0.230	0.053	96.270	11.18** (3,596)	-3.106(22) -2.588(28) -2.260(23)	2.50* 2.25* 2.25* (596)	1662.963	-0.116 -0.100 -0.095	-0.150	2.21 1.69 1.42

** Significant at 0.01 level.

* Significant at 0.05 level.

The second predictor variable that entered in this analysis is Attitude towards Pupils during practice teaching (variable No. 28 in Table 5.25). The values of R and R^2 are 0.212 and 0.045 respectively. The F-value of R is 14.15, which is significant at 0.01 level. The constant value is 1640.697. Thus the regression equation at this stage is

$$GT = 1640.697 - 3.890\ (TA_3) - 2.682\ (TA_9).$$

The third and the last step in this analysis is Attitude towards Low conceptual level (variable No. 23 in Table 5.25). The F-value of R is 11.18, which is significant at 0.01 level. The regression equation at this stage is

$$GT = 1662.963 - 3.106\ (TA_3) - 2.588\ (TA_9) - 2.260\ (TA_4)$$

PREDICTION OF TOTAL ACHIEVEMENT SCORE WITH THE HELP OF STUDY HABITS SCORES

In this section the dependent variable the total achievement score (GT) is predicted with the help of 10 Study Habit scores (Variable Nos. 32 to 41 in Table 5.25). The stepwise regression analysis is carried out and the results are presented in Table 5.59.

From Table 5.59, it is seen that the most important predictor variable that entered first into the stepwise multiple regression analysis is Home environment (S_1). The multiple R-value is 0.148. The F-value for R is 13.61, which is significant at 0.01 level for df 1,598. The multiple R^2 (0.022) indicates that this variable alone contributes 2.2 per cent of variance in GT. The value of b is 2.104 and 't' value for b is 3.69, which is significant at 0.01 level of confidence. GT value would change by 2.104 units for every unit of change in S_1. The constant value is 1376.439. The regression equation at this stage is

$$GT = 1376.439 + 2.104\ (S_1).$$

The second variable inserted into analysis is habits of concentration (S_4). The value of F for R is 8.40, which is significant at 0.01 level. The value of multiple R^2 is 0.027. The two variables S_1 and S_4 could explain 2.74 per cent of variance in total achievement score. Out of this 1.82 per cent of variance is accounted by S_1 and the remaining 0.92 per cent of variance is explained by S_4. The constant value of the prediction is 1344.037. The multiple regression equation at this stage is

$$GT = 1344.037 + 1.717\ (S_1) + 1.088\ (S_4).$$

Table 5.59: Prediction of Total Achievement Score with the Help of 10 Study Habits Variables

Step No.	*IV (VN)*	*R*	R^2	*SER*	*F Value For R*	*b(VN)*	*'t' Value for b*	*Constant*	*B*	*r*	*% of Variance*
1	2	3	4	5	6	7	8	9	10	11	12
1.	S_1(32)	0.148	0.022	97.671	13.61** (1,598)	2.104 (32)	3.69** (598)	1376.439	0.149	0.149	2.23
2.	S_4(35)	0.164	0.027	97.496	8.40** (2,597)	1.717(32) 1.088(35)	2.82** 1.77@ (597)	1344.037	0.122 0.077	0.120	1.82 0.92
3.	S_7(38)	0.184	0.034	97.254	6.95** (3,596)	1.928(32) 1.418(35) 1.849(38)	2.12* 2.24* 1.99* (596)	1371.923	0.137 0.100 -0.086	-0.016	2.04 1.20 0.14

* Significant at 0.05 level.

** Significant at 0.01 level.

@ Not Significant at 0.05 level.

The next and last variable entered in this analysis is Audio-Visual programmes (S_7). The values of Multiple R and R^2 are 0.184 and 0.034 respectively. The F value of R is 6.95, which is significant at 0.01 level of confidence. The regression analysis at this stage is

$$GT = 1371.923 + 1.928 (S_1) + 1.418 (S_4) + 1.849 (S_7).$$

PREDICTION OF TOTAL ACHIEVEMENT SCORE WITH THE HELP OF 16 PERSONALITY FACTORS (16 PF)

In this regression analysis the effect of 16PF (variable No's 42 to 57 in Table 5.25) on the dependent variable i.e. total achievement score (GT) is studied and the results obtained are presented in Table 5.60.

In Table 5.60, the first predictor variable that entered into the stepwise regression analysis is Factor E (PFE). The value of R is 0.138 and F value for R is 11.86, which is significant at 0.01 level. The partial regression co-efficient (b) is –6.972. The regression equation at this step is

$$GT = 1513.688 - 6.972 (PFE).$$

The second predictable variable in the stepwise regression analysis is Factor Q4 (PFQ4).

The values of R and R^2 are 0.195 and 0.038 respectively. The constant value is 1487.673. The contribution of PFE is 2.23 per cent and the remaining 1.54 per cent is contributed by PFQ4. The regression equation at this stage is GT = 1487.673 – 7.983 (PFE) + 5.547 (PFQ4).

The next predictor variable that entered in this analysis is Factor M (PFM i.e., variable No. 51 in Table 5.25). The value of R and R^2 are 0.219 and 0.048 respectively. The percentage of these predictor variables (PFE, PFQ4, PFM) is 4.8 per cent. The constant value in the regression is 1518.861. The regression equation with these 3 predictor variables PFE, PFQ4, PFM could be written as

$$GT = 1518.861 - 8.116 (PFE) + 5.662 (PFQ4) - 5.305 (PFM)$$

Table 5.60: Prediction of Total Achievement Score with the Help of 16 Personality Factors Variables

Step No.	*IV (VN)*	*R*	*R²*	*SER*	*F Value for R*	*b(VN)*	*'t' Value for b*	*Constant*	*B*	*r*	*% of Variance*
1	*2*	*3*	*4*	*5*	*6*	*7*	*8*	*9*	*10*	*11*	*12*
1.	PFE(45)	0.138	0.019	97.812	11.86** (1,598)	-6.972 (45)	3.44** (598)	1513.688	-0.139	-0.139	1.94
2.	PFQ4(57)	0.195	0.038	96.981	11.67** (2,597)	-7.983(45) 5.547(57)	3.93** 3.36** (597)	1487.673	-0.160 0.136	0.113	2.23 1.54
3.	PFM(51)	0.219	0.048	96.552	9.96** (3,596)	-8.116(45) 5.662(57) -5.305(51)	4.01** 3.44** 2.51* (596)	1518.861	-0.162 0.139 -0.101	-0.094	2.26 1.57 0.94
4.	PFI(48)	0.235	0.055	96.259	8.67** (4,595)	-8.749(45) 6.083(57) -4.932(51) -3.410(48)	4.30** 3.68** 2.34* 2.15* (595)	1497.297	-0.175 0.150 -0.094 0.87	0.058	2.44 1.69 0.87 0.51
5.	PFB(43)	0.251	0.063	95.936	7.99** (5,594)	-8.891(45) 6.238(57) -4.702(51) -3.815(48) -5.596(43)	4.38** 3.79** 2.23* 2.40* 2.24* (594)	1520.813	-0.178 0.153 -0.089 0.098 -0.090	-0.077	2.48 2.73 0.83 0.57 0.69

(Contd...)

1	2	3	4	5	6	7	8	9	10	11	12
6.	PFL(50)	0.265	0.070	95.683	7.38**	-9.061(45)	4.47**	1499.767	-0.181	0.098	2.53
					(6,593)	5.722(57)	3.44**		0.141		1.59
						-4.505(51)	2.14*		-0.085		0.80
						-3.981(48)	2.51*		0.102		0.59
						-5.164(43)	2.07*		-0.083		0.64
						3.970(50)	2.04*		0.082		0.81
							(593)				
7.	PFQ3(56)	0.274	0.075	95.460	6.90**	-8.580(45)	4.21**	1470.252	-0.172	0.065	2.39
					(7,592)	5.154(57)	3.68**		0.151		1.70
						-4.413(51)	2.10*		-0.084		0.78
						-3.687(48)	2.32*		0.095		0.55
						-5.464(43)	2.19*		-0.088		0.67
						4.542(50)	2.31*		0.094		0.93
						3.350(56)	1.64@		0.080		0.51
							(592)				
8.	PFA(42)	0.283	0.080	95.282	6.46**	-8.603(45)	4.23**	1491.423	-0.172	-0.077	2.40
					(8,591)	6.225(57)	3.73**		0.153		1.72
						-3.994(51)	1.89@		-0.076		0.71
						-3.972(48)	2.49*		0.102		0.59
						-5.371(43)	2.15*		-0.086		0.66
						4.236(50)	2.15*		0.088		0.86
						3.527(56)	2.05*		0.085		0.54
						-3.155(42)	1.79@		-0.072		0.55
							(591)				

(Contd...)

1	2	3	4	5	6	7	8	9	10	11	12
9.	PFQ1S(54)	0.290	0.084	95.191	5.99** (9,590)	-8.713(45) 6.254(57) -4.247(51) -3.930(48) -5.110(43) 4.233(50) 3.671(56) -3.205(42) 2.383(54)	4.28** 3.75** 2.01* 2.46* 2.17* 2.15* 2.13* 1.82@ 1.46@ (590)	1476.779	-0.174 0.154 -0.081 0.101 -0.087 0.088 0.088 -0.073 0.058	0.038	2.43 1.73 0.75 0.59 0.67 0.86 0.56 0.56 0.22

* Significant at 0.05 level.

** Significant at 0.01 level.

@ Not Significant at 0.05 level.

The ninth step is the last step in this analysis i.e., factor Q1 (PFQ1). The values of R and R^2 of this step are 0.290 and 0.084 respectively. The constant value is 1476.779. The end of this step the regression equation could be written as

GT = 1476.779 – 8.713 (PFE) + 6.254 (PFQ4) – 4.247 (PFM)- 3.930 (PFH) – 5.110 (PFB) + 4.233 (PFL) + 3.671 (PFQ3) – 3.205 (PFA) + 2.383 (PFQ1).

The other factors of 16PF have not significantly contributed anything to predict on the dependent variable GT.

PREDICTION OF TOTAL ACHIEVEMENT SCORE WITH THE HELP OF OBJECTIVE ACHIEVEMENT TEST SCORES

Prediction of Total achievement score (GT) with the help of Objective achievement test scores (variables Nos. 58 to 63 in Table 5.25) is studied and the results are presented in Table 5.61.

In Table 5.61, the predictor variable that entered first into the stepwise regression analysis is Elementary Education, Educational planning and management (A3 i.e., variable No. 60 in Table 5.25). The value of R is 0.207 and the F-value for R is 26.02, which is significant at 0.01 level. The value of b is – 4.385 and the constant value is 1560.363. The regression equation at this step is written as

GT = 1560.363-4.385 (A3)

The second predictable variable entered into the stepwise regression analysis is Teacher Education in Emerging India (A1 i.e., variable No.58 in Table 5.25). The value of R and R^2 are 0.230 and 0.053 respectively. The constant value is 1528.277. The regression equation at this stage is

GT = 1528.277 – 5.562 (A3) + 3.210 (A1)

The next and last predictable variable that entered in this analysis is perspectives in primary education (A4 i.e., variable No. 61 in Table 5.25). The value of R and R^2 are 0.249 and 0.062 respectively. The constant value is 1539.199. The regression equation for these three variables could be written as

GT = 1539.199 – 5.250 (A3) + 3.348 (A1) – 3.104 (A5) + 2.041 (A4)

Table 5.61: Prediction of Total Achievement Score with the Help of 6 Objective Achievement Test Variables

Step No.	*IV (VN)*	*R*	*R^2*	*SER*	*F Value for R*	*b(VN)*	*'t' Value for b*	*Constant*	*B*	*r*	*% of Variance*
1	2	3	4	5	6	7	8	9	10	11	12
1.	A_3(60)	0.207	0.042	96.695	26.02** (1.598)	-4.385(60)	5.10** (598)	1560.363	-0.204	-0.204	4.17
2.	A_1(58)	0.230	0.053	96.223	16.58** (2,597)	-5.562(60) 3.210(58)	5.76** 2.62** (597)	1528.277	-0.259 0.118	-0.002	5.29 -0.03
3.	A_5(62)	0.243	0.059	95.994	12.39** (3,596)	-4.336(60) 3.529(58) -2.439(62)	3.78** 2.86** 1.96* (596)	1545.993	-0.202 0.130 -0.101	-0.177	4.12 -0.03 1.78
4.	A_4(61)	0.249	0.062	95.902	9.85** (4,595)	-5.250(60) 3.348(58) -3.104(62) 2.041(61)	4.02** 2.71** 2.35* 1.46@ (595)	1539.199	-0.245 0.123 -0.128 0.089	0.115	4.99 -0.03 2.26 -1.02

@ Not Significant at 0.05 level.

PREDICTION OF TOTAL ACHIEVEMENT SCORE WITH THE HELP OF ACHIEVEMENT SCORES IN THEORY AND PRACTICALS

In this analysis the effect of students achievement scores in Theory and Practicals for first and second year (variable Nos. 64 to 69 in Table 5.25) on the dependent variable Total achievement score (GT) is studied and the results obtained are presented in Table 5.62.

In Table 5.62 the first predictor variable that entered into the stepwise regression analysis is the Total achievement score in Practicals for first and second year (AP i.e. variable No. 69 in Table 5.25). The value of t for b is 52.73, which is significant at 0.01 level. The regression equation at this step is

GT = 581.256 + 1.157 (AP).

The next predictable variable that entered in this analysis is Total achievement score in Theory for first and second year (AT i.e., variable No. 66 in Table 5.25). The 'F' value for R is 3482316.00, which is significant at 0.01 level. The constant value in this regression is 0.113. The regression equation at this stage is

GT = 0.113 + 1.000 (AP) + 1.000 (AT)

The other variables of achievement score in theory and practicals do not significantly contribute anything to predict on the dependent variable GT.

PREDICTION OF TOTAL ACHIEVEMENT SCORE WITH THE HELP OF 69 INDEPENDENT VARIABLES

In this analysis the effect of 69 independent variables on the dependent variable Total achievement score (GT) is studied and the obtained results are presented in Table 5.63.

In Table 5.63 the first predictor variable that entered into the stepwise regression analysis is the Total achievement score in Practicals for first and second year (AP i.e. variable No. 69 in Table 5.25). The value of t for b is 52.73, which is significant at 0.01 level. The regression equation at this stage is

GT = 581.268 + 1.157 (AP).

Table 5.62: Prediction of Total Achievement Score with the Help of Achievement Scores in Theory and Practicals

Step No.	*IV (VN)*	*R*	*R²*	*SER*	*F Value for R*	*b(VN)*	*'t' Value for b*	*Constant*	*B*	*r*	*% of Variance*
1	2	3	4	5	6	7	8	9	10	11	12
1.	AP(69)	0.907	0.823	41.556	2780.64* (1,598)	1.157 (69)	52.73* (598)	581.256	0.907	0.907	82.30
2.	AT(66)	1.000	1.000	0.915	3482316.00* (2,597)	1.000(69) 1.000(66)	1985.78* 1110.19** (597)	0.113	0.784 0.438	0.659	71.12 28.87

* Significant at 0.01 level.

@ Not Significant at 0.05 level.

Table 5.63: Prediction of Total Achievement Score with the Help of 69 Independent Variables

Step No.	*IV (VN)*	R	R^2	*SER*	*F Value For R*	*b(VN)*	*'t' Value for b*	*Constant*	*B*	*r*	*% of Variance*
1	2	3	4	5	6	7	8	9	10	11	12
1.	AP(69)	0.907	0.823	41.557	2780.39* (1,598)	1.157 (69)	52.73* (598)	581.268	0.907	0.907	82.30
2.	AT(66)	1.000	1.000	0.944	3272904.00* (2,597)	1.000(69) 1.000(66)	1925.12* 1076.30* (597)	0.117	0.784 0.438	0.659	71.12 28.87

* Significant at 0.01 level.

The next predictor variable that entered in this analysis is Total achievement score in Theory for first and second year (AT i.e., variable No. 66 in Table 5.25). The 'F' value for R is 3272904.00, which is significant at 0.01 level. The constant value in this regression is 0.117. The regression equation at this stage is

GT = 0.117 + 1.000 (AP) + 1.000 (AT)

The other independent variables are not significantly contributed anything to prediction the dependent variable GT.

PREDICTION OF ACHIEVEMENT SCORE IN THEORY WITH THE HELP OF DEMOGRAPHIC AND SOCIO-ECONOMIC VARIABLES

The relative contribution of 19 Demographic and Socio-Economic variables (Variable Nos. 1 to 19 in Table 5.25) to dependent variable i.e. achievement score in theory (variable No. 67 in Table 5.25) is studied with the help of multiple regression analysis. The results are presented in Table 5.64.

It is seen from Table 5.64 that the first variable entered into the stepwise multiple regression analysis are Caste (CA). The value of R is 0.161 indicating that the strength of the relationship between the two variables (AT and CA) is about 1.61 per cent. It is found that the 'F' value (16.12) is significant at 0.01 level for 1 and 598 df. The value of Multiple R^2 is 0.026 and therefore 2.63 per cent of the variance in achievement score in theory is accounted by Caste (CA). The Standard error of multiple R (SER) is 42.729. From this result it may be inferred that nearly 68 per cent of the actual AT value would lie within ± 42.729 points of AT value predicted with the help of variable CA.

The partial regression co-efficient (b) presented in column 7 of Table 5.64 are 6.954. This gives that the AT value would change by 6.954 units for every unit of change in CA. The t value for b is 4.02, which is significant at 0.01 level of confidence. The constant value is 683.270. The regression equation at this stage is

AT = 683.270 + 6.954 (CA)

Table 5.64: Prediction of Achievement Score in Theory with the Help of 19 Demographic and Socio-economic Variables

Step No.	*IV (VN)*	*R*	*R^2*	*SER*	*F Value For R*	*b (VN)*	*'t' Value for b*	*Constant*	*B*	*r*	*% of Variance*
1	*2*	*3*	*4*	*5*	*6*	*7*	*8*	*9*	*10*	*11*	*12*
1.	CA (15)	0.161	0.026	42.729	16.12** (1,598)	6.954(15)	4.02** (598)	683.270	0.162	0.162	2.63
2.	G(16)	0.212	0.045	42.349	14.09** (2,597)	7.128(15) -13.243(16)	4.15** 4.43** (597)	699.727	0.166 -0.137	-0.132	2.69 1.82
3.	A(4)	0.234	0.055	42.164	11.56** (3,596)	6.698(15) -13.127 (16) -6.446(4)	3.90** 3.39** 2.50* (596)	712.521	0.156 -0.135 -0.100	-0.118	2.53 1.79 1.18
4.	R(1)	0.249	0.062	42.033	9.91** (4,595)	6.709(15) -13.384(16) -6.116 (4) -4.179 (1)	3.92** 3.47** 2.37* 2.17* (595)	720.567	0.156 -0.138 -0.095 -0.086	-0.089	2.53 1.82 1.12 0.77
5.	C(2)	0.283	0.080	41.663	10.39** (5,594)	6.674(15) -13.023(16) -6.158(4) -21.139(1) -5.656(2)	3.93** 3.40** 2.41* 3.96** 3.41** (594)	785.313	0.156 -0.134 -0.096 -0.437 -0.376	0.033	2.52 1.77 1.13 1.26 3.87

(Contd...)

1	2	3	4	5	6	7	8	9	10	11	12
6.	FEM(10)	0.290	0.084	41.611	9.09** (6,593)	6.935(15) -13.231(16) -6.719(4) -21.087(1) -5.524(2) -3.202(10)	4.07** 3.46** 2.61** 3.96** 3.33** 1.58@ (593)	791.507	0.162 -0.136 -0.104 -0.436 -0.367 -0.064	-0.021	2.62 1.80 1.23 3.86 1.23 0.14
7.	FE(6)	0.295	0.087	41.577	8.09** (7,592)	6.710 (15) -13.255(16) -6.630(4) -21.316(1) -5.585(2) -6.013(10) 3.662 (6)	3.92** 3.47** 2.58** 4.00** 3.36** 2.11* 1.41@ (592)	790.829	0.156 -0.136 -0.103 -0.441 -0.371 -0.120 0.079	0.032	2.53 1.81 1.22 3.90 -1.24 0.25 0.26

* Significant at 0.05 level.

** Significant at 0.01 level.

@ Not Significant at 0.05 level.

The Group subject at Intermediate level (G) studied by the student teachers is the very significant variable in the stepwise regression analysis. The value of R between AT on one side and CA and G on the other side is 0.212. The strength of the relationship between AT and 2 independent variables CA and G put together is about 4.5 per cent. The 'F' ratio of R is 14.09, which is significant at 0.01 level for 2 and 597 df. Out of this 2.69 per cent of variance is explained by CA and the remaining 1.82 per cent variance is explained by G. These percentages can be obtained by multiplying the B (Beta) co-efficient, the corresponding symbol correlation between the dependent variable and the respective independent variable (shown in column–11). The 't' value for b is significant at 0.01 level for CA and G. The constant value is 699.727. The regression equation to predict AT with these two variables CA and G as predictor variable is

$$AT = 699.727 + 7.128\ (CA) - 13.243\ (G)$$

There are 7 steps in the stepwise regression analysis. Hence, demographic and Socio-Economic variables have their contribution to predict the dependent variable AT. The last variable entered into the analysis is Fathers Education (FE i.e. variable No. 6 in Table 5.25). The regression equation at the end of this step is written as

$$AT = 790.829 + 6.710\ (CA) - 13.255\ (G) - 6.630\ (A) - 21.316\ (R) + 5.585$$

$$(C) - 6.013\ (FEM) + 3.662\ (FE).$$

PREDICTION OF ACHIEVEMENT SCORE IN THEORY WITH THE HELP OF TEACHER ATTITUDE VARIABLES

This section deals with the help of 12 teacher attitude variables (variable Nos. 20 to 31 in Table 5.25). The stepwise regression analysis is carried out and the results are presented in Table 5.65.

Table 5.65: Prediction of Achievement Score in Theory with the Help of 12 Teacher Attitude Scores

Step No.	*IV (VN)*	*R*	*R^2*	*SER*	*F Value for R*	*b(VN)*	*'t' Value for b*	*Constant*	*B*	*r*	*% of Variance*
1	*2*	*3*	*4*	*5*	*6*	*7*	*8*	*9*	*10*	*11*	*12*
1.	TA_5(24)	0.084	0.007	43.139	4.51* (1,598)	-0.974(24)	2.12* (598)	724.816	-0.087	-0.086	0.75
2.	TA_2(21)	0.109	0.012	43.076	3.63* (2,597)	-1.324(24) -0.674(21)	2.63** 1.66@ (597)	710.350	-1.324 -0.674	0.025	1.02 0.19
3.	TA_{11}(30)	0.134	0.018	42.938	3.62 * (3,596)	-0.71(24) 1.237(21) -0.219(30)	1.19@ 2.46* 1.89@ (596)	730.639	-0.063 -0.136 -0.125	-0.072	0.55 0.34 0.90

* Significant at 0.05 level.

** Significant at 0.01 level.

@ Not Significant at 0.05 level.

From Table 5.65 it could be seen that the most important predictor variable that entered first in this analysis is Attitude towards High social approach (TA_5 i.e., variable No. 24 in Table 5.25). The value of R and R^2 are 0.084 and 0.007 respectively. The 'F' value for R is 4.51 at 0.05 level for 1 and 598 df. The t value of b is 2.12, which is significant at 0.05 level. The constant value is 732.819. Thus the regression equation at this stage is

$$AT = 724.816 - 0.974\ (TA_5)$$

The second predictor variable that entered in this analysis is attitude towards Need for content (TA_2 variable No. 21 in Table 5.25). The value of R and R^2 are 0.109 and 0.012 respectively. The 'F' value of R is 3.63, which is significant at 0.05 level. The constant value is 710.350. Thus the regression equation at this stage is

$$AT = 710.350 - 1.324\ (TA_5) - 0.067\ (TA_2)$$

The further and the last step in this analysis is Total score for attitude towards training (TA_{11} variable No. 30 in Table 5.25). The 'F' value of R is 3.62, which is significant at 0.05 level. The regression equation at this stage is

$$AT = 730.639 - 0.710\ (TA_5) + 1.237\ (TA_2) - 0.219\ (TA_{11})$$

PREDICTION OF ACHIEVEMENT SCORE IN THEORY WITH THE HELP OF STUDY HABITS SCORES

In this section the dependent variable Achievement score in theory (AT) is the predictor with the help of 10 Study habit areas (variable Nos. 32 to 41 in Table 5.25). The stepwise multiple regression analysis is carried out and the results are presented in Table 5.66.

From Table 5.66 it is seen that the most important predictor variable that entered first into the stepwise multiple regression analysis is Preparation for examinations (S_5). The multiple 'R' value is 0.122. The 'F' value for R is 9.31, which is significant at 0.01 level for df 1,598. The multiple R^2 is 0.015 indicating that this variable alone contributed 1.5 per cent of variance in AT. The value of b is 0.788 and t value for b is 3.05, which is significant at 0.01 level.

Table 5.66: Prediction of Achievement Score in Theory with the Help of 10 Study Habits Scores

Step No.	*IV (VN)*	*R*	*R^2*	*SER*	*F Value for R*	*b(VN)*	*'t' Value for b*	*Constant*	*B*	*r*	*% of Variance*
1	*2*	*3*	*4*	*5*	*6*	*7*	*8*	*9*	*10*	*11*	*12*
1.	S_5(36)	0.122	0.015	42.962	9.31** (1,598)	0.788(36)	3.05** (598)	668.198	0.124	0.124	1.53
2.	S_1(32)	0.141	0.02	42.894	6.21** (2,597)	0.629(36) 0.465(32)	2.30* 1.75@ (597)	652.012	0.099 0.075	0.108	1.22 0.81
3.	S_9(40)	0.158	0.025	42.824	5.13** (3,596)	0.708(36) 0.578(32) -0.638(40)	2.56* 2.12* 1.71@ (596)	661.275	0.111 0.094 -0.074	-0.018	1.38 1.01 0.13

* Significant at 0.05 level.

** Significant at 0.01 level.

@ Not Significant at 0.05 level.

It shows that for every unit of changing achievement score in theory (AT) there will be a change of 0.788 units in AT. The constant value is 668.198. Therefore, the multiple regression equation at the end of this step could be written as

$$AT = 668.198 + 0.788 (S_5)$$

The second variable that is inserted into analysis is Home environment (S_1). The value of F for R is 6.21, which is significant at 0.01 level of confidence. The value of Multiple R^2 is 0.02. The two variables S_5 and S_1 could explain 2.03 per cent of variance. The constant value of the prediction is 652.012. The multiple regressions at this stage is

$$AT = 652.012 + 0.629 (S_5) + 0.465 (S_1)$$

The next and last variable that inserted into analysis is College environment (S_9). The Multiple 'R' value is 0.158. The F value for R is 5.13, which is significant at 0.01 level for df. 3,596. The multiple R^2 is 0.025 and the constant value is 661.278. Therefore the multiple regression equation at the end of the step could be written as

$$AT = 661.278 + 0.708 (S_5) + 0.578 (S_1) - 0.638 (S_9)$$

PREDICTION OF ACHIEVEMENT SCORE IN THEORY WITH THE HELP OF 16 PERSONALITY FACOTRS (16 PF)

In this regression analysis the effect of 16 PF (variable Nos. 42 to 57 in Table 5.25) on the dependent variable Achievement score in Theory (AT) is studied and obtained results are presented in Table 5.67.

In Table 5.67, the first predictor variable that entered into the stepwise regression analysis is Factor L (PFL). The value of R is 0.104 and 'F' value for R is 6.43, which is significant at 0.01 level. The partial regression co-efficient (b) is 2.181. The regression equation at this stage is

$$AT = 692.398 + 2.181 (PFL).$$

The second predictor variable in the stepwise analysis is Factor E (PFE). The value of R and R^2 are 0.145 and 0.021 respectively. The constant value is 701.889. The contribution of PFL is 1.13 per cent and the remaining 0.96 per cent is contributed by PFE. The regression equation at this stage is

$$AT = 701.889 + 2.309 (PFL) - 2.223 (PFE)$$

Table 5.67: Prediction of Achievement Score in Theory with the Help of 16 Personality Factors Scores

Step No.	*IV (VN)*	*R*	*R^2*	*SER*	*F Value for R*	*b(VN)*	*'t' Value for b*	*Constant*	*B*	*r*	*% of Variance*
1	*2*	*3*	*4*	*5*	*6*	*7*	*8*	*9*	*10*	*11*	*12*
1.	PFL(50)	0.104	0.011	43.070	6.43** (1,598)	2.181(50)	2.54* (598)	692.398	0.103	0.103	1.06
2.	PFE(45)	0.145	0.021	42.882	6.37** (2,597)	2.309(50) -2.223(45)	2.69** 2.50* (597)	701.889	0.109 -0.101	-0.095	1.13 0.96
3.	PFQ4(57)	0.167	0.028	42.755	5.79** (3,596)	2.022(50) -2.492(45) 1.574(57)	2.34* 2.78** 2.14* (596)	695.903	0.096 -0.114 0.088	0.087	0.99 1.08 0.77

* Significant at 0.05 level.

** Significant at 0.01 level.

The next and last predictor variable that entered in this analysis is Factor Q4 (PFQ4) i.e., variable No. 57 in Table 5.25). The value of R and R^2 are 0.167 and 0.028 respectively. The percentage of these predictor variables (PFL, PFE and PFQ4) is 2.84 per cent. The constant value in the regression is 695.903. The regression equation with these 3 predictor variables PFL, PFE and PFQ4 could be written as

$$AT = 695.903 + 2.022 (PFL)-2.492 (PFE) + 1.574 (PFQ4)$$

The other factors of 16 PF have not significantly contributed any thing to predict the dependent variable AT.

PREDICTION OF ACHIEVEMENT SCORE IN THEORY WITH THE HELP OF OBJECTIVE ACHIEVEMENT TEST SCORE

In this regression analysis the effect of Objective Achievement test scores (variable Nos. 58 to 63 in Table 5.25) on the dependent variable achievement score in Theory (AT) is studied and the results obtained are presented in Table 5.68.

Table 5.68 the first predictor variable that entered into the stepwise regression analysis is Teacher education in emerging India (A_1 i.e., variable No. 58 in Table 5.25). The value of R is 0.094 and the 'F' value for R is 5.52, which is significant at 0.01 level. The value of b is 2.35. The constant value is 684.728. The regression equation at this stage is

$$AT = 684.728 + 1.141 (A_1)$$

The second predictor variable entered into the stepwise analysis is Elementary Education, Educational planning and management (A_3 i.e. variable No. 60 in Table 5.25). The value of R and R^2 are 0.126 and 0.016 respectively. The constant value is 691.960. The contribution of A_1 is 1.33 per cent and the remaining contribution 0.28 per cent is by the variable A_3. The regression equation at this stage is

$$AT = 684.702 + 1.663 (A_1) – 0.887 (A_3)$$

The next and the last predictor variable that entered in this analysis are Perspectives in primary education (A_4 i.e., variable No. 61 in Table 5.25). The value of R and R^2 are 0.155 and 0.024 respectively. The constant value is 684.702. The regression equation for these three variables could be written as

$$AT = 684.702 + 1.496 (A_1) – 1.666 (A_3) + 1.274 (A_4)$$

Table 5.68: Prediction of Achievement Score in Theory with the Help of 6 Objective Achievements Scores

Step No.	*IV (VN)*	*R*	*R^2*	*SER*	*F Value for R*	*b(VN)*	*'t' Value for b*	*Constant*	*B*	*r*	*% of Variance*
1	*2*	*3*	*4*	*5*	*6*	*7*	*8*	*9*	*10*	*11*	*12*
1.	A_1(58)	0.094	0.009	43.102	5.52** (1.598)	1.141(58)	2.35* (598)	684.728	0.096	0.096	0.92
2.	A_3(60)	0.126	0.016	42.987	4.89** (2,597)	1.663(58) -0.887(60)	3.04** 2.05* (597)	691.960	0.139 -0.094	-0.029	1.33 0.28
3.	A_4(61)	0.155	0.024	42.853	4.86** (3,596)	1.496(58) -1.666(60) 1.274(62)	2.72** 2.98** 2.18* (596)	684.702	0.125 0.177 0.126	0.053	1.20 0.52 0.67

** Significant at 0.01 level.

* Significant at 0.05 level.

PREDICTION OF ACHIEVEMENT SCORE IN THEORY WITH THE HELP OF THEORY, PRACTICALS AND TOTAL ACHIEVEMENT SCORES

In this analysis the effect of students Achievement score in Theory, Practicals and Total achievement score (for variable Nos. 64 to 65 and 67 to 70 in Table 5.25) on the dependent variable achievement score in Theory (AT) is studied and the obtained results are presented in Table 5.69.

In Table 5.69 the first predictor variable that entered into the stepwise regression analysis is the II year theory total score (AT_2 i.e., variable No. 65 in Table 5.25). The value of R and R^2 are 0.854 and 0.729 respectively. The value of t for b is 40.13, which is significant at 0.01 level. The regression equation at this stage is

$$AT = 204.134 + 1.423\ (AT_2).$$

The next predictor variable that entered into the analysis is I year theory score (AT1). The 'F' value for R is 34426.94, which is significant at 0.01 level. The constant value in this regression is 5.951. Thus the regression equation is

$$AT = 5.951 + 1.002\ (AT_2) + 0.982\ (AT1)$$

The next and the last variable that entered in this analysis are the total score of first and second year practicals (AP). The values of multiple R and R^2 are 0.999 and 0.999 respectively. The F value for R is 334204.30, which is significant at 0.01 level. Thus, the regression analysis at this stage is

$$AT = 0.165 - 1.124\ (AT_2) - 1.097\ (AT1) + 1.011\ (GT) - 1.011\ (AP).$$

PREDICTION OF THEORY SCORES WITH THE HELP OF 69 INDEPENDENT VARIABLES

In this analysis the effect of 69 Independent variables on the dependent variable achievement score in Theory (AT) is studied and the obtained results are presented in Table 5.70.

In Table 5.70 the first predictor variable that entered into the stepwise regression analysis is the II year theory total score (AT_2 i.e., variable No. 65 in Table 5.25). The value of R and R^2 are 0.854 and 0.729 respectively. The value of t for b is 40.13, which is significant at 0.01 level. The regression equation at this stage is

$$AT = 204.134 + 1.423\ (AT_2).$$

Table 5.69: Prediction of Achievement Score in Theory with the Help of Theory, Practicals and Total Achievement Score

Step No.	*IV (VN)*	*R*	*R^2*	*SER*	*F Value for R*	*b(VN)*	*'t' Value for b*	*Constant*	*B*	*r*	*% of Variance*
1	2	3	4	5	6	7	8	9	10	11	12
1.	AT_2(65)	0.854	0.729	22.533	1610.33* (1,598)	1.423 (65)	40.13* (598)	204.134	0.854	0.854	72.92
2.	AT_1(64)	0.995	0.991	4.018	34426.94* (2,597)	1.002(65) 0.982(64)	142.00* 134.94* (597)	5.951	0.601 0.571	0.837	51.32 47.82
3.	GT(70)	0.995	0.991	4.010	23039.83* (3,596)	0.992 (65) 0.979(64) 4.176(70)	112.17* 132.26* 1.81@ (596)	4.078	0.595 0.570 0.010	0.659	50.82 47.69 0.63
4.	AP(69)	0.999	0.999	0.916	334204.30* (4,595)	-1.124(65) -1.097(64) 1.011(70) -1.011(69)	1.14@ 1.14@ 104.39* 104.41* (595)	0.165	-0.007 -0.006 2.301 -1.808	0.281	-0.58 -0.53 151.89 -50.82

* Significant at 0.01 level.

@ Not Significant at 0.05 level.

Table 5.70: Prediction of Achievement Score in Theory with the Help of 69 Independent Variables

Step No.	*IV (VN)*	*R*	*R^2*	*SER*	*F Value for R*	*B(VN)*	*'t' Value for b*	*Constant*	*B*	*r*	*% of Variance*
1	2	3	4	5	6	7	8	9	10	11	12
1.	AT_2(65)	0.854	0.729	22.533	1610.38** (1,598)	1.428 (65)	40.13** (598)	204.123	0.854	0.854	72.92
2.	AT_1(64)	0.995	0.991	4.017	34452.49** (2,597)	1.002(65) 0.982(64)	142.00** 134.99** (597)	5.941	0.601 0.571	0.837	51.32 47.82
3.	TA_6(25)	0.995	0.991	4.008	23065.78** (3,596)	1.000 (65) 0.984(64) 4.100(25)	142.08** 134.40** 1.87@ (596)	3.660	0.601 0.572 0.007	-0.077	51.30 47.91 -0.05
4.	AFI(14)	0.996	0.992	4.000	17367.75** (4,595)	1.000(65) 0.984(64) 0.105(25) 0.324(14)	142.27** 134.51** 1.96* 1.82@ (595)	2.708	0.600 0.573 0.008 0.007	-0.009	51.27 47.95 -0.06 -0.01
5.	BE (8)	0.996	0.992	3.989	13976.01** (5,594)	1.000(65) 0.985(64) 0.102(25) 0.422(14) -0.264(8)	142.13** 134.91** 1.91@ 2.30* 2.11* (594)	3.431	0.600 0.573 0.007 0.009 -0.008	-0.070	51.21 47.95 -0.06 -0.01 0.06

(Contd...)

1	2	3	4	5	6	7	8	9	10	11	12
6.	SE (9)	1.000	1.000	3.974	11731.56** (6,593)	1.000(65) 0.984(64) 0.102(25) 0.538(14) -0.301(8) -0.296(9)	142.63** 135.27** 1.92@ 2.84** 2.40* 2.30* (593)	3.964	0.600 0.572 0.007 0.012 -0.009 -0.009	-0.033	51.21 47.93 -0.06 -0.01 0.07 0.03
7.	GT(70)	0.996	0.992	3.996	10097.58** (7,592)	0.990(65) 0.981(64) 0.103(25) 0.540(14) -0.307(8) -0.291(9) 0.004(70)	112.69** 132.70** 1.93@ 2.85** 2.45* 2.26* 1.86@ (592)	2.051	0.594 0.571 0.007 0.012 -0.010 -0.009 -0.010	0.659	50.70 47.80 -0.06 -0.01 0.07 0.03 0.64
8.	AP(69)	1.000	1.000	0.949	155710.00** (8,591)	0.004(65) 0.004(64) 0.001(25) 0.001(14) -0.0003(8) -0.001(9) 1.004(70) -1.004(69)	0.41@ 0.40@ 0.10@ 0.04@ 0.01@ 0.03@ 99.07** 98.79** (591)	0.209	-0.003 -0.002 -0.000 -0.000 0.000 0.000 2.290 -1.795	0.281	-0.21 -0.20 -0.00 -0.00 -0.00 -0.00 150.83 -50.47

* Significant at 0.05 level.

** Significant at 0.01 level.

@ Not Significant at 0.05 level.

The next predictor variable that entered into the analysis is I year theory score (AT1). The 'F' value for R is 34452.49, which is significant at 0.01 level. The constant value in this regression is 5.941. Thus, the regression equation is

$$AT = 5.941 + 1.002\,(AT_2) + 0.982\,(AT1)$$

The next and the last variable that entered in this analysis are the total score for first and second year practicals (AP). The values of multiple R and R^2 are 1.000 and 1.000 respectively. The F value for R is 155710.00, which is significant at 0.01 level of confidence. Thus, the regression analysis at this stage is

$$AT = 0.209 - 0.004\,(AT_2) - 0.004\,(AT1) - 0.001\,(TA6) - 0.001\,(AFI) + 0.003\,(BE) - 0.001\,(SE) + 1.004\,(GT) - 1.004\,(AP).$$

PREDICTION OF PRACTICALS SCORE WITHTHE HELP OF DEMOGRAPHIC AND SOCIO-ECONOMIC VARIABLES

The relative contribution of 19 demographic and Socio-Economic variables (variable Nos. 1 to 19 in Table 5.25) to the dependent variable i.e. achievement score in Practicals (variable No. 69 in Table 5.25) is studied with the help of multiple regression analysis. The results are presented in Table 5.71.

It is seen from Table 5.71 that the first variable entered into the stepwise multiple regression analysis is College (C) and its R-value is 0.499 indicating that the strength of the relationship between the two variables (AP and C) is about 40 per cent The value of Multiple R^2 is 0.249 and concluded that 24.9 per cent of the variance in achievement score in practicals is accounted by College (C).

The Standard error of Multiple R (SER) is 67.113. From this result it may be inferred that nearly 68 per cent of the actual AP value would lie within ± 67.113 points of AP value predictor with the help of variable C.

The partial regression co-efficient (b) is presented in Column 7 of Table 5.71 are 13.425. This gives the AP value would change by 13.425 units for every unit of change in C. The t value for b is 14.07, which is significant at 0.01 level. The constant value that could be written to predict AP at this stage is 704.40. The regression equation at the end of this step is

$$AP = 704.40 + 13.425\,(C)$$

Table 5.71: Prediction of Achievement Score in Practicals with the Help of 19 Demographic and Socio-economic Variables

Step No.	*IV (VN)*	*R*	*R^2*	*SER*	*F Value for R*	*b(VN)*	*'t' Value for b*	*Constant*	*B*	*r*	*% of Variance*
1	*2*	*3*	*4*	*5*	*6*	*7*	*8*	*9*	*10*	*11*	*12*
1.	C(2)	0.499	0.249	67.113	198.08** (1,598)	13.425 (2)	14.07** (598)	704.40	0.499	0.499	24.88
2.	OB(18)	0.546	0.298	64.910	127.01** (2,597)	31.700(2) -22.311(18)	14.83** 6.50** (597)	740.370	0.509 -0.223	-0.200	25.39 4.46
3.	R(1)	0.588	0.346	62.71	86.42** (3,596)	29.127(2) -22.866(18) 53.005(1)	11.65** 6.90** 6.60** (596)	550.445	1.082 -0.229 0.613	-0.390	53.98 4.57 -23.92
4.	G(16)	0.606	0.367	61.739	71.44** (4,595)	29.273(2) -16.927(18) 53.219(1) -27.322(16)	11.89** 4.80** 6.74** 4.46** (595)	573.981	1.088 -0.169 0.616 -0.157	-0.199	54.25 3.38 -24.01 3.13
5.	SEM(13)	0.613	0.376	61.397	71.44** (5,594)	28.962(2) -18.071(18) 52.281(1) -27.805(16) 8.508(13)	11.82** 5.12** 6.65** 4.56** 2.76** (594)	571.934	1.076 -0.181 0.605 -0.160 0.091	0.574	53.68 3.61 -23.59 3.18 0.67

(Contd...)

1	2	3	4	5	6	7	8	9	10	11	12
6.	ME(7)	0.619	0.384	61.026	61.64**	29.684(2)	12.12**	582.386	1.103	0.015	55.02
					(6,593)	-19.305(18)	5.46**		-0.193		3.86
						53.659(1)	6.85**		0.621		-24.21
						-27.713(16)	4.58**		-0.160		3.17
						9.063(13)	2.96**		0.097		0.72
						-9.816(7)	2.87**		-0.094		-0.14
							(593)				
7.	FE(6)	0.625	0.391	60.716	54.38**	29.708(2)	12.19**	572.748	1.104	0.109	55.06
					(7,592)	-18.159(18)	5.12**		-0.182		3.63
						53.963(1)	6.92**		0.624		24.35
						-28.363(16)	4.70**		-0.163		3.25
						8.119(13)	2.64**		0.087		0.64
						-15.639(7)	3.87**		-0.150		0.22
						8.581(6)	2.66**		0.104		1.13
							(592)				
8.	BEM(12)	0.628	0.395	60.607	48.144**	29.290(2)	11.99**	572.239	1.088	0.076	54.29
					(8,591)	-19.451(18)	5.38**		-0.195		3.89
						52.616(1)	6.73**		0.609		23.74
						-26.755(16)	4.39**		-0.154		3.06
						7.813(13)	2.55*		0.083		0.62
						-15.361(7)	3.80**		-0.148		-0.22
						8.516(6)	2.64**		0.103		1.12
						4.969(12)	1.77@		0.059		0.44
							(591)				

(Contd...)

1	2	3	4	5	6	7	8	9	10	11	12
9.	BE(8)	0.632	0.040	60.405	43.64**	29.412(2)	12.07**	573.052	1.093	-0.001	54.51
					(9,590)	-19.454(18)	5.40**		-0.195		3.89
						52.223(1)	6.83**		0.616		24.03
						-26.753(16)	4.23**		-0.148		2.95
						6.821(13)	2.21*		0.073		0.54
						-14.835(7)	3.68**		-0.143		0.21
						8.977(6)	2.79**		0.109		1.18
						12.433(12)	2.85**		0.146		1.11
						-6.451(8)	2.23*		-0.113		0.01
							(590)				
10.	SE(9)	0.634	0.402	60.350	39.55**	29.073(2)	11.89**	576.821	1.080	-0.017	53.88
					(10.589)	-19.293(18)	5.36**		-0.193		3.85
						52.403(1)	6.71**		0.606		-23.65
						-26.17(16)	4.12**		-0.145		-2.88
						12.380(13)	2.50*		0.132		0.98
						-14.225(7)	3.51**		-0.137		-0.20
						9.380(6)	2.90**		0.114		1.24
						11.744(12)	2.68**		0.138		1.05
						-6.302(8)	2.18*		-0.137		0.01
						-4.497(9)	1.44@		-0.110		0.13
							(589)				

(Contd...)

1	2	3	4	5	6	7	8	9	10	11	12
11.	CA(15)	0.635	0.402	60.295	36.21**	29.095(2)	11.91**	562.621	10.81	0.043	53.92
					(11,588)	-19.201(18)	5.34**		-0.192		3.84
						52.419(1)	6.72**		0.607		-23.65
						-25.423(16)	4.17**		-0.146		2.91
						12.802(13)	2.59**		0.136-		1.01
						-14.632(7)	3.61**		0.141		-0.21
						9.032(6)	2.79**		0.109		1.19
						11.384(12)	2.59**		0.134		1.01
						-5.900(8)	2.03*		-0.103		0.01
						-4.872(9)	1.55@		-0.083		0.14
						3.593(15)	1.45@		0.047		0.20
							(588)				

* Significant at 0.05 level.

** Significant at 0.01 level.

@ Not Significant at 0.05 level.

The Order of Birth (OB) of the student teacher in their family is very significant variable in the stepwise regression analysis. The value of R between AP on one side C and OB on the other side is 0.546. The strength of the relationship between AP and 2 independent variables C and OB put together is about 5.46 per cent. The F ratio of R is 127.01, which is significant at 0.01 level for 2 and 597 df.

The value of R^2 is 0.298. This shows that the two variables put together could explain 29.8 per cent of variance on the dependent variable (Achievement score in Practicals). Out of this 25.39 per cent of variance is explained by C and the remaining 4.46 per cent of variance is explained by OB. These percentages can be obtained by multiplying the B (Beta) co-efficient, the corresponding symbol correlation between the dependent variable and the respective independent variable (shown in column–12). The 't' value of b is significant beyond 0.01 level of confidence for C and OB. The constant value is 740.370. The regression equation to predict AP with these two variables C and OB as predictor variable is

AP = 740.370 + 31.700 (C) – 22.311 (OB).

The third predictor variable is entered in this analysis is Region (R) of the student (variable No. 1 in Table 5.25). The F value for R is 105.26, which is significant at 0.01 level. The regression equation at this stage is

AP = 550.445 + 29.127 (C) – 22.866 (OB) + 53.005 (R).

There are 11 steps in the stepwise regression analysis. Hence, the demographic and socio-economic variables have their contribution to predict the dependent variable AP.

The last variable entered into the analysis is Caste (variable No. 15 in Table 5.25). The regression equation at the end of this stage is

AP = 562.621 + 29.095 (C) – 19.201(OB) + 52.419 (R) – 25.423 (G) +12.802 (SEM) – 14.632 (ME) + 9.032 (FE) + 11.384 (BEM)- 5.900 (BE) – 4.872 (SE) + 3.593 (CA).

PREDICTION OF PRACTICAL SCORES WITH THE HELP OF TEACHER ATTITUDE VARIABLES

This section deals prediction of practical scores with the help of Teacher Attitude variables (Variable Nos. 20 to 31 in Table 5.25). The stepwise regression analysis is carried out and the results are presented in Table 5.72.

From Table 5.72 it could be seen that the most important predictor variable that entered first in this analysis is attitude towards profession and training (TA_{12} variable No. 31 in Table 5.25).

The value of R and R^2 are 0.20 and 0.040 respectively. F-value for R is 24.72, which is significant at 0.01 level for 1 and 598 df. The 't' value of b is 4.97, which is significant at 0.01 level. The constant value is 936.106. Thus, the regression equation at this stage is

$$AP = 936.106 - 0.499\ (TA_{12})$$

The second predictor variable that entered in this analysis is high intrinsic motivation (variable No. 25 in Table 5.25). The values of R and R^2 are 0.225 and 0.051 respectively. The F value of R is 16.18, which is significant at 0.01 level. The constant value is 927.552. Thus, the regression equation at this stage is

$$AP = 927.552 - 0.653\ (TA_2) + 3.120\ (TA_6).$$

The fifth and the last step in this analysis are attitude towards high conceptual level (variable No. 22 in Table 5.25). The F value of R is 9.51, which is significant at 0.01 level of confidence. The regression equation at this stage is

$$AP = 921.178 + 0.114\ (TA_{12}) + 2.710\ (TA_6) - 2.310\ (TA_9) - 2.221\ (TA_4) - 2.423\ (TA_3).$$

PREDICTION OF PRACTICALS SCORE WITH THE HELP OF STUDY HABITS AREAS

In this section the dependent variable Achievement score in practicals (AP) is predictor with the help of 10 Study habit scores (variable Nos. 32 to 41 in Table 5.25). The stepwise multiple regression analysis carried out and the results are presented in Table 5.73.

Table 5.72: Prediction of Achievement Score in Practicals with the Help of 12 Teacher Attitude Variables

Step No.	*IV (VN)*	*R*	*R^2*	*SER*	*F Value for R*	*B(VN)*	*'t' Value for b*	*Constant*	*B*	*r*	*% of Variance*
1	*2*	*3*	*4*	*5*	*6*	*7*	*8*	*9*	*10*	*11*	*12*
1.	TA_{12}(31)	0.20	0.040	75.882	24.72** (1,598)	-0.499(31)	4.97** (598)	936.106	-0.199	-0.199	3.97
2.	TA_6(25)	0.225	0.051	75.480	16.18** (2,597)	-0.653(31) 3.120(25)	5.69** 2.72** (597)	927.552	-0.261 0.125	-0.004	5.19 -0.05
3.	TA_9(28)	0.242	0.059	75.223	12.56** (3,596)	-0.579(31) 3.030 (25) -2.141(28)	3.87** 2.65** 2.26* (596)	930.609	-0.203 0.121 -0.106	-0.185	4.04 0.05 1.96
4.	TA_4(23)	0.259	0.067	74.984	10.68** (4,595)	-0.031(31) 2.685(25) -2.567(28) -2.056 (23)	1.87@ 2.33* 2.66** 2.19* (597)	921.658	-0.121 0.107 -0.127 -0.110	-0.181	2.40 -0.04 2.35 2.00

(Contd...)

1	2	3	4	5	6	7	8	9	10	11	12
5.	TA_3(22)	0.272	0.74	74.761	9.51** (5,594)	0.114(31) 2.710(25) -2.310(28) -2.221 (23) -2.423(22)	0.62@ 2.36* 2.38* 2.37* 2.13* (596)	921.178	-0.045 0.108 -0.114 -0.119 -0.115	-0.198	0.90 0.04 2.11 2.15 2.28

* Significant at 0.05 level.

** Significant at 0.01 level.

@ Not Significant at 0.05 level.

Table 5.73: Prediction of Achievement Score in Practicals with the Help of 10 Study Habits Variables

Step No.	*IV (VN)*	*R*	*R^2*	*SER*	*F Value for R*	*b(VN)*	*'t' Value for b*	*Constant*	*B*	*r*	*% of Variance*
1	*2*	*3*	*4*	*5*	*6*	*7*	*8*	*9*	*10*	*11*	*12*
1.	S_1(32)	0.130	0.017	76.777	10.28** (1,598)	1.437 (32)	3.21** (598)	706.218	0.130	0.130	1.69
2.	S_4(35)	0.148	0.022	76.636	6.76** (2,597)	1.131(32) 0.863(35)	2.36* 1.79@ (597)	680.509	0.102 0.078	0.114	1.33 0.89
3.	S_7(38)	0.173	0.030	76.411	6.04** (3,596)	1.307(32) 1.140(35) -1.548(38)	2.70** 2.29* 2.12* (596)	703.858	0.118 0.103 -0.092	-0.026	1.54 1.17 0.24

* Significant at 0.05 level.

** Significant at 0.01 level.

@ Not Significant at 0.05 level.

From Table 5.73 it is seen that the most important predictor variable that entered first into the stepwise multiple regression analysis is Home Environment (S_1). The multiple 'R' value is 0.130 and the F value for R is 10.28, which is significant at 0.01 level for df 1, 598. The Multiple R^2 is 0.017 indicating that this variable alone contributed 1.7 per cent of variance in AP. The value of b is 1.437 and t value for b is 3.21, which is significant at 0.01 level. It shows that for every unit of changing achievement score in practicals (AP) there will be a change of 1.437 units in AP. The constant value is 706.218. Therefore, the multiple regression equation at the end of this step could be written as

$$AP = 706.218 + 1.437 (S_1)$$

The second variable that is inserted into analysis is Habits of Concentration (S_4). The value of F for R is 6.76, which is significant at 0.01 level. The value of Multiple R^2 is 0.022. The two variables S_1 and S_4 could explain 0.24 per cent of variance on AP. The constant value of the prediction is 680.509. The multiple regression at this stage is

$$AP = 680.509 + 1.131 (S_1) + 0.863 (S_4).$$

The third variable that inserted into analysis is Audio-Visual programmes (S_7). The Multiple 'R' value is 0.173. The F value for R is 6.04, which is significant at 0.01 level for df 3, 596. The multiple R^2 is 0.030. The constant value is 703.858. Therefore, the multiple regression equation at the end of the step could be written as

$$AP = 703.858 + 1.307 (S_1) + 1.140 (S_4) - 1.548 (S_7)$$

PREDICTION OF PRACTICALS SCORES WITH THE HELP OF 16 PERSONALITY FACTORS (16 PF)

In this regression analysis the effect of 16 PF (variable Nos. 42 to 57 in Table 5.25) on the dependent variable achievement score in Practicals (AP) is studied and obtained results are presented in Table 5.74.

In Table 5.74, the first predictor variable that entered into the stepwise regression analysis is Factor E (PFE). The value of R is 0.126 and F value for R is 9.46, which is significant at 0.01 level. The partial regression co-efficient b is – 4.892. The regression equation at this stage is

$$AP = 800.569 - 4.892 (PFE).$$

Table 5.74: Prediction of Achievement Score in Practicals with the Help of 16 Personality Factors

Step No.	*IV (VN)*	*R*	*R^2*	*SER*	*F Value for R*	*b(VN)*	*'t' Value for b*	*Constant*	*B*	*r*	*% of Variance*
1	*2*	*3*	*4*	*5*	*6*	*7*	*8*	*9*	*10*	*11*	*12*
1.	PFE(45)	0.126	0.016	76.829	9.46**	-4.892(45)	3.08**	800.569	-0.125	-0.125	1.56
					(1,598)		(598)				
2.	PFQ4(57)	0.170	0.029	76.376	8.85**	-5.567(45)	3.48**	783.187	-0.142	0.095	1.77
					(2,597)	3.706(57)	2.85**		0.116		1.11
							(597)				
3.	PFH(48)	0.205	0.042	73.935	8.61**	-6.229(45)	3.88**	763.244	-0.159	0.081	1.98
					(3,596)	4.149(57)	3.18**		0.130		1.24
						3.512(48)	2.82**		0.115		0.94
							(596)				
4.	PFB(43)	0.230	0.053	75.524	8.41**	-6.367(45)	3.98**	787.223	-0.162	-0.091	2.03
					(4,595)	4.301(57)	3.32**		0.135		1.28
						3.887(48)	3.12**		0.127		1.03
						-5.379(43)	2.74**		-0.110		1.00
							(595)				
5.	PFQ3(56)	0.249	0.062	75.232	7.90**	-5.887(45)	3.67**	762.397	-0.150	0.094	1.87
					(5,594)	4.782(57)	3.66**		0.150		1.43
						3.580(48)	2.87**		0.117		0.95
						-5.720(43)	2.92**		-0.117		1.07
						3.186(56)	2.37*		0.097		0.92
							(594)				

(Contd...)

1	2	3	4	5	6	7	8	9	10	11	12
6.	PFA(42)	0.268	0.072	74.896	7.70** (6,593)	-5.927(45) 4.828(57) 3.871(48) -5.558(43) 3.418(56) -3.452(42)	3.71** 3.71** 2.10* 2.84** 2.55* 2.52* (593)	786.332	-0.151 0.151 0.127 -0.113 0.104 -0.010	-0.085	1.89 1.44 1.03 1.04 0.98 0.85
7.	PFM(51)	0.277	0.077	74.752	7.10** (7,592)	-5.966(45) 4.855(57) 3.654(48) -5.395(43) 3.361(56) -3.165(42) -2.995(51)	3.74** 3.74** 2.92** 2.76** 2.51* 2.30* 1.80@ (592)	802.522	-0.152 0.152 0.119 -0.110 0.103 -0.092 -0.072	-0.092	1.90 1.45 0.97 1.01 0.97 0.78 0.67
8.	PFF(46)	0.286	0.082	74.633	6.59** (8,591)	-6.023(45) 4.708(57) 3.257(48) -5.236(43) 3.621(56) -3.134(42) -2.913(51) 2.725(46)	3.78** 3.62** 2.56* 2.68** 2.69** 2.28* 1.76@ 1.70@ (591)	788.244	-0.154 0.148 0.106 -0.107 0.111 -0.091 -0.070 0.069	0.081	1.92 1.41 0.87 0.98 1.04 0.77 0.65 0.56

(Contd…)

1	2	3	4	5	6	7	8	9	10	11	12
9.	PFQ1(54)	0.293	0.086	74.539	6.15**	-6.117(45)	3.84**	775.739	-0.156	0.041	1.95
					(9,590)	4.731(57)	3.64**		0.148		1.41
						3.218(48)	2.53*		0.105		0.86
						-5.268(43)	2.70**		-0.108		0.98
						3.745(56)	2.78**		0.114		1.08
						-3.176(42)	2.31*		-0.093		0.78
						-3.126(51)	1.89@		-0.076		0.070
						2.747(46)	1.72@		0.70		0.57
						2.014(54)	1.58@		0.062		0.25
							(590)				
10.	PFL(50)	0.298	0.089	74.456	5.78**	-6.170(45)	3.88**	759.474	-0.157	0.068	1.96
					(10,589)	4.467(57)	3.41**		0.140		1.33
						3.263(48)	2.57*		0.107		-0.087
						-5.050(43)	2.59**		-0.103		0.94
						4.046(56)	2.98**		0.124		1.16
						-2.994(42)	2.17*		-0.087		0.74
						-3.027(51)	1.83@		-0.073		0.67
						2.797(46)	1.75@		0.071		0.58
						2.012(54)	1.58@		0.062		0.25
						2.351(50)	1.53@		0.062		0.42
							(589)				

* Significant at 0.05 level.

** Significant at 0.01 level.

@ Not Significant at 0.05 level.

The second predictor variable in the stepwise analysis is Factor Q4 (PFQ4). The value of R and R^2 are 0.170 and 0.029 respectively. The constant value is 783.187. The contribution of PFE is 1.77 per cent and the remaining 1.11 per cent contributed by PFQ4. The regression equation at this stage is

$$AP = 783.187 - 5.567\ (PFE) + 3.706\ (PFQ4).$$

The next predictor variable that entered in this analysis is Factor H (PFH i.e. variable No. 48 in Table 5.25). The values of R and R^2 are 0.205 and 0.042 respectively. The percentage of these predictor variables (PFE, PFQ4 and PFH) is 4.2 per cent. The constant value is 763.244. The regression equation with these 3 predictor variables PFE, PFQ4 and PFH could be written as

$$AP = 763.244 - 6.229\ (PFE) + 4.149\ (PFQ4) + 3.512\ (PFH).$$

The tenth step is the last step in this analysis i.e. Factor L (PFL). The values of R and R^2 0.298 and 0.089 respectively. The constant value is 759.474. The regression equation for this step is

$$AP = 759.474 - 6.170\ (PFE) + 4.467\ (PFQ4) + 3.263\ (PFH) - 5.050\ (PFB) + 4.046\ (PFQ3) - 2.994\ (PFA) - 3.027\ (PFM) + 2.797\ (PFF) + 2.012\ (PFQ1) + 2.351\ (PFL).$$

The other Factors of 16 PF have not significantly contributed any thing to predict on the dependent variable AP.

PREDICTION OF PRACTICALS SCORE WITH HE HELP OF OBJECTIVE ACHIEVEMENT TEST SCORES

In this regression analysis the effect of Objective achievement test scores (variable Nos. 58 to 63 in Table 5.25) on the dependent variable achievement score in Practicals (AP) is studied and the obtained results are presented in Table 5.75.

In Table 5.75 the first predictor variable that entered into the stepwise regression analysis is Elementary Education, Educational Planning and Management (A_3 i.e. variable No. 60 in Table 5.25). The value of R is 0.244 and the F value for R is 37.87, which is significant at 0.01 level. The value of b is – 4.109. The constant value is 851.791. The regression equation is

$$AP = 851.791 - 4.109\ (A_3)$$

Table 5.75: Prediction of Achievement Score in Practicals with the Help of 6 Objective Achievement Test Scores

Step No.	*IV (VN)*	*R*	R^2	*SER*	*F Value for R*	*b(VN)*	*'t' Value for b*	*Constant*	*B*	*r*	*% of Variance*
1	2	3	4	5	6	7	8	9	10	11	12
1.	A_3(60)	0.244	0.060	75.093	37.87** (1.598)	-4.109(60)	6.15** (598)	851.791	-0.244	-0.244	5.96
2.	A_5(62)	0.261	0.068	74.821	21.75** (3,596)	-2.886(60) -2.220(62)	3.40** 2.32* (596)	870.815	-0.171 -0.117	-0.223	4.18 2.61
3.	A_1(58)	0.272	0.074	74.645	15.84** (2,597)	-3.436(60) -2.468(62) 1.870(58)	3.85** 2.56* 1.95@ (597)	854.246	-0.204 -0.130 0.088	-0.056	4.98 2.90 -0.49

* Significant at 0.05 level.

** Significant at 0.01 level.

@ Not Significant at 0.05 level.

The second predictor variable entered into the stepwise analysis is Arts, Health, Physical and Computer education (A_5 i.e. variable No. 62 in Table 5.25). The values of R and R^2 are 0.261 and 0.068 respectively. The constant value is 870.815. The contribution of A_3 is 4.18 per cent and the remaining 2.61 per cent is contributed by the A_5. The regression equation at this stage is

$$AP = 870.815-2.886 (A_3) - 2.220 (A_5).$$

The next and the last predictor variable that entered in this analysis is Teacher education in emerging India (A_1 i.e. variable No. 58 in Table 5.25). The values of R and R^2 are 0.272 and 0.074 respectively. The constant value is 854.246. The regression equation for these three variables could be written as

$$AP = 854.246 - 3.436 (A_3) - 2.468 (A_5) + 1.870 (A_1)$$

PREDICTION OF PRACTICALS SCORES WITH THE HELP OF THEORY, PRACTICALS AND TOTAL SCORE

In this analysis the effect of students achievement scores in Theory, Practicals and Total score for I and II year (variable Nos. 64 to 68 and 70 in Table 5.25) on the dependent variable Achievement score in Practicals (AP) is studied and obtained results are presented in Table 5.76.

In Table 5.76 that the first predictor variable that entered into the step-wise regression analysis is I year Practicals score (AP_1 i.e. variable No. 67 in Table 5.25). The value of R and R^2 0.967 and 0.936 respectively. The value of t for b is 93.24, which is significant at 0.01 level. The regression equation at this stage is $AP = 143.846 + 1.613 (AP_1)$.

The next predictor variable that entered into the analysis is II year Practicals score (AP_2). The F value for R is 42000.58, which is significant at 0.01 level. The constant value is 1.361. Thus, the regression equation is $AP = 1.361 + 1.017 (AP_1) + 0.979 (AP_2)$.

The fourth step is the last step; the variable that entered in this analysis is the first and second year theory scores (AT). The values of multiple R and R^2 are 1.00 and 1.00 respectively. The F value for R is 1120970.00, which is significant at 0.01 level. Thus, the regression analysis at this stage is $AP = -0.004 + 0.003 (AP_1) + 0.030 (AP_2) + 0.970 (GT) - 0.970 (AT)$.

Table 5.76: Prediction of Achievement Score in Practicals with the Help of Theory, Practicals and Total Achievement Score

Step No.	*IV (VN)*	*R*	*R^2*	*SER*	*F Value for R*	*b(VN)*	*'t' Value for b*	*Constant*	*B*	*r*	*% of Variance*
1	*2*	*3*	*4*	*5*	*6*	*7*	*8*	*9*	*10*	*11*	*12*
1.	AP_1(67)	0.967	0.936	19.644	8693.90** (1,598)	1.613 (67)	93.24** (598)	143.846	0.967	0.967	93.56
2.	AP_2(68)	0.996	0.993	6.510	42000.58** (2,597)	1.017(67) 0.979(68)	98.72** 69.62** (597)	1.361	0.610 0.430	0.937	59.00 40.30
3.	GT(70)	0.996	0.993	6.465	28397.42** (3,596)	0.994 (67) 0.956(68) 0.019(70)	79.02** 60.60** 3.07** (596)	-9.841	0.596 0.420 0.025	0.907	57.69 39.37 2.24
4.	AT(66)	1.00	1.000	0.894	1120970.00** (4,595)	0.003(67) 0.030(68) 0.970(70) -0.970(66)	5.38** 5.16** 176.13** 174.83** (595)	-0.004	0.019 0.013 1.237 -0.542	0.281	1.80 1.22 112.21 -15.25

* Significant at 0.05 level.

** Significant at 0.01 level.

@ Not Significant at 0.05 level.

Table 5.77: Prediction of Achievement Score in Practicals with the Help of 69 Independent Variables

Step No.	*IV (VN)*	*R*	R^2	*SER*	*F Value for R*	*b(VN)*	*'t' Value for b*	*Constant*	*B*	*r*	*% of Variance*
1	2	3	4	5	6	7	8	9	10	11	12
1.	AP_1(67)	0.967	0.936	19.645	8692.75* (1,598)	1.613 (67)	93.23* (598)	143.848	0.967	0.967	93.56
2.	AP_2(68)	0.996	0.993	6.512	41978.80* (2,597)	1.017(67) 0.979(68)	98.70* 69.61* (597)	1.356	0.610 0.430	0.937	58.99 40.30
3.	GT(70)	0.996	0.993	6.467	28381.48* (3,596)	0.994 (67) 0.956(68) 0.019(70)	79.00* 60.58* 3.06* (596)	-9.832	0.596 0.420 0.025	0.907	57.69 39.37 2.24
4.	AT(66)	1.00	1.000	0.924	1050635.00* (4,595)	0.031(67) 0.030(68) 0.970(70) -0.970(66)	5.21* 5.00* 170.43* 169.17* (595)	0.004	0.019 0.013 1.237 -0.542	0.281	1.80 1.22 112.21 -15.25

* Significant at 0.01 level.

PREDICTION OF PRACTICALS SCORES WITH THE HELP OF 69 INDEPENDENT VARIABLES

This section deals with the prediction of practical scores with the help of 69 independent variables. The results are presented in Table 5.77.

In Table 5.77 that the first predictor variable that entered into the stepwise regression analysis is I year Practicals score (AP_1 i.e. variable No. 67 in Table 5.25). The value of R and R^2 are 0.967 and 0.936 respectively. The value of t for b is 93.23, which is significant at 0.01 level. The regression equation at this stage is

$$AP = 143.848 + 1.613 (AP_1).$$

The next predictor variable that entered into the analysis is second year Practicals score (AP_2). The F value for R is 41978.80, which is significant at 0.01 level. The constant value in this regression is 1.356. Thus, the regression equation is

$$AP = 1.356 + 1.017 (AP_1) + 0.979 (AP_2).$$

The fourth step is the last step; the variable that entered in this analysis is the first and second year theory scores (AT). The values of multiple R and R^2 are 1.00 and 1.00 respectively. The F value for R is 1050635.00, which is significant at 0.01 level. Thus, the regression equation at this stage is

$$AP = 0.004 + 0.031 (AP_1) + 0.030 (AP_2) + 0.970 (GT) - 0.970 (AT).$$

6

MAJOR FINDINGS, CONCLUSIONS RECOMMENDATIONS AND SUGGESTIONS FOR FURTHER RESEARCH

This chapter deals with major findings, conclusions, recommendations and suggestions for further research.

MAJOR FINDINGS OF THE STUDY

The statistical treatment of the data reveals the following major findings of the study.

1. The Mean total academic achievement of the DIET students is 1481.86 out of 2000 marks on the whole. The performance of the DIET students is good.
2. The sex does not have significant influence on the achievement in Theory, Practicals and total achievement of the DIET students.
3. Region has significant influence on the achievement in Theory, Practicals and total achievement of the DIET students, Andhra region students performed better than the Telangana and Rayalaseema students.
4. The students who scored better in achievement in Theory and Practicals also have scored better in total achievement.

5. The Teacher Attitude areas namely – High conceptual level, Low conceptual level, High social approach, Total attitude score for training, the total attitude score towards profession and training, Attitudes towards profession and classroom practice have significant influence on the total achievement of the DIET students.
6. The Study habit areas namely – Home environment, Reading, Listening and note taking techniques, General habits and attitude of work, Planning of work and subject, Habits of concentration, Preparation for examinations and total score of the study habits inventory have significant influence on the total achievement of the DIET students.
7. The Personality Factors B, E, F, M, Q2 and Q4 have significant influence on the total achievement of the DIET students.
8. The Objective achievement test score have significant influence on the total achievement of the DIET students.
9. The achievement in theory, practicals have significant influence on the total achievement of the DIET students.
10. The teacher attitude areas namely, High intrinsic motivation has significant influence in Theory.
11. The Study habit areas namely, Planning of work and subjects, Home environment, Preparation for examinations, General habits and attitude of work and study habits total score have significant influence on achievement in Theory.
12. The Personality Factors F, M and Q4 have significant influence on achievement in Theory.
13. The Objective achievement test areas namely: 1. Perspectives in Primary education; and 2. Educational Psychology, Measurement and Evaluation have significant influence on achievement in Theory.
14. The Teacher Attitude areas namely, High conceptual level, Low conceptual level, total score for attitudes towards training, total score for attitude towards

profession and training, attitudes towards profession, need for content, High social approach and classroom practice have significant influence on achievement in Practicals.

15. The Study habits areas namely – 1. Reading, Listening and note taking techniques; 2. Home environment; 3. Habits of concentration; and 4. General habits and attitude of work have significant impact on achievement in practicals.

16. The Personality Factors B, E, M, Q2 and Q3 have significant influence on achievement in Practicals.

17. The Objective achievement test areas namely – 1. Elementary Education, Educational Planning and Management; 2. Perspectives in Primary Education; 3. Art, Health, Physical and computer education; and 4. Total score of Objective achievement test have significant influence on achievement in Practicals.

18. Age has significant influence on achievement in theory.

19. Marital status does not have significant influence on achievement in Theory, Practicals and total achievement.

20. Father's and Mother's education have significant influence on achievement in Practicals and total achievement.

21. Brother's education has significant influence on the total achievement.

22. Sister's education does not have significant influence on achievement in Theory, Practicals and total achievement.

23. Father's employment, Brother's employment and Sister's employment have significant influence on achievement in Practicals.

24. Mother's employment does not have significant influence on achievement in Theory, Practicals and total achievement.

25. The variables Family Annual Income and Order of birth have significant influence on achievement in Practicals and total achievement.

26. Caste has significant influence on achievement in Theory and total achievement.

27. Place of birth does not have significant influence on achievement in Theory, Practicals and total achievement.

28. Group subjects in Intermediate, Socio-Economic status of the family has significant influence on achievement in Theory, Practicals and total achievement.

29. Out of 19 demographic and Socio-Economic variables, with the help of 9 variables, it is possible to explain 28 per cent of the variance in the total achievement. The multiple regression equation at step 9 would be written as:

    GT = 1342.532 +23.506 (C) – 40.922 (G) – 17.375 (OB) + 11.473 (CA) + 31.120 (R)-18.943 (ME) + 11.152 (FE) + 20.488 (SEM) – 9.051 (SE)

30. With the help of 12 Teacher attitude variables, it is possible to explain 5.3 per cent of the variance in the total achievement the multiple regression equation at step 3 would be written as:

    GT = 1662.963 – 3.106 (TA3) –2.588 (TA9) – 2.260 (TA4).

31. With the help of 10 Study habit variables it is possible to explain 3.4 per cent of the variance in the total achievement. The multiple regression equation at step 3 would be written as:

    GT = 1371.923 + 1.928 (S1) + 1.418 (S4) + 1.849 (S7)

32. With the help of 16 Personality Factors it is possible to explain 8.4 per cent of the variance in the total achievement. The multiple regression equation at step 9 would be written as:

GT = 1476.779 – 8.713 (PFE) + 6.254 (PFQ4) – 4.27 (PFM) – 3.930 (PFM) – 5.110 (PFB) + 4.233 (PFL) + 3.671 (PFQ3) –3.205 (PFA) + 2.388 (PFQ1)

33. With the help of Objective achievement variables it is possible to explain 6.2 per cent of the variance in the total achievement. The multiple regression equation at step 4 would be written as:

GT = 1539.199 -5.250 (A3) +3.348 (A1) –3.104 (A5) + 2.041 (A4).

34. With the help of Achievement scores in Theory and Practicals, it is possible to explain 100 per cent of the variance in the total achievement. The multiple regression equation at step 2 would be written as:

GT = 0.113 +1.00 (AP) +1.00 (AT).

35. With the help of Demographic and Socio-Economic variables, it is possible to explain 8.7 per cent of the variance in achievement in Theory. The multiple regression equation at step 7 would be written as:

AT = 790.829 +6.710 (CA) –13.255 (G) – 6.630 (A) – 21.316 (R) – 5.585 (C) – 6.013 (FEM) + 3.662 (FE)

36. With the help of Teacher attitude variables, it is possible to explain 1.8 per cent of the variance in achievement in Theory. The multiple regression equation at step 3 would be written as:

AT = 730.639 – 0.710 (TA5) + 1.237 (TA2) – 0.219 (TA11).

37. With the help of Study habit variables, it is possible to explain 2.5 per cent of the variance in achievement in Theory. The multiple regression equation at step 3 would be written as:

AT = 661.278 +0.708 (S5) + 0.578 (S1) – 0.638 (S9)

38. With the help of 16 Personality Factors, it is possible to explain 2.8 per cent of the variance in achievement in Theory. The multiple regression equation at step 3 would be written as:

AT= 695.903 + 2.022 (PFL) – 2.492 (PFE) + 1.574 (PFQ4)

39. With the help of objective achievement test variables, it is possible to explain 2.4 per cent of the variance in achievement in Theory. The multiple regression equation at step 3 would be written as:

AT = 684.702 +1.496 (A1) – 1.666 (A3) + 1.274 (A4)

40. With the help of Theory, Practicals and total achievement variables, it is possible to explain 99.9 per cent of the variance in achievement in Theory. The multiple regression equation at step 4 would be written as:

AT = 0.165 –1.124 (AT2) – 1.097 (AT1) + 1.011 (GT) – 1.001 (AP)

41. With the help of 69 independent variables, it is possible to explain 100 per cent of the variance in achievement in Theory. The multiple regression equation at step 8 would be written as:

AT = 0.209 – 0.0004 (AT2) – 0.004 (AT1) – 0.001 (TA6) – 0.001 (AFI) – 0.003 (BE) – 0.001 (SE) + 1.004 (GT) – 1.004 (AP).

42. With the help of Demographic and Socio-Economic variables, it is possible to explain 40.2 per cent of the variance in achievement in Practicals. The multiple regression equation at step 11 would be written as:

AP=562.629+29.095(C) –19.201 (OB) +52.419 (R) –25.423 (G) + 12.802(SEM) –14.632 (ME) +3.032(FE) +11.384 (BEM) – 5.900(BE) + 4.872 (S) + 3.593(CA)

43. With the help of Teacher Attitude variables, it is possible to explain 7.4 per cent of the variance in achievement in Practicals. The multiple regression equation at step 5 would be written as:

AP = 921.178 + 0.114 (TA12) + 2.710 (TA6) – 2.310 (TA 9) – 2.221 (TA4) – 2.423 (TA3)

44. With the help of Study habit variables, it is possible to explain 3.0 per cent of the variance in achievement in Practicals. The multiple regression equation at step 3 would be written as:

AP = 703.858 + 1.307 (S1) + 1.140 (S4) – 1.548 (S7).

45. With the help of 16 Personality Factors, it is possible to explain 8.9 per cent of the variance in achievement in Practicals. The multiple regression equation at step 10 would be written as:

AP = 759.474 – 6.170 (PFE) + 4.467 (PFQ4) + 3.263 (PFH) – 5.050 (PFB) + 4.046 (PFQ3) – 2.994 (PFA) – 3.027 (PFM) + 2.797 (PFF)+ 0.012 (PFQ1) + 2.35 (PFL).

46. With the help of Objective achievement test variable, it is possible to explain 7.4 per cent of the variance in achievement in Practicals. The multiple regression equation at step 3 would be written as:

AP = 854.246 – 3.436 (A_3) – 2.468 (A_5) + 1.870 (A_1)

47. With the help of Theory, Practicals and total achievement variables, it is possible to explain 100 per cent of the variance in achievement in Practicals. The multiple regression equation at step 4 would be written as:

AP = – 0.004 + 0.003 (AP_1) + 0.030 (AP_2) + 0.970 (GT) – 0.970 (AT).

48. With the help of 69 independent variables, it is possible to explain 100 per cent of the variance in achievement in Practicals. The multiple regression equation at step 4 would be written as:

AP = 0.004 + 0.031 (AP_1) + 0.030 (AP_2) + 0.970 (GT) – 0.970 (AT).

CONCLUSIONS

In the light of the findings present in preceding pages the following conclusions are drawn:

1. All the DIET students do not have same academic achievement.
2. Sex does not have significant influence on achievement.
3. Region has significant influence on achievement of the DIET students.

4. Some of the Teacher attitude variables towards profession and training have significant influence on achievement.

5. Some of the Study habit areas have significant influence on achievement.

6. Some of the 16 Personality Factors have significant influence on achievement of DIET students.

7. Some of the Objective achievement test variables have significant influence on achievement of DIET students

8. The variables Father's education, Mother's education, Brother's education, Father's employment, Brother's employment, Sister's employment, Family Annual income, Caste, Group subjects in Intermediate, Order of birth and Socio-Economics status have significant influence on achievement of DIET students.

9. The variables namely, Marital Status, Sisters education, Mother's employment, and Place of birth do not have significant influence on achievement of DIET students.

10. It is possible to predict the achievement in Theory, Practicals and total achievement with the help of: 1. Demographic and Socio-Economic variables; 2. Teachers attitude variables; 3. Study habits variables; 4. 16 Personality Factors; 5. Objective achievement test variables; and 6. Achievement scores in Theory, Practicals and total achievement.

EDUCATIONAL IMPLICATIONS AND RECOMMENDATIONS

The teacher serves the humanities and helps to shape the destiny of the society. The teacher has a powerful and abiding influence in the formation of the character of the future citizens. The teacher acts as a pivot for the transmission of intellectual and technical skills and cultural traditions from one generation to another. Hence, effective training has to be provided to the student teachers of DIETs.

On the basis of the results of this investigation the following recommendations are made:

1. Special care and extra coaching may be provided to the students of the DIETs, where the academic achievement is moderately low.

2. The Officials in the department of education have to take the special interest to remove the differences in achievement of DIET students in different regions.

3. Teacher attitude tests may be conducted before admitting the students to the DIETs. Those students who have better positive attitude towards teaching profession and training may be admitted into DIETs.

4. Better Study habits may be developed among the student teachers with necessary training in Study habits.

5. Necessary training may be provided to the student teachers in Personality development.

6. Objective achievement tests may be frequently conducted.

7. Some of the Demographic and Socio-Economic variables have significant influence on achievement of DIET students. Special care and training may be provided in order to overcome the effects of Demographic and Socio-Economic variables.

8. The majority of the DIETs are located in rural areas. The students and teacher educators are feeling difficulty for effective functioning.

9. Frequently the Faculty members are assigned various duties other than the regular academic work in the DIETs. This has to be minimised to the lowest possible extent.

10. Educational Technology inputs and Computers are essential for present day system of education. Hence, well equipped with Educational Technology laboratories and Computer laboratories may be established in DIETs.

11. It is observed that during most of the working hours the electric power facilities will not be available. The administrative authorities have to plan to overcome this difficulty.
12. The deficiencies in the Physical and infra-structural facilities can be provided as early as possible for effective functioning of the DIETs.
13. Congenial atmosphere is necessary for effective functioning. The government should take suitable steps in creating campus life both the student teacher and teacher educators.
14. It is observed that the hostels are in very bad shape with lack of clean surroundings, insufficient ventilation, furniture, water, low quality food etc. The administrators have to take necessary steps for better hostel facilities.
15. The co-curricular activities such as sports and games and cultural events (music, dance, drama, art, painting, clay-modelling etc.) have their own influence on the academic development of the student teachers. The administrators are advised to encourage the students to participate in co-curricular activities.
16. The SCERT should plan special training courses to the Principals for making their administrative styles more acceptable, more effective, more dynamic and more humane.
17. The NCERT, SCERT, NCTE and University departments of Education have to organise a series of workshops, seminars to re-orientation to the teacher educators to be committed to their profession.
18. Producing quality teachers has become a prerequisite to achieve quality to improvement in educatior..
19. Privatising the teacher education or allowing the existing self-finance institutions of teacher education has to be stopped at once and the Government should

establish in good number of teacher education institutions in accordance with the manpower requirement. Highly qualified and dedicated persons have to be recruited as teacher educators in DIETS.

LIMITATIONS OF THE STUDY AND SUGGESTIONS FORFURTHER RESEARCH

The following limitations and suggestions are considered for further investigation.

- The present study is limited to 600 student teachers of DIETs. It is suggested that the future researchers may undertake studies with large sample. Covering all the DIETs of the state, so as to make generalisations with regard to achievement of the DIET students.
- Similar studies may be conducted in other states of the country.
- Studies on achievement of B.Ed. students may be undertaken in future research studies.
- This is a presage-product study in the area of teacher training. Studies of presage-process, process-product and presage-process-product may be undertaken in the area of teacher training.
- Studies relating to achievement in teacher training and the actual job performance after appointment may be taken up in future research studies.
- This study is limited to some of the Demographic and Socio-economic variables, teacher attitude variables, study habits variables and 16 PF. It may be extended to other socio-psychological variables.
- Studies have hardly been longitudinal. In view of this fact that there is a serious need for taking up longitudinal studies with respect to all pupil outcomes. For example, the following directional relationship among the factors, would be taken up as a longitudinal study-teacher training programmes-regular teaching-

individual, group and community changes-their involvement, participation and productivity in respect of national development. This of course, ought to be planned as a national level research undertaking/ project.

- The educational innovations and the built-in-professional skills of the personnel working in the college of education in India; should rightly steer the vehicle of education, so that the passengers of students may reach their designated educational goals successfully.
- The study has not included any institutional variables such as year of establishment, results produced, titles and awards obtained etc., such institutional variables may help us to identify the variations between good and poor institutions. Studies in this direction may help us to improve the status of the teacher education.

APPENDIX–A

TEACHER ATTITUDE INVENTORY

The following statements express opinions on Teaching Profession deliberations in the classroom and your Training. You may like to agree with some statement and disagree with the others.

There are five alternative answers to every item. After careful study of the items, record your answers in the answer sheet provided to you against the relevant item number Please respond to each and every item without leaving any one.

If you

'Strongly Agree' with an item mark **'A'** in the bracket.

'Agree' with an item mark **'B'** in the bracket.

'Doubtful' with an item mark **'C'** in the bracket.

'Disagree' with an item mark **'D'** in the bracket.

'Strongly Disagree' with an item mark **'E'** in the bracket.

There is nothing like a right or wrong answer for these items and your opinion is correct by all means. So, please give your response freely without hesitation. Your responses will help to draw certain conclusions, which will benefit the future student teachers. Your responses will be useful for research work, and they will be kept confidential.

Please read the items and record your answers in the answer sheet provided to you.

Thanking you for your kind co-operation.

1. Teaching profession is interesting only in the initial stage.
2. Teaching is a cultured and well-mannered profession.
3. People in teaching profession are generally truthful.
4. There will be lot of dissatisfaction in teacher's profession than in any other profession.
5. Using teacher services in programmes not relevant to teaching pains me.
6. Teaching profession is only a source of livelihood.
7. Teaching profession decays dynamism.
8. Teaching profession is a quiet one.
9. People should not discriminate look down teachers.
10. Scope of corruption is very less in teaching profession.
11. Because of indifference of people and government towards teaching profession I am not interested in this profession.
12. There is lack of independence to teachers in expressing their views.
13. Every teacher should feel proud of his profession.
14. Trying to be an ideal teacher is deceiving one self.
15. Teachers should show more interest on pupil than earnings.
16. Teaching is a better profession than any other profession.
17. The main quality of a teacher must be to practice what be preaches.
18. National reconstruction depends on teacher's teaching.
19. Teaching profession is becoming a laughing stock day by day.

....

20. The syllabus framed for teacher education is suitable to meet our needs.
21. Theory papers in teacher's training are fresh and interesting.
22. Teaching methods explained in training are very much useful in practical teaching in classroom teaching.
23. There is dire need for teachers trained in computer education in our syllabus.
24. For most student teachers educational psychology is a subject causing difficulty.
25. Because of little leisure, there is no opportunity for teacher trainees to participate in co-curricular activities.
26. DIET plays a major part in developing standards in primary education.
27. There is no link between theoretical and practical aspects in teacher training.
28. Textbooks and reference books needed for teacher education are available

....

29. I wish to use teaching aids and teach the subject for easy understanding.
30. Pupils should actively participate in discussions during the training period.
31. The present system of teacher education neglects personality of student teachers.
32. I get satisfaction only when I teach difficult lessons very well.
33. Teachers have no sense of humour.
34. When a colleague teaches a lesson, I observe every aspect carefully and think how they will be useful for my teaching.

....

35. It is difficult for a rational teacher trainee to teach.
36. Lecturers are advise us about how to use library.

37. It causes disgust when the same teacher teaches many subjects.
38. There is no scope for entertainment or pleasure in this profession.
39. There is no need to give lot of importance to the pupil in teaching.
40. Lecturers supervising teaching activities are only an eyewash.

....

41. An ideal teacher is not fit for normal living in community.
42. There is scope for teacher trainees to participate in community activities during the period of training.
43. You can good marks if you are in good books of lecturers.
44. Teacher education does not attract intellectuals in society.
45. There is more sufficient freedom for teacher trainees in our training institute.
46. Good learning is possible only when there is strong and harmonious relation between teacher trainees.

....

47. The training period in DIET is enough to transform a trainee in to a good teacher.
48. I want to be a model by my good hand writing and painting.
49. I dislike students who ask questions when I teach.
50. There are no chances for conducting practicals in our computer lab.
51. Teacher training today fills teacher trainees with self-confidence.

....

52. Different aspects of teaching should be learnt one by one slowly, all can't be learnt in a single day.
53. Civic training is an important one in our training programme.

54. Ethical value should be taught in teacher training.
55. Standards of teacher education are deteriorating fast day by day.
56. Teachers decide ethical standards and intellectual wealth of a nation.
57. Teacher trainers are becoming inefficient due to lack of accountability.

....

58. Tables, maps and other paraphernalia are not necessary for an efficient teacher.
59. Audio-visual tools are not used for teacher trainees.
60. Training must be given for teacher trainees in using computers in classroom.
61. There are no teaching tools necessary for teacher trainees in our institute.
62. Demonstration and tape recorders are not much useful in classroom.
63. Pupils are feeling inconvenient because of teaching without teaching tools.
64. Teacher trainees should be given training in organisations that manufacture various teaching tools.
65. There are no critical classes after demonstration class.
66. Teacher trainees feel satisfy because of laboratory facilities in the training institute.

....

67. I feel afraid while conducting model classes.
68. Teacher should teach lessons so that they are interesting to pupils.
69. The teacher must explain the purpose of a topic and its use to pupils.
70. Teacher's need not be concerned about personal problems and needs of pupils.

....

71. It is much useful for pupil to repeat a lesson.

72. It is not possible to practice experimental teaching method in teaching of general science.

73. Teacher should give chance to pupils to express their opinions.

74. It is very interesting to observe teaching of my colleagues.

75. Teaching is classroom makes students disciplined.

76. To follow the prepared lesson plan in the classroom is difficult.

77. Lecture method is the best in classroom teaching.

78. Microteaching plan is not improving teaching capacities of teacher trainees.

79. There is not much encouragement for in service training in developing teaching skills.

80. Teacher does not show much interest in teaching exercises.

81. Pupils often talk in a meaningless manner in the classroom.

82. Teacher does not show enough interest on pupil in backside benches in the classroom.

83. Teacher education gives a chance to improve teacher's skill in conversation

* * * * * * * *

APPENDIX–B

STUDY HABITS INVENTORY

The following statements expressed an opinion relating to study habits of students are given. Read each statement carefully and express your attitude according to five-point scale. Record your answers in the answer sheet against the relevant number of the statement.

If particular study habit is present

'Always' in you, mark **'A'** in the corresponding bracket

'Often' in you, mark **'B'** in the corresponding bracket

'Sometimes' in you, mark **'C'** in the corresponding bracket

'Seldom' in you, mark **'D'** in the corresponding bracket

'Never' in you, mark **'E'** in the corresponding bracket

Do not leave any item. There is no right or wrong, while making the statements you should not make in terms of 'what you think you should be' or 'what you see others do'. You should mark the response that approximately refers to your case. Indicate the extent to which this practice applies to you.

This is not a test. This is only useful for the purpose of research. Your answers will be kept under confidential and shall not be disclosed to others. Your co-operation and help are essential for the research. This inventory is useful to know your study habits.

Please read the statements carefully and mark your correct response in the provided answer sheet.

1. All my family members cooperate regarding my studies.
2. I prepare my own plan for studies in my house/room.
3. My family members supervise my studies.
4. I study and learn lessons and subjects before I go to college.
5. My parents give enough money for me to purchase books.
6. I attend college because of force from my family members.
7. I complete my homework immediately on coming home from college.
8. My family members/room mates great obstacle for my studies.
9. It is inconvenient to study and take rest because of large number of people in my house/ room.
10. I cannot study well for lack of proper ventilation.
11. I cannot study well in the right because of the mosquitos in my house/room.
12. My studies are interrupted because of guests to my house/ room.
13. I cannot concentrate on my studies because of financial and other problem of my family

    ....
14. I note down important points while reading.
15. I have to read a second time because of not understanding lessons at first reading.
16. I note down important points when the teaching is going on in the class room and prepare notes afterwards.
17. I show much enthusiasm to study in the early morning time.
18. I try to link what I studied to a suitable topic.
19. I like to study with others than to study alone.

20. I understand while studying but cannot remember.
21. I study the second topic, only after completely understanding the first topic.
22. While writing running notes in the class some points explained by the lecturer get missed.

....

23. I study according to the plan prepared every month.
24. I try to study during the extra time also.
25. I divide my time to study all subjects.
26. I study the lessons taught on the same day.
27. I prepare a plan how to answer every question.
28. I postpone studies till the last minute.
29. I cannot study because of tiredness from writing lesson plans and records.
30. I wish to complete a subject in the allotted time.
31. There is not sufficient time to study theory papers.
32. Before beginning to study I gather the necessary materials.
33. I select important lessons in every subject and study them only.
34. I study material available with me and do not try for more information.
35. I concentrate on subjects difficult for me.
36. I study my favourite subjects and neglect others.
37. I am unable to correlate topics in one subject to topics in another subject.
38. I neglect studies for some time in the first quarter of the year.

....

39. I revise what I have learnt.
40. I can concentrate only at the examination time.

41. I repeat for my self what I studied.
42. The period of concentration on studies is less.
43. I can't study well during winter.
44. Several desires disturb my studies.
45. I can study well without being disturbed by every small thing.
46. I have proper knowledge of sex education.
47. I can't study well because of tiredness and excessive sleep.
48. I can't study well because of wayward thoughts.
49. With the purpose of reading quickly, I am unable to understand what I read.
50. I have waited sometime to get concentration.
51. I can remember that very well lessons learnt last month.
52. I learn everything by note.

....

53. I prepare answers for essay type of questions many days before the exams.
54. Important questions and suggestions reach one so I don't study always.
55. I prepare answers only for questions in the old question papers of previous years.
56. I feel disgust because of reading continuously for hours together at examination time.
57. I drink coffee or tea and read for many hours at night.
58. Because of confusion in examination hall I am unable to write what all I learn.
59. I decide the method of writing before writing an answer in the examination.
60. I study valued answer papers very well to know my mistakes.
61. I complete writing answers before the allotted time in any examination.

62. I study only side heading before the examination.
63. Once I study a paragraph, I memorise it.
64. I study more lessons only at the time of examinations.
65. I prepare answers for not only questions given at the end of the lessons but also other questions.

....

66. I always try to link the points in my textbooks with my surroundings.
67. I participate actively in programmes like Janmabhoomi, clean and green introduced by government.
68. I participate in social and cultural activities conducted in my college.
69. I consult teachers and others to understand difficult points.
70. I learn many things from nature and environment.
71. Social and cultural activities are helpful for my progress.
72. Social factors like strikes and boycotts are disturbing my studies.

....

73. I am unable to understand what is written on the block board because the black boards are not of good quality.
74. I cannot study well because of tiredness from seeing Television too much.
75. I use audio-visual materials to teach lessons to students.
76. I prepare graphs and tables to remember my lessons.
77. I like to listen to lessons over radio.
78. I read newspapers and magazines.
79. I prepare or collect charts, specimens, diagrams and models to remember points in my lessons.
80. I spend much time in seeing cinema.

....

81. I keep all my books neat and clean.

82. I study silently.

83. I like to participate in excursions etc.

84. I am unable to study properly because of psychological problems.

85. I show more interest in games and sports than studies.

86. I get sleep once I open the textbook.

87. I am able to study well because of nutritious diet I receive.

88. I daydream while studying.

....

89. I use books in the library of my training institute.

90. Facilities in training institute are satisfactory.

91. I have good relations with my lecturers.

92. As our training institute is adjacent to the main road sounds from vehicles are obstacles to teaching.

93. My teachers encourage some of my actions.

94. Some topics I dislike are thought in my institute, they are obstacles to my success.

95. All activities that related to teaching in my training institute is interesting.

* * * * * * * *

APPENDIX–C

DIET STUDNETS SCHOLASTIC OBJECTIVE ACHIEVEMENT TEST

The objective achievement test has been prepared for the purpose of educational research. The multiple-choice questions from first year syllabus of D.Ed. course have been given below. There are four alternative answers for each question and only one answer is correct. After careful study please note the correct answer against the question in the answer sheet. Your answers will not be revealed. They will be used only for research purpose. Your answers are kept confidential. Your heart felt co-operation is essential for this research.

SECTION – A

1. The main aim of the educational philosophy is
   (a) Creating theory of reality
   (b) Empirical belief in knowledge
   (c) Belief in rational reconstruction
   (d) all the above

2. Father of kindergarten is
   (a) Froebel
   (b) Rousseau
   (c) Montessori
   (d) Plato

3. Which philosophical theory is centre to all action of men
   - (a) Realism
   - (b) Humanism
   - (c) Idealism
   - (d) Naturalism
4. Five Principles theory in education was proposed by
   - (a) Ravindranath Tagore
   - (b) Swamy Vivekananda
   - (c) Sri Aurobindo Ghosh
   - (d) Ramakrishna Paramahamsa
5. The main feature of basic education of Gandhi is
   - (a) Strict discipline and punishment
   - (b) Strict control and opposition to punishment
   - (c) Strict supervision and control overall activities
   - (d) Imparting education through training five senses.
6. According to which educational philosophy 'values are changing'.
   - (a) Idealism
   - (b) Realism
   - (c) Sri Pragmatism
   - (d) Naturalism
7. We want not rural and urban societies but only human society —. This was said by
   - (a) Vivekananda
   - (b) Radhakrishnan
   - (c) Tagore
   - (d) Gandhi

8. The following explains characteristics of social change
   (a) Westernization
   (b) Modernization
   (c) Urbanization
   (d) all the above
9. Ecology studies the following
   (a) Ancient family life
   (b) Relationship between living beings and their environment
   (c) Sociological problems in the society
   (d) None of the above
10. The main topic of study in sociology is
   (a) Individual
   (b) Group
   (c) Pre-literate society
   (d) Political institution
11. A teacher makes the students to have social thought by the following method
   (a) By imparting knowledge about their level
   (b) By encouraging to share experiences with sympathy
   (c) By encouraging the feeling of courage to live and let live
   (d) By concentrating their attention and focus on differences in society
12. "Family is the first school for a child". Therefore
   (a) All parents must become graduates
   (b) Children need not attend nursery school
   (c) School and college should introduce courses on educating parents
   (d) Children should not be admitted into public schools

13. What is the meaning of education
    (a) Wisdom
    (b) Knowledge
    (c) Character
    (d) Wealth
14. The following supported Naturalism
    (a) Rousseau
    (b) Pestolozee
    (c) Herbert
    (d) Dewey
15. Education is that system; it gives knowledge to adjust with environment and men's nature.
    (a) Idealism
    (b) Pragmatism
    (c) Realists
    (d) Naturalists
16. The word Sociology is suggested by the following.
    (a) Emile Durkhalm
    (b) Talkot Parsons
    (c) Herbert mead
    (d) Agust Komte
17. The institution that conducted research on Microteaching in India
    (a) NCERT
    (b) CASE
    (c) SCERT
    (d) NCTE

18. From which Latin word is the word education derived
    (a) Educare
    (b) Educate
    (c) Education
    (d) Educere
19. The teaching aspect of a teacher must be
    (a) Limited to lessons
    (b) Stagnant
    (c) Provoking good thoughts in a students
    (d) Not limited to lessons
20. Modern teacher requires this attitude
    (a) Dictatorial
    (b) Democratic
    (c) Disciplinary
    (d) None of the above
21. According to Vivekananda aim of education is
    (a) Building up the nation
    (b) Literacy
    (c) Individual wealth of character and building of nation
    (d) Discipline
22. Main aim of the socialization of the child
    (a) Individual adjustment with society
    (b) Development of beliefs and interests
    (c) Development of desirable change which was aspire by society
    (d) Producing individual learning according needs

23. Main aim of the Sociometry
    (a) Formulation of group construction
    (b) To recognize the capable leader
    (c) To recognize friendship
    (d) None of the above
24. The steps used for teacher training were proposed by
    (a) Pestolozee
    (b) Herbert
    (c) Rousseau
    (d) Froebel
25. The script for blind was invented by
    (a) Luwie Braille
    (b) Luwie Pasteur
    (c) Rutherford
    (d) Newton
26. Population theory was proposed by
    (a) Graham Bell
    (b) Copernicus
    (c) Malthus
    (d) Mendel
27. "Cultural lag" is linked to
    (a) William Auburn
    (b) Max Weber
    (c) Agust Komte
    (d) Karl Marx
28. The theory in epistemology is related to
    (a) Values
    (b) Knowledge
    (c) Thoughts
    (d) Social standards

29. Naturalistic stress on the content is
    (a) Science
    (b) Religion
    (c) Languages
    (d) Psychology
30. Which of the following can modernize education
    (a) Constitution
    (b) Government
    (c) Technology
    (d) Philosophy

SECTION – B

31. Psychology is the science of consciousness
    (a) Fraud
    (b) Woundt
    (c) Aristotle
    (d) James
32. Developmental activities means
    (a) Skills required for Pre-Primary education
    (b) Stages of development
    (c) Learning skills to particular age group persons in the society
    (d) Development of skills during childhood
33. The first emotional feeling expressed by an infant is
    (a) Feeling
    (b) Enthusiasm
    (c) Anger
    (d) None of the above

34. The source from which school students get their information about sex is

    (a) Peer students

    (b) Books

    (c) Parents

    (d) Teachers

35. The aim of Sex education is

    (a) To develop interest towards the opposite sex

    (b) To develop correct aims regarding various aspects of sex

    (c) To learnt knowledge regarding sex relationships

    (d) To inform about dangers from sexual relationships

36. That which explains the bahaviour of an infant is

    (a) Special

    (b) Integration

    (c) Ordinary

    (d) Distinctive

37. Which is not important process of development in the Adolescent stage

    (a) Receiving emotions independent from adults

    (b) Development of individual style

    (c) Relieving from adult domination

    (d) Developing social efficiency

38. The correct definition of learning is

    (a) Improving skills

    (b) Earning knowledge

    (c) Knowledge of problem solving

    (d) Relative permanent change of behaviour

39. Transfer of learning depends upon
    (a) Learner's intelligence
    (b) Nature of topic of learning
    (c) Generalization of learning
    (d) Teaching method
40. Main aim of the creative activities in the school is
    (a) Providing chances to self expressions
    (b) Providing good learning activities
    (c) Providing mental relaxation and happiness
    (d) Remove daydreams
41. Differences in various aptitudes within the individual are represented by
    (a) Trait characteristics
    (b) Individual differences
    (c) Differential indicator aptitude
    (d) Intra differences
42. Maladjustment means
    (a) Socially adjustable
    (b) Fail in adjustment
    (c) Dissatisfaction in individual and socially needed adjustment
    (d) Inconsistency in adjustment
43. Direction is
    (a) Advise the pupil
    (b) Tell him what to do it
    (c) Help in total development of a pupil
    (d) Do something for a pupil

44. Modern research has decided the following as the maximum limit of development

(a) 18 years

(b) 21 years

(c) 40 years

(d) Till death

45. "Learning is a complex personal information activity". This is the opinion of

(a) Behaviourists

(b) Symbolists

(c) Social Psychologists

(d) All the above

46. Beating a pupil is

(a) Physical punishment

(b) Negative punishment

(c) Removing from practice

(d) None of the above

47. Individual study method observes

(a) Present experience

(b) Past experience

(c) Present and past experience

(d) Future experience

48. Democratic leadership in classroom improves the following

(a) Collective following

(b) Close contact with the group

(c) Size of production

(d) Collective formation

49. Dull pupils can be defined to have
    (a) Low level of mental development
    (b) Mental illness
    (c) Lack of mental development and behavioural adjustment
    (d) All the above

50. "Meritorious" means
    (a) Mentally at a high level
    (b) Capacity of perform any human activity easily and capably
    (c) Healthy morally
    (d) Capable physically and purpose-wise

51. A student who is backward in studies but he has merit in games is called as
    (a) Projection
    (b) Compensation
    (c) Displacement
    (d) Repression

52. The method of recording history of persons is
    (a) Observation method
    (b) Case method
    (c) Experimental method
    (d) Introspection method

53. The reason for plateau in learning is
    (a) Loss of interest
    (b) Fatigue
    (c) Lack of revision
    (d) Lack of encouragement

54. This can be reduced in pupils by playing method
   (a) Wish
   (b) Eagerness
   (c) Balance
   (d) Anger
55. The memory activity of remembering a content by perfectly understanding it is called
   (a) Memory by note
   (b) Memory by logic
   (c) long time memory
   (d) None of the above
56. I.Q. of people with average intelligence is
   (a) 140
   (b) 70-79
   (c) 90-109
   (d) 110-119
57. Laziness and tardiness in an individual are the result of lack of this Harmon
   (a) Insulin
   (b) Thyroxin
   (c) Pancreatic juice
   (d) Bile
58. "Adolescence is a stage involving pressure as well as mental ups and downs". This is the opinion of
   (a) W.C. Bhagghle
   (b) Stanley Hall
   (c) Kohler
   (d) Woodworth

59. Trying to forget painful incidents is called
    (a) Compensation
    (b) Repression
    (c) Change
    (d) None of the above

60. What will you do as a teacher of Psychology to remove the feeling of fear in pupils?
    (a) Slowly habituate them to situations causing fear
    (b) Keep them away from situations causing fear
    (c) See that such situations do not arise
    (d) None of the above

SECTION – C

61. The ideal of work experience in schools in India was formulated by
    (a) Secondary Education Commission
    (b) Kothari Education Commission
    (c) Zakir Hussain Commission
    (d) University Education Commission

62. According to 1986 National Education Policy work experience is considered compulsory at this level.
    (a) At all levels of education
    (b) Primary and Secondary education level
    (c) Secondary education level
    (d) Primary education level

63. The Committee constituted by the government in 1991 to review recommendations of Prof. Ramamurthy Education Committee is
    (a) Eswaribhai Patel Committee
    (b) Janardhana Reddy Committee
    (c) National Education Committee
    (d) None of the above

64. International Literacy day is observed on
    (a) 15 August
    (b) 18 August
    (c) 8 September
    (d) 18 September
65. The first state in India to introduce Non-Detention system is
    (a) Tamil Nadu
    (b) Madhya Pradesh
    (c) Uttar Pradesh
    (d) Andhra Pradesh
66. The first state to introduce education through Television in India is
    (a) Karnataka
    (b) Madhya Pradesh
    (c) Uttar Pradesh
    (d) Andhra Pradesh
67. The main aim of distance education is
    (a) To bring education to reach of less number of students
    (b) To bring education within the reach of large number of students
    (c) To bring education within the reach of distant students
    (d) B and C
68. The meaning of Team teaching is
    (a) A process of teaching to small group
    (b) A process of teaching to larger group
    (c) Panel discussion
    (d) None of the above

69. Diorama means
    (a) Two dimensional map
    (b) Three dimensional map
    (c) Working model
    (d) Real life activity which plays in classroom
70. The Time-Table to be found in a school is
    (a) Class Time-Table
    (b) Teacher's Time-Table
    (c) Master Time-Table
    (d) All the above
71. Financial assistance extended by the government to recognized educational institutions is
    (a) Financial assistance
    (b) Donation
    (c) Grant-in-aid
    (d) Loan
72. The report that gave official recognition to Pre-Primary Education.
    (a) Saddler Committee report
    (b) Woods report
    (c) Hunter Commission Report
    (d) Sargeant Report
73. The duty with heavy responsibility for a headmaster is
    (a) Supervision
    (b) Teaching
    (c) Division of work
    (d) None of the above

74. Main aim of the brain storming is
    (a) Identify individual differences
    (b) Training to mental parts
    (c) Development to adequate skill in speaking
    (d) Creating a new creative ideas
75. The table giving various weightages in preparation of a question paper is called
    (a) Evaluation
    (b) Topics to be examined
    (c) Blue print
    (d) Question bank
76. The organization that conducts training classes for education officials at various levels in the state is
    (a) SCERT
    (b) NCERT
    (c) NCTE
    (d) CASE
77. The principle used in the curriculum framework is
    (a) Correlational principle
    (b) Learning principle
    (c) Activity
    (d) Difficulty principle
78. The following method is student centre curriculum
    (a) Logical psychological approach
    (b) Concentric approach
    (c) Topical approach
    (d) None of the above

79. According to which educational plan, students were introduced in the class according to their mental stability
    (a) Topical approach
    (b) Concentric approach
    (c) Spiral approach
    (d) None of the above
80. The main aim of the school is
    (a) To prepare pupils for examinations
    (b) To teach various subjects
    (c) To prepare students for jobs
    (d) To help students for all their all round development
81. "Education is a Tri-polar process". This was stated by
    (a) Adamson
    (b) Morgan
    (c) Gandhi
    (d) Montessori
82. Chief characteristics of good evaluators is
    (a) Managing flexibility
    (b) Objectivity
    (c) Depends upon individual interest
    (d) None of the above
83. Meritorious students taking part in teaching is called
    (a) Monitorial system
    (b) Instructional system
    (c) Open Education system
    (d) Memory system

84. Teaching skills depend on the following

(a) Physical ability of a teacher

(b) His ability to explain the subject

(c) His ability to control the pupils

(d) His intimacy with pupils

85. Following are largely found at primary education level in our country

(a) Wastage and Stagnation

(b) Poverty

(c) Apathy

(d) Worry

86. Ashram schools were started for the following

(a) City level students

(b) Girls

(c) Rural areas

(d) Tribals

87. Difference between community school and progressive school is

(a) Reveals individual merit

(b) More life-centered then pupil-centered

(c) More book-centered then life-centered

(d) Proposes same curriculum for all pupils

88. A fundamental principle in educational administration is

(a) Follow the same method always

(b) Exhibit an inflexible attitude

(c) Change according to circumstances

(d) None of the above

89. School supervisor is
    (a) An inspector only
    (b) Should not observe teaching
    (c) Must be a guide
    (d) Just to show authority

90. Rate of literacy in India is
    (a) 42%
    (b) 52%
    (c) 62%
    (d) 32%

SECTION – D

91. Tri-polar Process of education involves
    (a) Teacher – School – Community
    (b) Teacher – School – Pupil
    (c) Pupil – School – Community
    (d) None of the above

92. The system that is an obstacle to the spirit of the constitution to provide equal educational opportunities for all is
    (a) Navodaya schools system
    (b) Progressive schools system
    (c) Women's education system
    (d) Public schools system

93. O.B.B. plan was started in the year
    (a) 1986
    (b) 1987
    (c) 1985
    (d) 1990

94. Which education structure is in force as per New National Education Policy 1996?

(a) 10+3+2

(b) 10+2+3

(c) 10+5

(d) 10+2+4

95. Teaching tools are used mainly for this purpose

(a) For entertainment of pupils

(b) To Encourage pupils

(c) To develop interests and understand in pupils

(d) For showing something new

96. The Committee that suggested the formation of a Centre at State level and State Educational Institutions for development of Pre-Primary Education is

(a) Mudaliar

(b) Kothari

(c) Radhakrishnan

(d) Eswaribhai Patel

97. The state level organisation related to educational research and training is

(a) DIET

(b) SCERT

(c) NCERT

(d) SIET

98. Engineering and Medicine belong to

(a) Social Education

(b) General Education

(c) Professional Education

(d) None of the above

99. What is the function held in the ancient period to indicate the completion of education
    - (a) Samavasthana
    - (b) Parivarthana
    - (c) Aswasam
    - (d) Parikalpitham

100. The Commission that gave importance to vocational education
    - (a) Radhakrishnan Commission
    - (b) Kothari Commission
    - (c) Mudaliar Commission
    - (d) RamaMurthy Commission

101. In an country, there are generally given a place in the framing of Educational plans
    - (a) Teachers
    - (b) Intellectuals
    - (c) Educationists
    - (d) None of the above

102. The first state to impart free education to women in India
    - (a) Andhra Pradesh
    - (b) Himachal Pradesh
    - (c) Tamil Nadu
    - (d) Kerala

103. The utility of Janmabhoomi was started in Andhra Pradesh
    - (a) To teach working hard
    - (b) To teach dignity of labour
    - (c) Rebuilding of villages
    - (d) None of the above

104. The article in the constitution of India that expresses teaching in Mother Tongue in primary education is

(a) 350A

(b) 332

(c) 45

(d) 356

105. The district with the lowest literacy rate in Andhra Pradesh

(a) Anantapur

(b) Mahaboobnagar

(c) Guntur

(d) Kadapa

106. A picture book for teaching was prepared for the first time by

(a) Comenius

(b) Columbus

(c) Skinner

(d) None of the above

107. The age for Pre-Primary education is

(a) 6-11

(b) 3-8

(c) 2-6

(d) 3-5

108. Balwadis are within the scope of this education

(a) Pre-Primary

(b) Primary

(c) Secondary

(d) None of the above

109. Main steps in Morison plan
    (a) Follow the directions prescribes for them
    (b) Divided into two groups
    (c) Providing directions according their interests
    (d) Creating small groups including to learning
110. Which theory is a source for introducing aptitude test
    (a) Unifactor theory
    (b) Two factor theory
    (c) Primary mental ability
    (d) All of the above
111. Benjamin Blooms in his Taxonomy divided results of learning experiences into the following types
    (a) 3
    (b) 2
    (c) 4
    (d) 5
112. This is called the second clock of a school
    (a) School Time Table
    (b) Pupil Time-Table
    (c) Check List
    (d) None of the above
113. The best method for teaching at Pre-Primary level is
    (a) Narrative method
    (b) Lecture method
    (c) Playing method
    (d) Discussion method

114. The five districts selected for DPEP in 1996-97 are
   (a) Vizianagaram, Nellore, Warangal, Karimnagar, Kurnool
   (b) Warangal, Karimnagar, Anantapur, Srikakulam, Krishna
   (c) Guntur, Krishna, Mahaboobnagar, Visakhapatnam, Hyderabad
   (d) Nellore, Vizianagaram, Hyderabad, Nalgonda, Khammam

115. The Executive Officer for school education in the state is
   (a) Director of Higher Education
   (b) Director of School Education
   (c) Minister of Education
   (d) None of the above

116. The type of question paper that gives the same result for students irrespective of the evaluation is
   (a) Essay type test paper
   (b) Objective type test paper
   (c) Completion type test paper
   (d) None of the above

117. The main aim of social sciences is
   (a) Improve human relationships in community
   (b) To prepare syllabus easily
   (c) Because textbook is a must
   (d) None of the above

118. The year in which NCERT was started
   (a) 1961
   (b) 1962
   (c) 1952
   (d) 1970

119. Audio-visual education has been imparted in primary schools in A.P. from

   (a) 1964- 65
   (b) 1952-53
   (c) 1986-87
   (d) 1971-72

120. Core curriculum means

   (a) Preparation of integrated education plan
   (b) Main component of integrated education plan
   (c) Integrated education plan itself
   (d) None of the above

SECTION – E

121. International charter for physical education and sports was framed by

   (a) America
   (b) India
   (c) Canada
   (d) UNESCO

122. Maintaining health records of pupils in a school is the responsibility of

   (a) Class teacher
   (b) Headmaster
   (c) Physical education teacher
   (d) Science teacher

123. The system of each team competing against other teams in a combination is known as

   (a) League competitions
   (b) Combination competitions
   (c) Knock out competitions
   (d) Challenge competitions

124. Kinesiology explains the following
    - (a) Different activities in human body
    - (b) Movements in human body
    - (c) Structure of human body
    - (d) Human health
125. Bull fighting belongs to this country
    - (a) Italy
    - (b) USA
    - (c) France
    - (d) Spain
126. The year in which the first computer was introduced
    - (a) 1945
    - (b) 1950
    - (c) 1970
    - (d) 1975
127. The name of the computer introduced in India with Indigenous technology
    - (a) Param
    - (b) Vikranth
    - (c) Croe
    - (d) Atlus
128. Wimbledon is associated with
    - (a) Volleyball
    - (b) Football
    - (c) Hockey
    - (d) Tennis

129. Durand cup is associated with

(a) Football

(b) Hockey

(c) Cricket

(d) Tennis

130. The organization that worked for use of Hindi in computer

(a) National council for technology

(b) International software technology

(c) Department of electronics

(d) None of the above

131. The presiding Diety in Konark temple is

(a) Shiva

(b) Bramha

(c) Surya

(d) Vishnu

132. Yakshagana means

(a) Vocal music

(b) Dance drama

(c) Folk dance

(d) Classical dance style of Karnataka

133. Vivekananda Rock Memorial is located at

(a) Cochin

(b) Bhuvanagiri

(c) Calcutta

(d) Kanniyakumari

134. Lepakshi temple is in this district

(a) Kadapa

(b) Anantapur

(c) Chittoor

(d) Kurnool

135. Playing method was designed by
    (a) Froebell
    (b) Kilpatrick
    (c) Montessori
    (d) John Lewie

136. A sound mind in a sound body — This was stated by
    (a) William
    (b) Aristotle
    (c) Tagore
    (d) Rousseau

137. Which theory of learning supports skill
    (a) Law of exercise
    (b) Law of readiness
    (c) Law of effect
    (d) Law of Identical elements

138. In the education system Play way method is supported by
    (a) Pragmatists
    (b) Naturalists
    (c) Idealists
    (d) Realists

139. 2000 Olympic games were held in
    (a) Athence
    (b) Atlanta
    (c) Las Angels
    (d) Sydney

140. The cricketer who received Rajiv Gandhi Khale Ratna award (2001)
    (a) Tendulkar
    (b) Srinath
    (c) Dravid
    (d) Ganguly

141. Branching programme technique was prepared by
 (a) Rober. F. Major
 (b) Norman A. Croder
 (c) F.S. Keller
 (d) Pavolov

142. What is CLASS plan
 (a) Creation o facilities to students
 (b) Readmission of drop outs
 (c) Imparting computer knowledge to pupils
 (d) None of the above

143. Super computer is used in this field in India
 (a) Game of Chess
 (b) Difference
 (c) Atmospheric research
 (d) Multimedia

144. DIETS are meant for
 (a) College teachers
 (b) University teachers
 (c) Primary teachers
 (d) Officials of Education Department

145. Vishwanthan Anand is associated with
 (a) Chess
 (b) Cricket
 (c) Khabadi
 (d) Football

146. Penicillin was invented by
 (a) Fleming
 (b) Pasture
 (c) Edison
 (d) Newton

147. The instrument that recognizes growth in plants
   (a) Epidiascope
   (b) Criscograph
   (c) Microscope
   (d) Cardiograph

148. Night blindness is caused by shortage of
   (a) A vitamin
   (b) B vitamin
   (c) C vitamin
   (d) K vitamin

149. William Harvey is associated with
   (a) Blood circulation
   (b) Malaria
   (c) Cholera
   (d) T.B.

150. The writer of Vandemataram is
   (a) Bankim Chandra Chatterjee
   (b) Tagore
   (c) Tilak
   (d) Patel

* * * * * * * *

APPENDIX–D

FORM C

(1969 EDITION)

SRI VENKATESWARA UNIVERSITY COLLEGE: TIRUPATI
DEPARTMENT OF EDUCATION
16 PERSONALITY FACTORS QUESTIONNAIRE

Dear Sir/Madam,

"Accurate information is the backbone of any useful research work".

In connection with my research work...for the award of Ph.D. degree in Education, I am supplying this questionnaire to the student teachers of DIETs. Each person has his own mental make-up and Psychology. The items in this questionnaire are intended to find out your likes and dislikes, tastes and attitudes. You must note that all people differ in opinions about an item. Therefore there is no question of saying 'right' or wrong' you opinion expressed on an item.

Whatever you find convincing to you is your correct opinion. I request you to answer this questionnaire freely and frankly according to the directions given below:

Inside this booklet are some questions to find your attitudes and interests. Please pick up your choice among the three alternatives. To be able to get the advice from your results, you will want to answer them exactly and truly.

Examples:

1. I like to watch team games.

   (a) Yes

   (b) Occasionally

   (c) No.

2. Woman is to child as cat is to:

   (a) Kitten

   (b) Dog

   (c) Boy

Separate answer sheet is provided for answering the questions. If your answer choice is the 'a', write letter 'a', in the bracket against the corresponding question number in the answer sheet. If your answer choice is the 'b', write letter 'b', in the corresponding question number in the answer sheet, and if your answer choice is the 'c', write letter 'c' in against the corresponding question number in the answer sheet.

When you answer, keep these four points in mind:

1. You are asked not to spend time pondering. Give the first, natural answer as it comes to you. Of course, the questions are too short to give you all the particulars you would sometimes like to have. For instance, the above question asks you about "team games" and you might be found of football than basketball. But you are to reply "for the average game", or to strike an average in situations of the kind stated. Give the best answer you can at a rate not slower than five or six a minute, You should finish in a little more than half an hour.

2. Try not to fall back on the middle, "uncertain" answers except when the answer at either end is really impossible for you.

3. Be sure not to skip anything, but answer every question, somehow. Some may not apply to you very well, but give your best guess. Some may seem personal, but remember that the answers are kept confidential. Answers to particular questions are not inspected.

4. Answer as honestly as possible what is true of you. Do not merely mark what seems "the right thing to say " to impress the examiner.

The information required is purely for academic purpose and the responses given by you will be kept strictly confidential.

Thanking you for your kind co-operation.

1. I think my memory is better than it ever was.
   (a) Yes
   (b) In between
   (c) No.
2. I could happily live alone far from anyone, like a hermit.
   (a) Yes
   (b) Occasionally
   (c) No.
3. If I say the sky is "down" and winter is "hot", I would call a criminal:
   (a) Gangster
   (b) A Saint
   (c) A could.
4. When going to bed, I:
   (a) Drop off to sleep quickly
   (b) In between
   (c) Have difficulty falling asleep.
5. When driving a car in a line of traffic, I feel satisfied:
   (a) To remain behind most of the other cars
   (b) In between
   (c) Only after I've reached the front of the line.
6. At a party I let others keep the jokes and stories going.
   (a) Yes
   (b) Sometimes
   (c) No.

7. It's important to me not to live in messy surroundings.

   (a) True

   (b) Uncertain

   (c) False.

8. Most people I meet at a party are undoubtedly glad to see me.

   (a) Yes

   (b) Sometimes

   (c) No.

9. I would rather exercise by:

   (a) Fencing and dancing,

   (b) in between

   (c) Wrestling and baseball.

10. I smile to myself at the big difference between what people do and what they say they do.

    (a) Yes

    (b) Occasionally

    (c) No.

11. In reading about an accident I like to find out exactly how it happened.

    (a) Always

    (b) Sometimes

    (c) Seldom.

12. When friends play a joke on me, I usually enjoy it as much as the others, without feeling at all upset.

    (a) True

    (b) In between

    (c) False.

13. When someone speaks angrily on me, I can forget the matter quickly.

    (a) True

    (b) Uncertain

    (c) False.

14. I like to "dream up" new ways of doing things rather than to be a practical follower of well-tried ways.

    (a) True

    (b) Uncertain

    (c) False.

15. When I plan something, I like to do so quite alone without any outside help.

    (a) Yes

    (b) Occasionally

    (c) No.

16. I consider myself less "high strung" than most people.

    (a) True

    (b) In between

    (c) False.

17. I get impatient easily with people who don't decide quickly.

    (a) True

    (b) In between

    (c) False.

18. I have sometimes, even if briefly, has hateful feelings towards my parents.

    (a) Yes

    (b) In between

    (c) No.

19. I would rather tell my innermost thoughts to:
    (a) My good friends
    (b) Uncertain
    (c) Diary.

20. I think the opposite of the opposite "inexact" is:
    (a) Casual
    (b) Accurate
    (c) Rough.

21. I always have lots of energy at times when I need it.
    (a) Yes
    (b) In between
    (c) No.

22. I am more annoyed by a person who:
    (a) Tells off-colour jokes and embarrasses people
    (b) Uncertain
    (c) Is late for an appointment and inconveniences me.

23. I greatly enjoy inviting guests and amusing them.
    (a) True
    (b) Uncertain
    (c) False.

24. I feel that:
    (a) Some jobs just don't have to be done so carefully as others
    (b) In between
    (c) Any job should be done thoroughly if you do it at all.

25. I have always had to fight against being too shy.
    (a) Yes
    (b) In between
    (c) No.

26. It would be more interesting to be:

    (a) A priest

    (b) Uncertain

    (c) A colonel.

27. If a neighbour cheats me in small things, I would rather humour him than show him up.

    (a) Yes

    (b) Occasionally

    (c) No.

28. I like a friend who:

    (a) Is efficient and practical in his interests

    (b) In between

    (c) Seriously thinks out his attitudes toward like.

29. It bothers me if I hear others expressing ideas that are contrary to those that I firmly believe.

    (a) True

    (b) In between

    (c) False.

30. I am over-conscientious, worrying over my past acts or mistakes.

    (a) Yes

    (b) In between

    (c) No.

31. If I were good at both, I would rather:

    (a) Play chess

    (b) In between

    (c) Go bowling.

32. I like to join with people who show lively group enthusiasm.
    (a) Yes
    (b) In between
    (c) No.
33. I put my faith more in:
    (a) Insurance
    (b) In between
    (c) Good fortune.
34. I can forget my worries and responsibilities whenever I need to.
    (a) Yes
    (b) Sometimes
    (c) No.
35. It's hard for me to admit it when I am wrong.
    (a) Yes
    (b) Sometimes
    (c) No.
36. In a factory it would be more interesting to be in charge of:
    (a) Machinery or keeping records
    (b) In between
    (c) Talking to and hiring new people.
37. Which word does not belong with the other two?
    (a) Cat
    (b) Near
    (c) Sun.
38. Minor distractions seem:
    (a) To irritate me
    (b) In between
    (c) Not to bother me at all.

39. I am quite happy to be waited on at appropriate times, by personal servants.

    (a) Often

    (b) Sometimes

    (c) Never.

40. I would rather live in a town:

    (a) Artistically laid out, but relatively poor

    (b) Uncertain

    (c) That is rough, prosperous, and booming.

41. People should insist more than they now do that moral law be followed.

    (a) Yes

    (b) Sometimes

    (c) No.

42. I have been told that, as a child, I was rather:

    (a) Quit and kept to myself

    (b) In between

    (c) Lively and always active.

43. I enjoy routine, constructive work, using a good piece of machinery or apparatus

    (a) Yes

    (b) Sometimes

    (c) No.

44. I think most witnesses tell the truth even if it becomes embarrassing.

    (a) Yes

    (b) In between

    (c) No.

45. When I meet a new person I would rather:

(a) discuss his politics and social views

(b) In between

(c) Have him tell me some good, new jokes.

46. I try to make my laughter at jokes quieter than most people's.

(a) Yes

(b) In between

(c) No.

47. I never feel so wretched that I want to cry.

(a) True

(b) Uncertain

(c) False.

48. In my music I enjoy:

(a) Military band marches

(b) Uncertain

(c) Violin solos.

49. I would rather spend two weeks in the summer:

(a) Bird-watching and walking in the country with a friend or two

(b) Uncertain

(c) Being a leader of a group in a camp.

50. The effort taken in planning ahead:

(a) Is never wasted

(b) In between

(c) Is not worth it.

51. In considerate acts or remarks by my neighbours do not make me touchy an unhappy.

(a) True

(b) Uncertain

(c) False.

52. When I know I'm doing the right thing, I find my task easy.
    (a) Always
    (b) Sometimes
    (c) Seldom.
53. I would rather be:
    (a) In a business office, organizing and seeing people
    (b) In between
    (c) An architect, drawing plans in a quiet room.
54. "House" is to "room" as "tree" is to:
    (a) Forest
    (b) Plant
    (c) Leaf.
55. Things go wrong for me:
    (a) Rarely
    (b) Occasionally
    (c) Frequently.
56. In most things in life, I believe in:
    (a) Taking a gamble
    (b) In between
    (c) Playing it safe.
57. Some people may think I talk too much.
    (a) Likely
    (b) Uncertain
    (c) Unlikely.
58. I admire more:
    (a) A clever, but undependable man
    (b) In between
    (c) A man who is average, but strong to resist temptations.

59. I make decisions:

    (a) Faster than many people

    (b) Uncertain

    (c) Slower than most people.

60. I am more impressed by:

    (a) Acts of skill and grace,

    (b) In between

    (c) Acts of strength and power.

61. I am considered a co-operative person.

    (a) Yes

    (b) In between

    (c) No.

62. I enjoy talking more with polished, sophisticated people than with outspoken, down-to-earth individuals.

    (a) Yes

    (b) In between

    (c) No.

63. I prefer to:

    (a) Keep my problems to myself

    (b) In between

    (c) Talk about them to my friends.

64. If a person doesn't answer when I make a suggestion, I feel I've said something silly.

    (a) True

    (b) In between

    (c) False.

65. I learned more in my school days by:

    (a) Going to class

    (b) In between

    (c) Reading books.

66. I avoid getting involved in social responsibilities and organisations.
    (a) True
    (b) Sometimes
    (c) False.

67. When a problem gets hard and there is a lot to do, I try:
    (a) A different problem
    (b) In between
    (c) A different attack on the same problem.

68. I get strong emotional mood-anxiety, anger, laughter, etc. that seem to arise without much actual cause.
    (a) Yes
    (b) Occasionally
    (c) No.

69. My mind doesn't work so clearly at some times as it does at others.
    (a) True
    (b) In between
    (c) False.

70. I am happy to oblige people by making appointments at times they prefer, even if it is a bit inconvenient to me.
    (a) Yes
    (b) Sometimes
    (c) False.

71. I think the proper number to continue the series 1, 2, 3, 6 and 5 is:
    (a) 10
    (b) 5
    (c) 7.

72. I have occasionally had a brief touch of faintness, dizziness, or light-headedness for no apparent reason.

(a) Yes

(b) Uncertain

(c) No.

73. I would rather do without something than put a waiter or waitress to a lot of extra trouble.

(a) Yes

(b) Occasionally

(c) No.

74. I live for the "here and now" more than most people do.

(a) True

(b) Uncertain

(c) False.

75. At a party, I like:

(a) To get into worthwhile conversation

(b) In between

(c) To see people relax and completely let go.

76. I speak my mind no matter how many people are around.

(a) Yes

(b) Sometimes

(c) No.

77. If I could go back in time, I'd rather meet:

(a) Columbus

(b) Uncertain

(c) Shakespeare.

78. I have to stop myself from getting too involved in trying to straighten out other people's problems.

(a) Yes

(b) Sometimes

(c) No.

79. In a store or market, I would prefer to:
    (a) Design and do window displays
    (b) Uncertain
    (c) Be a cashier.

80. If the people think poorly of me, I can still go on calmly
    (a) Yes
    (b) In between
    (c) No.

81. If an old friend seems cold and reserved to me, I usually:
    (a) Just think "He's in a bad mood"
    (b) Uncertain
    (c) Worry about what I may have done wrong.

82. More trouble arises from people.
    (a) Changing and meddling with ways that are already satisfactory
    (b) In between
    (c) Turning down new, promising methods.

83. I greatly enjoy talking to people about local problems:
    (a) Yes
    (b) Sometimes
    (c) No.

84. Prim, strict people don't seem to get along well with me.
    (a) Yes
    (b) Sometimes
    (c) False.

85. I guest I'm less irritable than most people.
    (a) True
    (b) Uncertain
    (c) False.

86. I may be less considerate of other people than they are of me.

(a) True

(b) Sometimes

(c) False.

87. I would just as soon let someone else have all the worry of being in charge of an organisation of which I am a member.

(a) True

(b) Uncertain

(c) False.

88. If the two hands on a watch come together exactly every 65 minutes (according to an accurate watch) the watch is running:

(a) Slow

(b) On time

(c) Fast.

89. I am bored

(a) Often

(b) Occasionally

(c) Seldom.

90. People say that I like to have things done my own way.

(a) True

(b) Occasionally

(c) False.

91. I find it wise to avoid too much excitement because it tends to wear me out.

(a) Yes

(b) Occasionally

(c) No.

92. At home, with a bit of spare time, I:
    (a) Use it chatting and relaxing
    (b) In between
    (c) Arrange to fill it with special jobs.

93. I am shy, and careful, about making friends with new people.
    (a) Yes
    (b) Occasionally
    (c) No.

94. I think that what people say in poetry could be put just as exactly in plain prose.
    (a) Yes
    (b) Sometimes
    (c) No.

95. I suspect that people who act friendly to me can be disloyal behind my back.
    (a) Yes, generally
    (b) Occasionally
    (c) No, rarely.

96. I think that even the most dramatic experiences during the year leave my personality much the same as it was.
    (a) Yes
    (b) Sometimes
    (c) No.

97. It would seem more interesting to be a:
    (a) Naturalist and work with plants
    (b) Uncertain
    (c) Public accountant or insurance man.

98. I get unreasonable fears or distaste's for something for examples, particular animals, plants, and so on.

    (a) Yes

    (b) Sometimes

    (c) No.

99. I like to think out ways in which our world could be changed to improve it.

    (a) Yes

    (b) In between

    (c) No.

100. I prefer games where:

    (a) You're on a team or have a partner

    (b) Uncertain

    (c) Each person is his own.

101. At night I have rather fantastic or ridiculous dreams.

    (a) Yes

    (b) Occasionally

    (c) No.

102. If left in a lonely house I tend, after a time, to feel a bit anxious or fearful.

    (a) Yes

    (b) Sometimes

    (c) No.

103. I may deceive people by being friendly when I really dislike them.

    (a) Yes

    (b) Sometimes

    (c) No.

104. Which word does not belong with the other two?

(a) Think

(b) See

(c) Hear.

105. If Mary's mother is Fred's father's sister, what relation is Fred to Mary's father?

(a) Cousin

(b) Nephew

(c) Uncle.

* * * * * * * *

APPENDIX – E

DEMOGRAPHIC AND SOCIO-ECONOMIC SCALE

(Please Fill the Following Particulars)

1. Name :
2. Age :
3. Male/Female :
4. Married/Un Married :
5. Fill up the particulars of your family members in the table (Put mark on related column):

Relation	*Age*	*Education*	*Profession/ Employment*	*Annual Income*
Father				
Mother				
Brothers				
1.				
2.				
3.				
Sisters				
1.				
2.				
3.				

6.	Caste	:	OC/BC/SC/ST/Minority
7.	Group subjects in the Intermediate (10+2 Level)	:	
8.	Place of Birth	:	City/Town/Small Town Village
9.	Order of Birth	:	
10.	Type of Family	:	Combined/Nuclear
11.	Economic status of the family	:	Rich/Middle/Poor

TAI-A

1. Teaching profession is interesting only in the initial stage.
2. Teaching is a cultured and well-mannered profession.
3. People in teaching profession are generally truthful.
4. There will be lot of dissatisfaction in teacher's profession than in any other profession
5. Using teacher services in programmes not relevant to teaching pains me.
6. Teaching profession is only a source of livelihood.
7. Teaching profession decays dynamism.
8. Teaching profession is a quiet one.
9. People should not discriminate look down teachers.
10. Scope of corruption is very less in teaching profession.
11. Because of indifference of people and government towards teaching profession I am not interested in this profession.
12. There is lack of independence to teachers in expressing their views.
13. Every teacher should feel proud of his profession.
14. Trying to be an ideal teacher is deceiving oneself.
15. Teachers should show more interest on pupil than earnings.

16. Teaching is a better profession than any other profession.
17. The main quality of a teacher must be to practice what be preaches.
18. National reconstruction depends on teacher's teaching.
19. Teaching profession is becoming a laughing stock day by day.

....

20. The syllabus framed for teacher education is suitable to meet our needs.
21. Theory papers in teacher's training are fresh and interesting.
22. Teaching methods explained in training are very much useful in practical teaching in classroom teaching.
23. There is dire need for teachers trained in computer education in our syllabus.
24. For most student teachers educational psychology is a subject causing difficulty.
25. Because of little leisure, there is no opportunity for teacher trainees to participate in co-curricular activities.
26. DIET plays a major part in developing standards in primary education.
27. There is no link between theoretical and practical aspects in teacher training.
28. Text books and reference books needed for teacher education are available

....

29. I wish to use teaching aids and teach the subject for easy understanding.
30. Pupils should actively participate in discussions during the training period.
31. The present system of teacher education neglects personality of student teachers.

32. I get satisfaction only when I teach difficult lessons very well.
33. Teachers have no sense of humour.
34. When a colleague teaches a lesson, I observe every aspect carefully and think how they will be useful for my teaching.

....

35. It is difficult for a rational teacher trainee to teach.
36. Lecturers are advise us about how to use library.
37. It causes disgust when the same teacher teaches many subjects.
38. There is no scope for entertainment or pleasure in this profession.
39. There is no need to give lot of importance to the pupil in teaching.
40. Lecturers supervising teaching activities are only an eyewash.

....

41. An ideal teacher is not fit for normal living in community.
42. There is scope for teacher trainees to participate in community activities during the period of training.
43. You can good marks if you are in good books of lecturers.
44. Teacher education does not attract intellectuals in society.
45. There is more sufficient freedom for teacher trainees in our training institute.
46. Good learning is possible only when there is strong and harmonious relation between teacher trainees.

....

47. The training period in DIET is enough to transform a trainee in to a good teacher.
48. I want to be a model by my good handwriting and painting.
49. I dislike students who ask questions when I teach.
50. There are no chances for conducting practicals in our computer lab.

51. Teacher training today fills teacher trainees with self-confidence.

    ....

52. Different aspects of teaching should be learnt one by one slowly, all can't be learnt in a single day.
53. Civic training is an important one in our training programme.
54. Ethical value should be taught in teacher training.
55. Standards of teacher education are deteriorating fast day by day.
56. Teachers decide ethical standards and intellectual wealth of a nation.
57. Teacher trainers are becoming inefficient due to lack of accountability.

    ....

58. Tables, maps and other paraphernalia are not necessary for an efficient teacher.
59. Audio-visual tools are not used for teacher trainees.
60. Training must be given for teacher trainees in using computers in classroom.
61. There are no teaching tools necessary for teacher trainees in our institute.
62. Demonstration and tape recorders are not much useful in classroom.
63. Pupils are feeling inconvenient because of teaching without teaching tools.
64. Teacher trainees should be given training in organisations that manufacture various teaching tools.
65. There are no critical classes after demonstration class.
66. Teacher trainees feel satisfy because of laboratory facilities in the training institute.

    ....

67. I feel afraid while conducting model classes.
68. Teacher should teach lessons so that they are interesting to pupils.
69. The teacher must explain the purpose of a topic and its use to pupils.
70. Teacher's need not be concerned about personal problems and needs of pupils.

....

71. It is much useful for pupil to repeat a lesson.
72. It is not possible to practice experimental teaching method in teaching of general science.
73. Teacher should give chance to pupils to express their opinions.
74. It is very interesting to observe teaching of my colleagues.
75. Teaching is classroom makes students disciplined.
76. To follow the prepared lesson plan in the classroom is difficult.
77. Lecture method is the best in classroom teaching.
78. Microteaching plan is not improving teaching capacities of teacher trainees.
79. There is not much encouragement for in service training in developing teaching skills.
80. Teacher does not show much interest in teaching exercises.
81. Pupils often talk in a meaningless manner in the classroom.
82. Teacher does not show enough interest on pupil in backside benches in the classroom.
83. Teacher education gives a chance to improve teacher's skill in conversation.

* * * * * * * *

SHI-B

1. All my family members cooperate regarding my studies.
2. I prepare my own plan for studies in my house/room.
3. My family members supervise my studies.
4. I study and learn lessons and subjects before I go to college.
5. My parents give enough money for me to purchase books.
6. I attend college because of force from my family members.
7. I complete my homework immediately on coming home from college.
8. My family members/room mates great obstacle for my studies.
9. It is inconvenient to study and take rest because of large number of people in my house/ room.
10. I cannot study well for lack of proper ventilation.
11. I cannot study well in the right because of the mosquitos in my house/room.
12. My studies are interrupted because of guests to my house/ room.
13. I can not concentrate on my studies because of financial and other problem of my family.

....

14. I note down important points while reading.
15. I have to read a second time because of not understanding lessons at first reading.
16. I note down important points when the teaching is going on in the class room and prepare notes afterwards.
17. I show much enthusiasm to study in the early morning time.
18. I try to link what I studied to a suitable topic.
19. I like to study with others than to study alone.
20. I understand while studying but cannot remember.

21. I study the second topic, only after completely understanding the first topic.
22. While writing running notes in the class some points explained by the lecturer get missed.

. . . .

23. I study according to the plan prepared every month.
24. I try to study during the extra time also.
25. I divide my time to study all subjects.
26. I study the lessons taught on the same day.
27. I prepare a plan how to answer every question.
28. I postpone studies till the last minute.
29. I cannot study because of tiredness from writing lesson plans and records.
30. I wish to complete a subject in the allotted time.
31. There is not sufficient time to study theory papers.
32. Before beginning to study I gather the necessary materials.
33. I select important lessons in every subject and study them only.
34. I study material available with me and do not try for more information.
35. I concentrate on subjects difficult for me.
36. I study my favourite subjects and neglect others.
37. I am unable to correlate topics in one subject to topics in another subject.
38. I neglect studies for some time in the first quarter of the year.

. . . .

39. I revise what I have learnt.
40. I can concentrate only at the examination time.
41. I repeat for my self what I studied.

42. The period of concentration on studies is less.
43. I can't study well during winter.
44. Several desires disturb my studies.
45. I can study well without being disturbed by every small thing.
46. I have proper knowledge of sex education.
47. I can't study well because of tiredness and excessive sleep.
48. I can't study well because of wayward thoughts.
49. With the purpose of reading quickly, I am unable to understand what I read.
50. I have waited sometime to get concentration.
51. I can remember that very well lessons learnt last month.
52. I learn everything by note.

....

53. I prepare answers for essay type of questions many days before the exams.
54. Important questions and suggestions reach one so I don't study always.
55. I prepare answers only for questions in the old question papers of previous years.
56. I feel disgust because of reading continuously for hours together at examination time.
57. I drink coffee or tea and read for many hours at night.
58. Because of confusion in examination hall I am unable to write what all I learn.
59. I decide the method of writing before writing an answer in the examination.
60. I study valued answer papers very well to know my mistakes.
61. I complete writing answers before the allotted time in any examination.
62. I study only side heading before the examination.

63. Once I study a paragraph, I memorise it.
64. I study more lessons only at the time of examinations.
65. I prepare answers for not only questions given at the end of the lessons but also other questions.

....

66. I always try to link the points in my textbooks with my surroundings.
67. I participate actively in programmes like Janmabhoomi, clean and green introduced by government.
68. I participate in social and cultural activities conducted in my college.
69. I consult teachers and others to understand difficult points.
70. I learn many things from nature and environment.
71. Social and cultural activities are helpful for my progress.
72. Social factors like strikes and boycotts are disturbing my studies.

....

73. I am unable to understand what is written on the blockboard because the blackboards are not of good quality.
74. I cannot study well because of tiredness from seeing Television too much.
75. I use audio-visual materials to teach lessons to students.
76. I prepare graphs and tables to remember my lessons.
77. I like to listen to lessons over radio.
78. I read newspapers and magazines.
79. I prepare or collect charts, specimens, diagrams and models to remember points in my lessons.
80. I spend much time in seeing cinema.

....

81. I keep all my books neat and clean.
82. I study silently.
83. I like to participate in excursions etc.
84. I am unable to study properly because of psychological problems.
85. I show more interest in games and sports than studies.
86. I get sleep once I open the textbook.
87. I am able to study well because of nutritious diet I receive.
88. I daydream while studying.

....

89. I use books in the library of my training institute.
90. Facilities in training institute are satisfactory.
91. I have good relations with my lecturers.
92. As our training institute is adjacent to the main road sounds from vehicles are obstacles to teaching.
93. My teachers encourage some of my actions.
94. Some topics I dislike are thought in my institute, they are obstacles to my success.
95. All activities that related to teaching in my training institute is interesting.

* * * * * * * * * * *

BIBLIOGRAPHY

Abraham, M. (1974), Some Factors Relating to Under Achievement in English of Secondary School Pupils. Ph.D. (Education), Kerala University.

Adinarayana Reddy, P. and Indira, K. (1993), *Reading Interests of Adults*, New Delhi: Uppal Publishing House.

Aggarwal, Y.P., and Saini .V.P. (1969), "Pattern of Study Habits and its Relationship with Achievement and Parents Economic and Educational Status", *Journal of Educational Research and Extension*, Vol. 5, No. 4, pp. 161-165.

Ahman, J., Smith, S. and Glack, M.D. (1958), "Predicting Academic Success in College by Means a Study and Attitudes Inventory", *Educational Psychology Management*, Vol. 18, pp. 553-557.

Ahuliwalia, S.P. and Shyam. D. (1975), "A Study of Relationship Between Socio-economic Status and Academic Achievement of High School Students", *Journal of Educational Research and Extension*, Vol. 12, No. 1, pp. 1-5.

Al-Hilawani,Yasser, S., and Aziz, A. (1997),"Study Skills and Habits of Female University Students", *College Student Journal*, Vol. 31, No. 4, pp. 537-544.

Anuradha Joshi, (1990), "Teaching Elements of Science to Class IX Students of Madhya Pradesh State: Evolvement of an Instructional Strategy", *Indian Education Review*, Vol. 25, No. 1, pp. 56-62.

Aruna, R. (1994), Study Habits of IX Class Pupils. M.Ed. Dissertation, Tirupati: Sri Venkateswara University. (Unpublished).

Asha Bhatnagar (1980), "A Study of Some Factors Affecting Student Involvement in Studies", *Journal of Educational Research, Indian Educational Review*, Vol. 15, No. 3, pp. 70-75.

Balasubramanian, P., and Sivakumar, R. (2001), "A Comparative Study of Academic Achievement of Primary Teachers Training Students", *The Educational Review*, Vol. No. 7, pp. 6-8.

Benerjee, D., and Geetha Papneja (1975), "Relationship Between Motivational Pattern and Study Habits of Selected College Students", *Mana*, Vol. 22, No. 2, pp. 205-218.

Best, J.W. (1959), *Research in Education*, USA: Prentice Hall Inc., Engle wood Cliffs, p. 31.

Best, J.W. (1977), *Research in Education*, New Delhi: Prentice Hall.

Bernstein, B. (1968), "Some Sociological Determinants of Perception—An Enquiry into Sub-cultural Differences", *British Journal of Sociology*, Vol. 9, p. 159.

Bhatia, I. (1976-77). "A Study of Relationship Between Academic Achievement Competence and Level of Aspiration", *Research Journal of Educational Psychology*, Vol. 7, pp. 9-14.

Biswas, A. and Aggarwal, J. (1971), *Encyclopedic Dictionary and Directory of Education*, New Delhi (India): Academic Publishers.

Brown, W.F. and Holtzman W. (1955), "A Study Attitude Questionnaire for Predicting Academic Success", *Journal of Education Psychology*, Vol. 46, pp. 75-84.

Brown, W.F. and Holtzman W. (1956 and 64), *Survey of Study Habits and Attitudes*, The New York, Psychological Corporation, p. 9.

Brown, F.G. and Dubois (1964), "Study Habits and Attitudes, College Experience and College Success", *Personal and Guidance Journal*, Vol. 43, pp. 287-292.

Burnet, C.W. (1951), "Study Skills and Counselor Training, A Two Way Teaching Programme", *California Journal of Educational Research*, Vol. 2, pp. 18-21.

Burt, C. (1937), *The Backward Child*, London: University of London Press.

Carol, C.A. (1991), "Cognitive Strategies and Study Habits: Analysis of the Measurement of Tertiary Students' Learning", *British Journal of Educational Psychology*, Vol. 61(3), pp. 290-299.

Carter, H.D. (1948), "Methods of Learning as Factors of Prediction of School Success", *Journal of Psychology*, Vol. 26, pp. 249-262.

Carter, H.D. (1950), "The Mechanism of Study Procedure", *California Journal of Educational Research*, Vol. 9, pp. 8-13.

Carter, H.D. (1950), "Correlation Between Intelligence Test and Study Habits and Skills in a College Course", *Journal of Psychology*, Vol. 30, pp. 333-49.

Carter, H.D. (1953), "Cross Validation of a Study Method Test", *Journal of Educational Research*, Vol. 4, pp. 32-36.

Carter, H.D. (1955), "Development of a Diagnostic Scoring Scheme for a Study Method Test", *California Journal of Educational Research*, Vol. 6, pp. 26-32.

Cattell, R.B. (1946), *The Description and Measurement of Personality*, New York: World.

Cattell, R.B. (1969), *Handbook for Junior-Senior High School Personality Questionnaire*, Ellinois: Institute of Personality and Ability Testing.

Cattell, R.B., Sealey. A.P. and Sweeney. A.B. (1966), "What can Parents and Motivation. Source Trait Measurements Add to the Prediction of School Achievement", *British Journal of Educational Psychology*, Vol. 36, pp. 280-295.

Chabra, S. (1990), *Academic Achievement in Relation to Self Deal Discrepancy and Socio-economic Status*, M.Ed. Dissertation, Chandigarh: Punjab University (Unpublished).

Chauhan, S.S. and Singh H. (1982), "An Investigation in to the Study Habits of 10 to 12 Years of Children with Regard to Their Parental Profession", *Indian Educational Review*, NCERT, New Delhi.

Chopra, P.C. (1964), *A Study of Relationship of Socio-economic Factors with Achievement of Students in Secondary Schools*, Ph.D. Thesis, Lucknow: Lucknow University.

Chopra, S.L. (1966). "Socio-economic Background and Failure in the High School Examination", *Education and Psychological Measurements*, Vol. 2, pp. 495-97.

Clarke, R.M. (1981), "Student Approaches to Learning in An Innovative Medical School: A Cross Sectional Study", *The British Journal of Educational Psychology.*

Cuff, N.B. (1937), "Study Habits in Grades Four to Twelve", *Journal of Educational Psychology*, Vol. 28, No. 4, pp. 295-301.

Deb, M. and Grewal, H.P. (1990), "Relationship Between Study Habits and Academic Achievement of Undergraduate Home Science Final Year Students", *Journal of Educational Research*, Vol. 25, No. 3, pp. 71-74.

Desai, B.D. (1971), *Achievement Motivation in High School Pupils in Kaira District*, NCERT Project Report, Vallabh (Vidya Nagar): M.B. Patel College of Education.

Dev Mohan (1972), *Dev Mohan Socio-economic Status Scale. Department of Education*, Chandigarh: Punjab University.

Diener, C.L. (1960),"Similarities and Differences Between Over Achieving and Underachieving Students", *Personal Guide Journal*, Vol. 38, No. 5, pp. 396-400.

Edwards, A.L. (1957), *Techniques of Attitude Scale Construction*, New York: Appleton Century Crofts Inc.

Edwards, A.L. (1969), *Statistical Analysis*, New York: Holt, Rinehard and Winston Inc.

Edwards, A.L. (1969), *Techniques of Attitude Scale Construction*, Bombay: Vakils, Feffer and Simons.

Ekins, Judith. M. (1992), *Study Approaches of Distance Learning Study, Studying in a Second Language*, Paper Presented at an International Conference for Distance Education, Thailand.

Elliott, C.D. (1972), "Personality Factors and Scholastic Attainment", *British Journal of Educational Psychology*, Vol. 42, pp. 23-32.

Entwistle, N.J., Nisbet. J., Entwistle. D. and Cowell .M.D. (1971), "The Academic Performance of Students", *British Journal of Educational Psychology*, pp. 258-67.

Entwistle, N.J. (1972), "Personality and Academic Achievement", *British Journal of Educational Psychology*, Vol. 42, pp. 137-151.

Eysebtg, H.J. and Cookson, D. (1969), "Personality in Primary School Children", *British Journal of Educational Psychology*, Vol. 40, pp. 117-131.

Finlayson, D.S. (1970), "A Follow-up Study of School Achievement in Relation to Personality", *British Journal of Psychology*, Vol. 40, pp. 344-348.

Florence, P.S. and Ronald, R.S. (1971), *Relationship of Study Habits and School Attitudes to Achievement in Mathematics and Reading*, Vol. 65, No. 2, pp. 71-73.

Ford Dawson (1970), "An Analytical Study of the Effects of Material Employment of Some Sex Denials in Pre-adolescence and of Residential Mobility on Self-Actualisation Achievement in a Sample of Adolescents". *Dissertation Abstracts International*, Vol. 3, p. 924.

Fraser Elizabeth (1959), *Home Environment and the School*, London: University of London Press.

Fruntera, Lucy and Rosalind Horowitz (1995), "Reading and Study Behaviours of Fourth Grade Hispanics Can Teachers Assess Risk?", *Hispanic Journal of Behavioural Sciences*, Vol. 17, No. 1, pp. 100-120.

Gadzella Bernadette and James David (1984), "Study Skills, Self Concept and Academic Achievement for High School Students", *Resources in Education*, Vol. 19, No. 12, p. 34.

Ganapathy, M. and Raghuram Singh, (1981), "The Impact of Socio-economic Conditions on Achievement", *Experiments in Education*, Vol. 9, No. 8, pp. 144-177.

Ganguly, Malabika (1989), "Socio-economic Status and Scholastic Achievement", *Indian Educational Review*, Vol. 24, No. 1 pp. 84-95.

Garrett, H.E, (1973), *Statistics in Psychology and Education*, Bombay: Vikalls Feffer and Simmons Pvt. Ltd.

Gary Lee (1990), "The Learning and Study Strategies of College Freshmen", *Dissertation Abstracts International*, Vol. 51, No. 12.

Gaur, C.B., Amritha Murtthy and Nathawat. S.S. (2001), "Intelligence and Scholastic Achievement as Determinants of Stress and Adjustment in Adolescent Male and Female Students", *Indian Journal of Clinical Psychology*, Vol. 28, No. 2, pp. 257-263.

Girija, P.R., Bhadra, B.P and Ameerjan, M.S. (1975). "The Relationship of Study Habits with Study Skills, Academic Achievement Motivation and Academic Achievement", *Journal of Educational Psychology*, Vol. 33, No. 1, pp. 47-53.

GoldFried Marvin, R. and D'Zurilla, Thomas J, (1973), "Prediction of Acaddemic Competence by Means of the Survey of Study Habits and Attitudes", *Journal of Educational Psychology*, Vol. 64, No. 1, pp. 116-122.

Gordon, H.P. (1941), "Study Habit Inventory Scores and Scholarship", *Journal of Applied Psychology*, Vol. 25, pp. 101-107.

Gordan, D. (1998), "The Relationship Among Academic Self Concept, Academic Achievement and Persistence with Self-attribution, Study Habits and Perceived School Environment", *Dissertation Abstracts International*, Vol. 58, No. 12, p. 26.

Guilford, J.P., (1950), *Fundamental Statistics in Psychology and Education: International Student Edition*, New York: McGraw Hill.

Guilford, J.P. (1954), *Psychometric Methods*, London: Unwin, p. 47.

Gupta, S.P.(1974), *Statistical Methods*, Delhi: Sultan Chand.

Gupta, P.L. (1983), A Study of Personality Characteristics of Ninth Grade Over and Underachieving Boys and Girls at Different Levels of Achievement Motivation, Ph.D. Thesis, Punjab: Punjab University (unpublished).

Hugh, M. Bell (1931), "Study Habits of Teachers College Students", *Journal of Educational Psychology*, Vol. 22, No. 7, pp. 538-43.

Jagannadhan, K. (1986), "Socio-economic Status and Academic Achievement", *Journal of Educational Research and Extension*, Vol. 22, No. 3, pp. 141-49.

Jammur, K.K. (1961), Investigation of Some Psychological Factors Underlying Study Habits of College Students, Ph.D. Thesis, Bihar: Patna University, (Unpublished).

Kamala, S.P. (1990), "Interactive Effect of Science Aptitude and Attitude Towards Science on Biology Achievement", *Journal of Educational Research and Extension*, Vol. 26, No. 4, pp. 206-10.

Kohli, T.K. (1977), "Characteristic Behavioural and Environmental Correlates of Academic Achievement", *A Review of Research Bulletin*, Vol. 18, No. 12, pp. 87-121.

Kothleenorme, (1974), "Personality, Ability and Achievement in Primary School Children", *Educational Research*, Vol. 17, No. 3, pp. 199-201.

Krishnamurthy, S. (2000), "Achievement in History as Related to Academic Achievement Motivation", *Experiments in Education*, Vol. 28, No.1, pp. 9-14.

Krishna Murthy, S. and Raja Rao, T.S. (1969), "A Comparative Investigation of the Study Habits of Sub-Urban and Urban Children in Some High Schools in Coimbatore", *Journal of Educational Research and Extension*, Vol. 6, No. 1, pp. 32-41.

Lakshmi Devi, S. (2002), *Vidyajyothi (DIET Calendar)*, Bukkapatnam: DIET Handbook pp. 42-43.

Likert, R. (1932), "A Technique for Measurement of Attitudes", *Archieves of Pschology*, 140.

Lindblam-Yalamne (1999), "Individual Ways of Interacting with the Learning Environment-Are They Related to Study Success?", *Learning and Instruction*, Vol. 9, No. 1, pp. 1-18.

Lynn, D.J. (1976). A Study of the Effectiveness of Guided Note Taking and Study Skill Systems Upon the Level of Academic Success Among Entering University of Idaho Freshmen, Dissertation, Idaho: University of Idaho.

Marentic-Pozaranik, B. (1974), "Study Habits and Attitudes Towards Learning as a Factor of Scholastic Achievement", *Psychological Abstracts*, Vol. 51, No. 2, p. 480.

Mary Esther, St. (1945), *An Analysis of the Study Habits of Catholic High School Students*, London: Catholic Educational, pp. 542-49.

Mavi, N.S. and Iswar Patel. (1997), "A Study of Academic Achievement in Relation to Selected Personality Variables of Tribal Adolescents", *Experiments in Education*, Vol. 25, No. 10, pp. 9-11.

McClelland, D.C. (1961), *The Achieving Society*, Princeton: D Van Nostrand.

McCausland and Stewart, N.E. (1974), "Academic Aptitude, Study Skills and Attitudes and College GPA", *Journal of Educational Research*, Vol. 67, No. 8, pp. 354-357.

Mortan Friedman, (1977), *Teachers' Cognitive Emphasis and Pupil Achievement*, Vol. 2, No. 1, pp. 42-47.

Nanda, Ashok Kumar (2000), "Study Habits of Socially Advantaged and Disadvantaged School Students", *The Educational Review*, Vol. 106, No. 10, pp. 173-174.

Narayana Koteswara (1997), Reading Achievement in Relation to Personality Factors, Study Habits and Other Variables, Ph.D. Thesis. Tirupati: Sri Venkateswara University. (Unpublished).

Norton, D.F. (1959), "The Relationship of Study Habits and Other Measures of Achievement of IX Grade General Sciences", *Journal of Experiments in Education*, Vol. 27, pp. 211-17.

NCTE, (2001), *Teacher Education in Andhra Pradesh*, New Delhi: NCTE Document, pp. 5-7.

On Tse Ka and Walkins David (1994), "Doing Living and Study Habits and the Academic Achievements of Secondary School Students in Hong Kong", *Perceptual and Motor Skills*, Vol. 79, No. 1, pp. 231-34.

Palaniappan, V.P. (1999), "Effectiveness of in Service Training Programmes to Teachers on the Achievements of the Students at Primary Level in Coimbatore District", *Journal of Educational Research and Extension*, Vol. 36, No. 3, pp. 2-11.

Passi, R.K., and Sharma, S.K. (1982), "A Study of Teaching Competency of Secondary School Teachers", *A Document*, Indore: Indore University.

Patel, B.V. (1976), "A Study of the Reading Ability and Intelligence in the Context of Study Habit", *Journal of Education and Psychology*, Vol. 34, No. 1, pp. 19-29.

Patel, D.N. (1981), "The Impact of Study Habits of Intellectually Backward Pupil Upon Their Academic Achievement", *The Progress of Education*, Vol. 56, No. 2, pp. 33-37.

Patnaik, S.P., and Basavayya, D. (1991), "Study Habits and Achievement in Mathematics", *The Progress of Education*, Vol. 45, No. 6, pp. 142-144.

Pavithran, A.N., and Feroze, M. (1965), "Influence of Socio-economic Factors on the Scholastic Achievement of Tenth Standard of Pathanamthitta Educational District", *Journal of Educational Research and Extension*, Vol. 1, No. 4, pp. 6-12.

Perumal, N., and Visvesvaran, H (1968), "A Study of Scientific Attitude of Pupils of Standard IX in Relation to Their Achievement in Science, in Some High Schools in Coimbatore", *Journal of Educational Research and Extension*, Vol. 1, pp. 24-31.

Praveena, V. (1990), "A Study of the Effect of Cognitive Variable on Achievement in Mathematics of Secondary School Students", *Journal of Educational Research and Extension*, Vol. 26, No. 3, pp. 140-148.

Premalathasarma, (1984), "Study Habits and Academic Achievement Among Rural Girls", *Journal of Educational Research and Extension*, Vol. 22, No. 4, pp. 220-24.

Quraishi, Z.M., and Bhat, V.D. (1986), "Academic Achievement in Relation to Socio-economic Status, Age and Sex", *Indian Journal of Psychometry and Education*, Vol. 17, No. 1 and 2, pp. 57-66.

Ram Mishra, (1985), "A Study of Professional Attitude of Teachers in Relation to Their Teaching Behaviour", *Journal of Educational Research and Extension*, Vol. 21, No. 3, pp. 165-69.

Ramakumar, Vasantha (1969), Self-concept and Achievement in School Subject of Prospective University Entrance, Ph.D. Thesis. Kerala: Kerala University.

Ramana Sood (1990), "A Study of Academic Achievement Pre-engineering Students in Relation to Socio-economic Status", *Journal of Educational Research and Extension*, Vol. 26, No. 4, pp. 223-27.

Ramaswamy, R. (1990), "Study Habits and Academic Achievement", *Experiments in Education*, Vol. 18, No. 10, pp. 255-259.

Rangaswamy, S.P., and Visvesvaran (1977), "A Comparative Study of the Academic Achievement of High School Sportsmen and Other Students in Coimbatore District", *Journal of Educational Research and Extension*, Vol. 13, No. 4, pp. 239-40.

Rao, D.G. (1965), *A Study of Some Factors Related to Scholastic Achievement*, Ph.d. Thesis, Delhi: Delhi University.

Rawat Leela (1995), A Study of the Effect of Parental Absence on Adjustment, Study Habits and Academic Development of Students of High School Classes. Ph.D. Thesis. Hemawati Nandan Bahuguna Garhwal University, (Unpublished).

Reddy, A.V. (1972), An Investigation into Guidance Needs of Pupils Studying in VIII, IX and X Class in the Secondary Schools of Chittoor District, Andhra Pradesh, M.Ed. Dissertation. Tirupati. Sri Venkateswara University. (Unpublished)

Reddy, M.V.S. and Basavanna, M. (1978), "A Study of Self-confidence and Achievement Motivation in Relation to Academic Achievement, Combined Annual Convention of Indian Psychological Association, National Vocational and Educational Guidance Association, Indian Academy of Applied Psychology.

Richard, G.W., and Virginia, M.W. (1967), "The Relationship of Knowledge and Usage of Study Skill Techniques to Academic Performance", *Journal of Educational Research*, Vol. 61, No. 2, pp. 78-80.

Richard, D.B. Donald and Morely, R. (1971), "Study Habit Modification and Its Effect on Academic Performance: A Behavioural Approach", *Journal of Educational Research*, Vol. 64, No. 8, pp. 347-50.

Richardson, J.T (1995), "Cultural Specificity of Approaches to Studying in Higher Education: A Comparative Investigation Using the Approaches to Studying Inventory", *Educational Psychological Measurement*, Vol. 55, No. 2, pp. 300-308.

Roach, D.A. (1979), "The Effects of Conceptual Style Preference, Related Cognitive Variables and Sex on Achievement in Mathematics", *British Journal of Educational Psychology*, Vol. 49, pp. 79-82.

Ruth Lee, F. (1992), "Development of Study Skills Pocket to Improve Grades in IX and X Standard Students", *ERIC*, Vol. 281, No. 3, p. 137.

Saini, B.K. (1977), "Academic Achievement as a Function of Economic Status and Educational Standard of Parents", *Psychological Studies*, Vol. 22, No. 2, pp. 24-27.

Sam Sundar Raj, H., and Sreethi. S. (2000), "Academic Achievement As Related to Procrastination Behaviour and Study Habits", *Journal of Psychological Reseaches*, Vol. 44, No. 2, pp. 82-87.

Samuel, T.M. and Rao, T.R.S. (1967), "An Investigation of the Study Habits of the Pre-University Colleges Students in Coimbatore", *Journal of Educational Research and Extension*, Vol. 5, No. 4, pp. 18-28.

Shanmugasundaram (1983), "An Investigation into Factors Related to Academic Achievement Among Undergraduate Students Under Semester System", *Fourth Survey of Educational Research*, p. 850.

SCERT (2001), *Teacher Education (With Reference to Andhra Pradesh)*, Hyderabad: SCERT Document, pp. 1-2, 8-33.

Selvam, M. and Soundaravalli, S. (2002), "An Empirical Study of Problems of Higher Secondary Students and Their Achievement", *Recent Researches in Educational Psychology*, Vol. 7, No. 324, pp. 102-04.

Sharma, V.P. and Bhargava, M. (1980), "Academic Attainment and Prolonged Deprivation", *Journal of Education and Psychology*, Vol. 37, p. 4.

Shaw, M.C. and Mccum, J.T. (1960). "The Onset of Academic Under-achievement, *Journal of Educational Psychology*, Vol. 51, pp. 103-07.

Silverman, M.S., and Riodens K. (1974), "Study Skills Training for High Risk Freshmen", *Journal of College Students Personal*, Vol. 15, No. 1, p. 63.

Singh (1984), "A Survey of the Study Habits of High, Middle and Low Achievers Adolescents in Relaticn to Their Sex, Intelligence and Socio-Economic Status", *Fourth Survey of Educational Research*, p. 895.

Singh, H. (1987), "Study Habits of Scheduled Tribe Students in Relation to Their Concept and Level of aspiration", *Journal of Educational Research and Extension*, Vol. 24, No. 3, pp. 165-172.

Skaalvik, E. M. (1983), "Academic Achievement, Self-Esteem and Valuing of the School–some Sex Differences", *British Journal of Educational Psychology*, Vol. 53 , pp. 299-306.

Smith, H.C. (1961), *Personality and Adjustment*, New York: McGraw Hill.

Spaights, E. (1967), "Students Appraise, Teachers' Methods and Attitudes Improving College and University Teaching, *British Journal of Educational Psychology*, Vol. 15, pp. 15-17.

Stella and Purushothaman (1993), "Study Habits of the Underachievers", *Journal of Educational Research and Extension*, Vol. 29, No. 4, pp. 206-14.

Sten, C.P. (1970), *Study Skills and Mathematics Achievement*, Report No. 2, ERIC, Part III.

Srivastava, A.K. (1967), *An Investigation into the Factors Related to Educational Under Achievement*, Ph.D. Thesis, Patna: Patna University.

Stock (1989), "The Effects of Performance Expectation and Question Difficulty on Text Study Time, Response Certitude and Correct Responding", *Bulletin of the Psychonomic Society*, Vol. 27, No. 6, pp. 567-69.

Sudamma, G.R. (1973), *A Study of the Effect of Library Use on Academic Achievement of Post-graduate Students in the M.S. Univeristy of Baroda*, Ph.D. Thesis. Baroda: Maharaja Sayaji Rao University.

Sukhia, S.P. (1980), *Elements of Educational Research*, New Delhi: Allied Publications, pp. 101-07.

Tiwari (1982), *Study Habits and Scholastic Performance at Three Levels of Education*, Ph.D.Thesis, Varanasi: Banaras Hindu University.

Tuli, N.R. (1980), "Study Habits as Correlates of Achievement in Mathematics", *Journal of Educational Psychology*, Vol. 38, No. 3, pp. 141-148.

Vanden Hurk (1998), "The Impact of Student Generated Learning Issued on Individual Study Time and Academic Achievement", *RIE Journal*, Vol. 34, No. 9.

Ved Prakash Gupta, (1968), "Intelligence, Economic Status , Sex, and Academic Success", *Journal of Educational Research and Extension*, Vol. 5, No. 2, pp. 81-87.

Vedavalli, H.C. (1953), "Study Habits of College Students in Tirupati", *The Education and Psychology*, Vol. 3, No. 3, pp. 42-50.

Verma, D. (1971), "Student Failure: A Few Observations". The Progress of Education, Vol. 46, No. 3, p. 82-85.

Verma, B.P., Sheikh, G. and Sangita (1996), "Study Habits of Adolescent Students in Relation to Academic Motivation and Test Anxiety", *Psycho-Lingua*, Vol. 27, No. 2, pp. 107-10.

Vijayakumari, L. (2002), *Jnanadeepika (DIET Calendar)*, Medak: DIET Handbook: pp. 20-24.

Viswanadhan Nair, P. and Bindu, T.V. (1998). "Association Between Certain Demographic Variables and Discrepant Achievement in Six School Projects of Secondary Pupils", *Experiments in Education*, Vol. 26, No. 7, pp. 13-20.

Vivian Ridler, (1961) (Ed.), *The Oxford Dictionary*. Great Britain: Oxford University Press.

Warkins, D., Hattie , J. and Astilla, E. (1984), "Approaches to Study by Fillipino Students. A Longitudinal Investigation", *The British Journal of Educational Psychology*.

Wrenn, C.G. (1933), *Study Habits Inventory*, California: Stanford University Press.

Wrenn, C.G. and Humber, W.J. (1941), "Study Habits Associated with High and Low Scholarship", *Journal of Educational. Psychology*, Vol. 32, No. 8, pp. 611-15.

Index

❑❑❑